Johnson & Johnson

FROM BABY TO TODDLER

EDITED BY

JOHN J. FISHER

PHOTOGRAPHS BY

BILL PARSONS

*Developed by Johnson & Johnson
in arrangement with
The Child Growth & Development
Corporation*

A PERIGEE BOOK

Perigee Books
are published by
The Berkley Publishing Group
200 Madison Avenue
New York, NY 10016

The author gratefully acknowledges permission from the following
sources to reprint material in their control:
Excerpt from *Listen to Your Child*, by David Crystal (Penguin, 1986).
Copyright © David Crystal, 1986. Reproduced by permission of
Penguin Books Limited. *The Journal of Genetic Psychology*, 134,
Table 1, page 173, 1979. Reprinted with permission of the Helen
Dwight Reid Educational Foundation. Published by Heldref
Publications, 4000 Albemarle St., N.W., Washington, D.C. 20016.
Copyright © 1979

Library of Congress Cataloging-in-Publication Data

Johnson & Johnson from baby to toddler
month-by-month resource on your child's first two years of life/
edited by John J. Fisher: photographs by Bill Parsons.

p.   cm.
"A Perigee book."
1. Infants—Development.   2. Child development.
I. Fisher, John J.
II. Title: Johnson and Johnson from baby to toddler.
III. Title: From baby to toddler.
RJ134.J64   1987   87-38207 CIP
649'.122—dc19
ISBN 0-399-51393-0

Book design and typography by The Sarabande Press

Printed in the United States of America
11   12   13   14   15   16   17   18   19   20

CONTENTS

Contents

INTRODUCTION

New baby, new parents! Congratulations as you begin this marvelous adventure together.

Over the past fifteen years, I've had the privilege—and delight—of working with hundreds of families in their homes, observing daily activities. I've watched how parents and children handle occasional ups and downs, what play materials they use (and why), and how they deal with their common challenges. One concern frequently rises to the forefront: "Am I doing the best for my baby?"

It's a concern without a clear-cut answer. Certainly, there are many ways—and no single "right" way—to approach most issues of child care and rearing, from feeding to bathing to handling crying and night waking. Research and common sense tell us that there are also many ways parents can enhance development. But what is truly best for each baby? Only parents can answer that. And the best advice I've heard for parents to heed is this:

1. Always look at your own baby. He or she is an *individual*, with individual needs and interests, individual skills and talents, even individual limitations. You should think about the things you read regarding infant behavior and stimulation, and then determine how you might best apply such information to your own family.

2. Try your best—and it *is* difficult—not to compare your child with any other, especially with a sibling. You'll undoubtedly be pleased if your child is the first in his or her group to sit without help, take a first step, say a first word, master a simple puzzle. Yet when you consider that this child will be developing and learning throughout an entire lifetime, momentary precociousness isn't all that important. Secretly punishing yourself—or worse, your child—for occasional slowness or setbacks is a defeating exercise. It's far more vital to let your child know how much you love him—for himself. This feeling of being loved, this security, is the best way to help ensure a happy, confident child.

A NOTE ON ORGANIZATION

This book is organized into chapters by a baby's monthly age. Please remember that this is somewhat arbitrary, and that every baby develops on his or her own schedule. Don't be concerned if your baby isn't doing everything when this book "says" he or she should be; the inclusion of a certain behavior in a specific month is usually based on "average" development, and no baby is exactly average. Care information is also included where it is usually most appropriate, but again the month in which a specific topic is placed is somewhat arbitrary.

HE OR SHE?

In *From Baby to Toddler*, as in the Johnson & Johnson Child Development Publications, we acknowledge that children come in two genders. So half these chapters call the child *he*, the other half *she*.

ABOUT THIS BOOK

Raising a child is a collaborative effort involving family and friends. Creating this book was a collaborative effort, too, involving pediatricians, researchers, writers, editors, professionals in early child development, education, and play, and hundreds of parents like yourself. Ellen Sackoff, director of research for The Child Growth & Development Corporation, organized and managed a staff of freelance researchers; the manuscript was reviewed by parents and members of our Editorial Advisory Board, whom I especially want to thank. We've tried to incorporate the best, most current, and most scholarly research studies into a readable book that, I hope, truly does help you enjoy and enhance your young child's development.

John J. Fisher
Editor

About the Editor

John J. Fisher, Director of Publications for The Child Growth & Development Corporation, is a writer and editor specializing in early childhood. He helped create the line of Johnson & Johnson Child Development Toys, and authors the Play and Learning Guides that accompany each. He is also coauthor of three child development books sponsored by Johnson & Johnson: *Your Baby, Your Toddler,* and *Your Preschooler,* and writer/editor of many other Johnson & Johnson publications. He holds undergraduate and graduate degrees from The Johns Hopkins University. His latest book, also from Perigee, is *More Toys to Grow With: Infants & Toddlers.*

About The Child Growth & Development Corporation

The Child Growth & Development Corporation was founded nearly twenty years ago to integrate applied research techniques in the behavioral sciences with sophisticated product design. It possesses a unique combination of resources that enable it to develop innovative products for children, including:

- A fully integrated team of highly experienced research and design professionals, representing a wide range of disciplines.
- A research library of over forty thousand books, journals, and reprints related to all areas of child development, with on-line access to outside data bases.
- A photography library with more than one hundred thousand still photographs of children and their families.
- A network of twenty-five hundred families with young children, representing a broad range of backgrounds; and a network of over one hundred schools and day-care centers serving children of all ages.
- A product testing laboratory, two design studios, and two prototype shops.

EDITORIAL ADVISORY BOARD

The Editorial Advisory Board consists of professionals representing the fields of psychiatry, developmental psychology, pediatrics, and early childhood education. These board members, who reviewed and commented on drafts of this manuscript, include:

Larry Aber, Ph.D., Assistant Professor of Clinical and Developmental Psychology, Barnard College, New York, NY

Marc Bornstein, Ph.D., Senior Research Scientist and Head of Child and Family Research, National Institute of Child Health and Human Development

Richard Chase, M.D., President, The Child Growth & Development Corporation, New York, NY; Associate Professor of Psychiatry and Behavioral Sciences, The Johns Hopkins University School of Medicine, Baltimore, MD

Margery Franklin, Ph.D., Professor of Psychology, Sarah Lawrence College, Bronxville, NY

Irving Sigel, Ph.D., Distinguished Research Scientist, Educational Testing Service, Princeton, NJ

William Waldman, M.D., Pediatrician in private practice, Baltimore, MD

Sara Wilford, Director, Sarah Lawrence Early Childhood Center; Director, Sarah Lawrence Art of Teaching Graduate Program, Sarah Lawrence College, Bronxville, NY

1

BECOMING PARENTS

New Baby, New Parents

In many ways, becoming a new parent is like starting any completely new job. You're happy and excited about the possibilities, yet nervous about whether you'll be able to handle this major, somewhat unfathomable new responsibility. You can, undoubtedly. It just takes time to learn your new role and adjust to it. And this adjustment period might be marked by more rough spots than you had anticipated.

Parents-to-be often have romantic visions of life with baby: a smiling face beaming up at them, a tender body snuggling in their arms, a few tears that are quickly dried with a gentle kiss. Yes, these are some of the good times. But there is another side to reality. First and foremost, caring for a new baby takes a lot of time—in fact, much more than every parent we interviewed had imagined. Second, a new baby has a very erratic schedule, eating and sleeping and crying at all hours of the day and night. Put these together and you're bound to be exhausted. Lack of sleep is by far the most difficult hurdle parents tell us they must overcome. Since everything about taking care of a baby is more difficult when you're fatigued, do whatever you can to get sleep.

For many parents, this newness and lack of sleep are compounded by uncertainty about the burgeoning parent-baby relationship. This usually translates to: Am I doing the best for my baby? Try to relax. There is no single way to make this relationship prosper. It takes things like mutual respect, understanding, acceptance, and plenty of affection. These are expressed uniquely in every family. Also, remember that you're not alone. Your baby takes an active part in this unfolding relationship. He lets you know what he wants and how he feels, so pay attention to his cries and coos and body language. You'll find that he guides you almost as much as you guide him.

Psychologists and other experts on family life have studied the factors that help ensure a positive parent-baby relationship. As you might expect with such a broad undertaking, no set of absolute *dos* and *don'ts* has emerged. Each baby, each family, is unique. Nonetheless, there *are* some guidelines on which most experts agree.

Let Your Baby Know How Much You Love Him.   This most emphatically will *not* spoil him. Tell him with your eyes, your smiles, your tender words and loving touches. Physical contact is very important. Your baby picks up messages of your affection from the way you handle him, just as adults form opinions of other people based on a handshake or embrace.

Respect Your Baby's Limited Ability to Interact.   Many people become so excited about having a newborn respond to them that they forget to consider his limited ability to interact. Parents or relatives trying to establish eye contact with the baby should remember not to put their heads so close that he can't withdraw his attention when he wants. (He signals his desire to withdraw by breaking eye contact, yawning, or turning away.) Also, keep his limited skills in mind regarding your own relationship with him. Right now you'll be doing a lot of giving with very little receiving. But soon he'll tell you with eyes and smiles how much he loves you, too.

Respect Your Baby's Uniqueness. Your baby has his own personality and temperament right from the beginning (see "Your Baby's Personal Style," page 58). You'll notice this more demonstrably over the coming months. Life is easier if you take into account his ways of doing things. For instance, even though physical contact is important, some babies don't particularly enjoy being held close or cuddled. If yours isn't a cuddler, you can convey your love in other ways.

Try to Be Consistent. Routines are comforting. Just as you enjoy reading the paper over your morning coffee, or eating at a prescribed time, your baby feels secure when there are things that he can count on. Establish a ritual at bath time, for example—a game or two, a wash, a massage, possibly some exercises. Or maybe nursing is always accompanied by rocking in a favorite chair, or a loving lullaby. Inserting some routine into the daily schedule teaches your baby a bit about orderliness and helps him make sense of those many impressions that fill his waking time. You needn't settle into an unchanging daily routine, of course; flexible consistency is the key.

Established patterns are particularly important when someone else cares for your baby. If the sitter follows the routine you and your baby have worked out, your baby will adjust more easily to this new person and to his time without you.

How Your Baby Changes You

Having a baby certainly heightens the feelings of love a couple share. However, this new addition, delightful as he is, brings countless changes to the husband-wife relationship. There's bound to be a period of adjustment—even conflict—before a couple can relate as they did before. In fact, many parents tell us that adjusting to the baby was in many ways harder than adapting to married life.

Parents we've interviewed agree that most conflicts center around four issues.

Not Enough Time Alone. The number one complaint was that parents have far less time to spend alone together. Second, and related, was the loss of closeness and relaxation even when the time is there.

Watching television, going out, taking long walks—there are hundreds of ways couples enjoy each other's company. But a baby cuts down dramatically on this freedom to come and go. At home you can no longer count on the peaceful, quiet times you used to enjoy. A baby's schedule is pretty irregular, particularly during the early months. He may well demand your attention at the most awkward moments.

Jealousy and Envy. Parents are apt to feel a little jealous when a new person enters their lives. A baby often directs parents' attention away from each other and toward him. A husband may envy the large amounts of time and attention his wife gives the baby, or the affection she displays. She may resent it when her husband returns from work and dashes to see the baby instead of spending time with her. And if the mother was working before the baby came, she may also envy her husband's freedom to leave the house while she stays at home.

Irritability. New parents are often overwhelmed by the new pressures and responsibilities. They frequently lack time to talk things out. They *never* get enough sleep. Stress may come from a tighter budget, a messy home that no one has time to clean, any number of obligations over which a new baby takes priority.

Changes in the Sexual Relationship. The disruption of a couple's sexual relationship presents an added pressure. New parents may worry that sex may never again be as spontaneous or passionate.

YOU'RE NOT ALONE

If you're having problems you didn't anticipate, remember that *you're not alone.* Don't let unexpected problems undermine your confidence. Most parents we talk to have trying times. As the seasoned ones tell us, you'll begin to relax as you grow into your new roles. They also offer suggestions that might ease your adjustment.

Be Open with Each Other. Parents usually experience new and conflicting emotions during the first months after a baby's arrival. That is why you talk together, sharing hopes for your baby as well as practical problems you face. Some people we consulted set aside a time each day to discuss the things they experience as new parents. Talking together helps you see the lighter side of parenting, too, when things are rough. Shared laughter helps lighten your load.

Share Responsibilities. A new baby takes lots of work; traditionally, most of this falls on one parent, usually the mother. And admit it or not, many mothers resent this imbalance. Take turns diapering. If your baby is bottle-fed, trade feeding times—especially that disruptive middle-of-the-night one. In many families we talked to, the father took responsibility for the baby's bath. Be sure each parent spends time alone playing with the baby, too. This will also help promote your baby's attachment to *both* parents.

Accept Interruptions as a Given. Interruptions are a way of life for new parents, especially for mothers at home with an infant. Try to schedule your time by accepting and anticipating these interruptions. As one mother related with a laugh, it took her three days just to vacuum her apartment.

Take Time Away from Your Baby. Although they might hate to admit it, most new parents get cabin fever at times. They need to get away, to forget about diapers and crying and the next feeding. First, find yourself a trustworthy babysitter. Then visit friends, take in a movie, treat yourself to dinner (so nice, as one mother grinned, to "have someone else take care of *you* for a change"), go dancing, do some of the things you especially enjoyed before your baby was born. You'll probably find, as did the parents we talked to, that these breaks from parenthood go far to raise your spirits.

EVERYONE BENEFITS

Working through difficulties so you can enjoy a close, loving relationship is as important for your baby as for you. Even very young children are sensitive to the emotions flowing around them. When there are loving feelings that reflect mutual trust and a positive way of working out problems, your baby will sense he's growing up in an atmosphere of love and security.

Handling "Baby Blues"

"Baby blues"—that sudden, temporary depression that strikes many new mothers—can set in anywhere from a few days to a few months after the baby is born, and last anywhere from a day to several weeks. Its causes seem to be a mixture of the physical and the psychological. Some contributing factors:

Hormonal changes: Pregnancy and readjustment to the no-longer-pregnant body can throw a woman's hormonal system out of balance, causing dramatic mood swings.

Fatigue: As we said before, most new mothers are overtired, so even the slightest things can set them off.

Feelings of being overwhelmed: As one mother told us, "At first I was exhilarated, but the abrupt transition of stopping work, being tied to the house, and having this tiny creature completely dependent on me hit like a lead balloon. I felt totally overwhelmed. Besides the baby, I still had a house to clean and meals to cook—and little of my old strength and enthusiasm."

Diminished attention: Some mothers we interviewed were likewise upset by how other adults suddenly behaved differently toward them. As one expressed it: "When I was pregnant, I was the center of attention. I loved the baby showers, the whole rigamarole. Lots of people called or dropped by to see how things were going, particularly as I was nearing delivery. This attention helped ease some of my apprehension. But soon after Andrew was born, my friends stopped calling nearly as much. It's not that they weren't interested. I think they were afraid of interrupting me or waking the baby—or waking me; it's true that I usually sounded tired on the phone. Still, I missed them. And I missed their support when I felt vulnerable. Another thing—when you're no longer pregnant, people who visit only pay attention to the baby. Sometimes it feels like your husband only pays attention to the baby, too."

THE CURE: TIME AND SUPPORT

"Baby blues" is one case where time truly *does* heal. As your hormones readjust themselves and you get used to the new responsibilities a baby brings, the dark times will subside. Parents tell us that understanding and support make all the difference. The mothers who talked about these feelings with their partners, and whose partners accepted the temporary blues as real and justified, felt far less alone and overwhelmed. If you're feeling the blues, you might also talk to your baby's pediatrician or the pediatric nurse practitioner in the pediatrician's practice or clinic. These professionals are well-versed in the troubles new mothers face, and can help you come to terms with the sometimes bewildering changes a new baby brings.

> Some new mothers suffer from postpartum depression, which is more severe, longer lasting, and usually more psychologically debilitating than the more common and less troubling "baby blues." If you have serious difficulty accepting your baby and new role as parent, do talk to your baby's pediatrician or your own doctor about the possibility of professional help. Don't be ashamed; a new baby *is* a huge change in your life, and unique factors both in your family and your own psychological makeup might render it a bigger adjustment than you can make without help.

If Your Baby Was Preterm

If your baby was preterm or ill at birth, you and he have already been through some tough times together. Coming home from the hospital—always an exciting event—likely had extra meaning as you left behind the very anxious days and institutional setting. Many parents of babies who have had a difficult start take special pride in watching their babies' accomplishments and progress. They can have special questions, too, says Joy Goldberger, a former child life teacher for infants and toddlers at The Johns Hopkins Hospital. She offers the following advice.

• Preterm infants are individuals, just as are all newborns. Preterm babies, like full-term ones, develop in a fairly predictable sequence, each on his own timetable. However, unlike most full-term babies, some of your baby's developmental processes may be affected by his unique medical history and hospital experience.

· It's best not to measure your preterm infant's development against that of a full-term baby. A baby born a month early and discharged from the hospital about three or four weeks later is not at the same developmental point as a full-term infant. Also, preterms often find it harder to "organize" themselves into predictable and regular patterns of waking, sleeping, hunger, and alert times.

· You and your baby may find, each in your own way, that you miss aspects of the hospital life. You probably felt some safety with the medical monitoring and always-available professional staff. That's quite understandable, and you can expect to go through an anxious transition. Your baby may seem to miss the noise and lights of the hospital; for instance, he may fuss when all is quiet and appear more content when surrounded by bustle. He might also expect that touching often means hurting. Some parents have found that gentle massage and extra rocking and cuddling have helped relax their baby into being handled. For other babies, talking and singing to them without holding may be more comfortable initially. Also, you may need to "wean" your baby gradually from the bustle of the hospital to the quieter sounds of home. Radio, television, noisy household appliances, and adult voices might help your baby get used to this new environment.

· You might be tempted to be overprotective, to respond almost before your baby asks for help. But it's best to avoid being so responsive that he rarely has a chance to express himself. All babies need a balance of time with parents and time to explore and play on their own. Preterm babies, like full-term ones, learn best through doing. Of course, you should respond to his cues and overtures just as you would with a full-term baby.

· Some basic aspects of a preterm baby's care are different from a full-term baby's. For example:

· Be especially sure he is kept warm, and sleeps in a draft-free area. He tends to have trouble maintaining his internal temperature and loses body heat more rapidly than a full-term baby because his circulatory system is still adapting to life out of the womb, and because he has less body fat.
· He may require some dietary supplements, such as iron and certain vitamins. A premature baby grows faster than a full-term one, and his intestines absorb certain nutrients less completely. Discuss your preterm baby's diet with his doctor

and make sure you follow the doctor's advice exactly.

· He may also require smaller, more frequent feedings. Charts of how much and how often a "typical" baby feeds don't always apply to a preterm baby. It's best to feed him "on demand" rather than by any schedule you may wish to set. And if he seems to be having trouble feeding, or appears to lose weight, be sure to contact his doctor.

· A preterm baby often sleeps more than a full-term one, and may take longer than "normal" to settle into a sleep-wake routine. He is also usually less active; this benefits him, since he needs to conserve his energy in order to gain weight. For this reason, you should keep active play to a minimum until it's clear your baby is thriving.

· A preterm baby rarely needs a full tub bath for the first weeks or even months, as long as he is cleaned well at diapering and is sponged off every day or so. Some sources we consulted say you can give him a real bath when he reaches about 7 pounds, which is about the average birth weight of a full-term baby. However, we recommend you ask your baby's doctor when it is wise to introduce a baby bathtub (and also ask about early sponge baths and other cleaning procedures). The doctor may have good reasons for recommending a real bath before or after this 7-pound rule of thumb. (See "Baths" on page 44.)

· Occasionally, preterm babies experience some developmental lags that bear looking at more closely. At the advice of your baby's doctor, you might explore the services of a special developmental pediatrician or developmental center. These can help with problems. In fact, if you're unsure about any aspect of your baby's growth, ask his pediatrician or the staff of the neonatal unit who helped to care for him. They are likely to be the best qualified to answer most questions about *your* baby's needs.

Good Book

Parenting a premature baby can raise many more questions than we have room to deal with here. If you would like more information, we recommend the following book:

The Premature Baby Book, by Helen Harrison (with Ann Kositsky). New York: St. Martin's Press, 1983.

2

YOUR NEWBORN

Overview

Looking at your tiny, wrinkled newborn, you might naturally assume that she's essentially helpless. Indeed, babies were long described this way even by professionals. Yet this fragile appearance belies many innate abilities that help her adjust to life outside the womb and survive in this brand-new environment. Some are reflex movements directly related to life-supporting activities. For instance, she automatically turns her head when an object presses against her nose or mouth and interferes with her

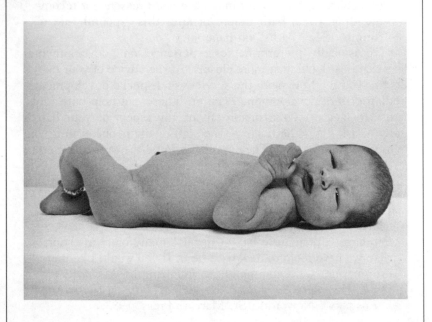

breathing. When you stroke a newborn's cheek or a corner of her mouth, she automatically turns her head toward your hand. This rooting reflex helps her find the nipple for sucking. And should she catch up with your finger, she'll suck it vigorously, as she does almost any appropriately sized object placed into her mouth. This sucking reflex helps assure successful feeding in the newborn period. Press an object into her palm and she grasps it, again, automatically. This reflex helps her hold on to you, contributing to her safety and sense of security.

Your newborn likewise has a repertoire of social behaviors. She's born with a fascination for human faces and voices, and demonstrates even in the delivery room her interest in others of her species. She communicates her needs—albeit clumsily at first—with cries that soon turn into a language of their own, alerting her parents to what she needs to feel comfortable. Soon, too, she recognizes her mother out of all the other faces she sees in a typical day. A baby's senses—sight, hearing, smell, taste, touch—work from birth, although not all are as finely developed as they will be later in life. Still, they help her form attachments to her parents and allow her to start learning about her world.

GETTING SETTLED

If this is your first baby, the first week or so after her birth will be among the most confusing and unsettling of your lifetime together. Nothing you've read or will read adequately prepares you for the enormous responsibility this new person brings—or for the almost total lack of confidence you are likely to feel at times. Her every sneeze or cough stops your heart, her "cheesing" up milk during a burp makes you doubt your feeding prowess. You're bound to question her every behavior, such as sleeping patterns or sudden cries that seemingly come out of nowhere. Despite how much you may know about newborns in general, you know almost nothing about this *particular* baby. She's too young to have demonstrated how much sleeping or eating is normal for *her.* You don't know her well enough to determine whether a cry signals hunger or some other discomfort. Much of your care will involve guessing until she settles somewhat into life outside the womb, and you can understand—at least a little—her general ways of behaving.

New parents are usually the most anxious about the following behaviors.

Breathing. Your newborn's lungs are small. Her breathing may seem very shallow, which is normal. It's also normal for her breathing to be a little irregular, or for her to make snuffling sounds when she breathes, sometimes caused by mucus in the nasal passages. (NOTE: A baby breathes through her nose.) This does not necessarily indicate a cold. Newborns also cough and sneeze to clear air passages. They frequently sneeze, too, when they open their eyes in bright light the first few days. According to British pediatrician Miriam Stoppard, this is because the light stimulates the nerves to the nose as well as the eyes.

Hiccups. Newborns often hiccup, which is caused by a sudden, irregular contraction of the diaphragm. You do not need to do anything—hiccups go away all by themselves. Do not try to give your baby water to "calm" hiccups. By about five or six weeks of age, a baby's frequency of hiccuping decreases significantly.

"Cheesing." It's also normal for a young baby to bring up some milk when being burped. This "cheese" may be lumpy rather than purely liquid, since she may have already started digesting the milk, causing it to curdle.

Moro Reflex. When a newborn baby is startled—by a sudden sharp sound, or because her position is shifted so abruptly that she feels a loss of support—she often responds with what is called the *Moro reflex.* She extends her arms, opening and closing the fingers, and alternately draws up and extends her legs while crying. It looks almost like she's trying to grab something with her hands and legs. Some experts believe that this reflex is left over from the time, earlier in human evolution, when human babies clung to their mothers very much like monkeys do today. If faced with a sudden startling sound or a sensation that they may fall, these baby forebears instinctively clutched their mothers more tightly. Nowadays, the Moro reflex helps your baby tell you about her own sensitivities. It's a hint to be a little more careful when handling her, so that you don't startle her unnecessarily.

Feeding. It will take several days—or even weeks—for your baby to settle into some sort of predictable feeding schedule. She may be hungry every half hour or every two hours or every three hours; or after a half hour now, then again two hours later, then four hours after that. Don't worry if she takes a while to slip into a feeding schedule. It's also quite normal for a baby to lose weight for the first few days after birth, then to start gaining it back. However, if you have any concerns about your child's nutrition, contact her pediatrician.

Sleeping. A newborn regulates her own need for sleep. It's quite difficult to keep her awake, and equally as difficult to wake her up for more than a few moments, when she needs to sleep. During the early weeks, she'll likely appear to make little distinction between day and night and will spend most of the twenty-four hours sleeping, awakening to eat and for other caretaking routines. She's likely to be alert just a few minutes at a time, often before eating or during her bath, and will drift in and out of sleep without much advance warning. As she grows older she stays awake more and more during the day, and sleeps for longer periods at night.

That's the "typical" baby, but in researching sleep patterns particularly, we've found almost no "typical" baby. Some babies, right from the start, sleep for only about fourteen hours out of twenty-four, and have several minutes of alertness several different times throughout the day. Others sleep almost twenty-two hours a day, and are fairly groggy even when awake. Because your baby regulates her own sleeping, there's little to do this month but go along with her self-imposed behaviors.

GETTING ACQUAINTED

Relationships between baby and parents start right from birth or even earlier; some parents claim to "bond" to the baby in utero. But it's the baby's emergence into the world that sets the stage for a mutual love affair. Yes, the first month of life is a monumental beginning in every sense of the word.

Tuned In from Birth

The more researchers study newborns, the more we learn how even the youngest infants are tuned in to people. A classic study by Peter Eimas, Einar Siqueland, and Lewis Lipsitt at Brown University found that right in the delivery room, a newborn becomes especially alert when she hears a human voice. These scientists have also shown, through another experiment, that babies prefer human sounds to pure tones. The infants sucked on a pacifier while listening to sounds. They paused briefly after hearing the pure tone, then continued sucking steadily. But when these same babies heard a human voice instead, their sucking pattern was different. They paused as before, but then they resumed a pattern of sucking . . . pausing . . . sucking . . . pausing—as if they expected more information to follow and thereby paused frequently to pay attention. Is also seems that very young infants find human speech reinforcing. Sandra Trehub and Hsing-Wu Chang of the University of Toronto found that when they presented speech to a sucking baby, the baby increased her sucking. But presenting nonspeech sounds or speech that was not tied to sucking had no effect on the babies' motivation to suck.

A newborn not only likes voices, but from just a few hours old can also distinguish between her mother's voice and that of another woman. In a study at the University of North Carolina, Greensboro, Anthony DeCasper and William Fifer tried another sucking experiment. By sucking one way on a pacifier, an infant could listen to a recording of her mother; another way, she heard a similar female voice. These babies showed, through their sucking, that they could tell the difference between the two voices—and they definitely preferred listening to their own mothers.

NEWBORNS LIKE FACES, TOO

Very young babies are also tuned in to human sights. A newborn pays special attention to faces and pictures of faces. She'll move her eyes—and sometimes her whole head—to follow a picture of a face as it moves past her line of vision. The same newborn will also stare at a picture of a human face with its features rearranged, but she's far less likely to follow its movement.

Research has found more facts about babies and faces:

- Until about two months most babies tend to scan the edges of a face and the hairline more than the eyes and other internal features. Soon afterward, though, the eyes become their most favorite feature.
- Babies look more at faces that talk than faces that are silent.
- By about three months, babies can discriminate among different degrees of smiling, and by about five months can distinguish among the facial expressions of anger, fear, and sadness.

As with voice, a baby learns to discriminate her mother's face at a very tender age. In a study at the University of Miami Medical School, researchers Tiffany Field, Debra Cohen, Robert Garcia, and Reena Greenberg found that infants less than two days old could tell the difference between their mother's face and the face of another woman. These infants preferred looking at their mothers, too. A study by I. W. R. Bushnell, at the University of Glasgow, Scotland, found that four-week-olds can discriminate between a photograph of their mother and that of another woman.

SMELLS AND TASTES

A baby's senses of taste and smell are also specially tuned to people. In a classic study, Dr. Aidan MacFarlane, at Oxford University, England, found that very young babies prefer milk smells over those of sugar water. Babies also suck differently on a bottle containing human milk than on formula made with cow milk. Also, as is the case with voice and appearance, a baby quickly learns to single out her mother on the basis of her distinctive smell. Another study by Dr. MacFarlane found that a baby tends to prefer her own mother's breast pads over those of another nursing mother. A study in France found that a very young baby could also tell the difference between a cotton gauze pad that had been worn on her mother's neck and a pad from another lactating woman's neck. In a study at Vanderbilt University, Jennifer Cernoch and Richard Porter found that breastfeeding babies could distinguish between gauze pads worn in the underarm region by their mothers and those worn by their fathers and by strangers. Interestingly, all these findings are based on breastfed babies. The study by Cernoch and Porter also found that bottlefed babies could *not* distinguish between the smells of their mother, their father, and a stranger. And neither breastfed nor bottlefed babies recognized their fathers preferentially.

A HEALTHY START

There is other evidence of the newborn's special adaptation to people, and no doubt future research will reveal additional inborn or quickly learned skills. Taken together, these findings paint a portrait of the special link between a baby and other humans, most particularly her mother. We can only speculate why this exists. One theory suggests that such skills help ensure a baby's survival— emotional as well as physical. It's possible that in the early ages of the human race, babies who recognized and adapted quickly to people—especially their mothers—were most likely to survive and pass these abilities along to their own offspring. Nowadays, of course, this isn't as necessary for physical survival, but it still lays the foundation for other aspects of development. Parents are by far the richest source of help, stimulation, and care in a baby's world. Inborn adaptation skills help guarantee that parents and baby will start right at the beginning to enjoy their special relationship.

When—and What—Do Newborns See?

Unlike a puppy or kitten, a newborn can see from the moment she's born. Her vision, however, is far from perfect. It's believed that for the first weeks, a baby sees most clearly objects that are about eight to twelve inches from her eyes. Those closer or farther away are visible but blurry, because in the early weeks, the lenses in her eyes can't adjust to different distances.

Normal vision develops with maturation and experience using the eyes. At first, a baby tends to move her eyes in jerky rather than fluid movements. By about two or three months, she can control her eye movements better. She can also focus on objects as close as a few inches and as far away as several feet. By three or four months, she can move her eyes toward one another (*converge*) to keep an object in focus as it slowly approaches her face. This control over *eye motility* develops faster than *visual acuity*. A normally sighted adult is said to have 20–20 vision; this is the measure of visual acuity (or clarity). Although a six-month-old has good vision, and can see most things in the immediate environment fairly clearly, she still lacks perfect acuity. In fact, most children don't develop what is called 20–20 vision until about four years of age.

DO NEWBORNS SEE COLOR?

The answer, apparently, is yes. However, color vision is not easy to study because colors vary on three dimensions: hue, saturation, and brightness.

So-called "color-blind" people make identifiable color discrimination errors, and they also confuse certain wavelengths with white. Marc Bornstein at New York University studied both these characteristics to assess color vision. He found that three-month-olds could discriminate blue-green from white and could discriminate between yellow and green. Individuals with the two major types of color blindness (red-green) fail at these discriminations. Davida Teller and her colleagues at the University of Washington,

Newborns prefer looking at faces and high-contrast patterns—such as checkerboards.

Seattle, later confirmed these findings, and extended them down to infants only one month old. Russell Adams and his colleagues in Canada showed that neonates only hours old could discriminate red, yellow, and green from gray. Teller has also found that one-month-olds give evidence that they are not blue-blind, a third and rare kind of color blindness. In overview, babies one month old and certainly babies two months old give evidence that they have largely normal color vision. By four months (and possibly earlier) babies easily differentiate among red, blue, green, and yellow and probably many other colors. They also tend to prefer bright shades over duller ones (even at younger ages) and prefer red and blue to green and yellow.

VISUAL PREFERENCES

It seems that newborns have definite visual preferences. In his pioneering vision studies at Case Western Reserve in the 1950s, Robert Fantz found that infants prefer faces and simple, high-contrast patterns (like a checkerboard or bull's-eye) to a solid color. Simple, high-contrast patterns are popular because the newborn tends to look most at the line where one color meets another. In tests with black-and-white checkerboards, babies looked more at the edges where black meets white than at the separate squares themselves. Faces are popular for the reasons discussed in the section "Tuned In from Birth," on page 26. Here, too, very young babies look at the edge rather than the center. This changes over time, as babies come to favor facial features. In studies at the University of Denver, Marshall Haith found that:

- Three- to five-week-olds looked at the edge or outline of a face 57 percent of the time, eyes 30 percent, nose 8 percent, and mouth 5 percent.
- Seven-week-olds looked at eyes 55 percent of the time, edges 34 percent, nose 7 percent, and mouth 4 percent.
- Nine- to eleven-week-olds looked at eyes 49 percent of the time, edges 33 percent, nose 13 percent, and mouth 6 percent.

Faces generally attract more attention when they're active. Haith found that when the person talked, infants looked at eyes slightly more time than when the person was quiet. In studies at the Boston University Medical Center, Genevieve Carpenter found that babies pay more attention to a moving face than a stationary one.

ADDING VISUAL VARIETY

Your newborn certainly has an appetite for looking at things. In fact, looking is a primary way she explores this new world around her. But since she can focus clearly only on nearby things (and since she can't get to things herself!), she depends on you to provide visual variety. So keep your face near hers when you look at and talk to her. Hold her close to interesting objects in the environment: patterned wallpaper, simple pictures on the wall, and so forth. Bring toys and other objects close to her eyes. Choose things that have bright colors, bold patterns, and faces. You'll find some other suggestions in "Growing through Play," near the end of this chapter.

In general, let your baby see how interested *you* are in her exploring her world visually. Talk about the things she is looking at, and show your pleasure as she examines her close surroundings. She won't understand your words, naturally, but she'll sense your enthusiasm and encouragement. And you'll help build her interest in the world—an interest that presumably provides a basis for her future enjoyment and learning.

Bottlefeeding

There are three basic types of commercial formula, all of which are equally nutritious:

1. *Ready-to-feed*. This usually come in eight- or thirty-two-ounce cans. As the name implies, it is *not* to be mixed with water. Ready-to-feed is the most convenient, but is usually the most costly. Always follow package directions regarding storage, particularly after a can has been opened. Instructions typically say that opened cans must be covered with a piece of aluminum foil, for instance, and be refrigerated and used within forty-eight hours.
2. *Concentrated*. This generally comes in thirteen-ounce cans, and must be mixed with water, usually at a 1:1 ratio. Be sure to follow package directions exactly regarding how much water to add to concentrate. Otherwise the formula could be too rich or too lean, which could result in overfeeding or underfeeding your baby.
3. *Powdered*. This come in large cans, generally with a scoop. Again, follow package directions regarding the correct proportion of water to powder (usually one scoop of formula for every two ounces of water).

Some formulas come fortified with iron. Use these only if instructed by your baby's doctor, because too much dietary iron can be harmful.

Because some babies are allergic to cow milk, formulas also come with a soy base. It's best to use soy-based formula only when recommended by your baby's doctor, because some babies do not tolerate soy well. Symptoms of allergy to cow milk include the following:

- · Vomiting
- · Diarrhea
- · Cramps
- · Excessive gas
- · Irritability
- · Wheeziness
- · Runny nose and sniffles

However, there is no unanimous agreement among the medical profession regarding exactly which symptoms indicate an allergy, so if you suspect your baby has trouble with cow milk formula, be sure to discuss it with the pediatrician.

STERILIZING BOTTLES

Not all pediatricians agree that you *need* to sterilize bottles as long as you wash them well, particularly in a dishwasher; the high heat of the dry cycle kills potentially troublesome germs. However, ask your baby's doctor. If he or she recommends sterilizing bottles, here are some techniques.

METHOD A
1. Wash bottles and nipples well.
2. Boil nipples, empty bottles, can opener, measuring devices, funnels, and any other formula-making equipment for twenty minutes. Let cool.
3. Open can of ready-to-feed formula or prepare powder or concentrate formula with sterile water.
4. Fill bottles and refrigerate.

METHOD B
1. Wash bottles and nipples.
2. Open can of ready-to-feed formula or prepare powder or concentrate formula in a large container.
3. Wash bottles and nipples. Fill bottles, invert the nipples (or leave them upright and cover with nipple domes), and loosely screw on the nipple rings.
4. Put the bottles in a large pot, add about three inches of water, cover, and boil for about twenty-five minutes. Or use a special bottle sterilizer.
5. Turn off the heat and let the bottles stand, still covered, for about one hour.
6. Remove the bottles from the pot, tightly screw on the nipple rings, and refrigerate.

METHOD C
If you use formula powder or concentrate, you can try this method:
1. Wash bottles and nipples. Fill each bottle with the amount of water necessary for one feeding, invert the nipples (or leave them upright and cover with nipple domes), and loosely screw on the nipple rings.

2. Put the bottles in a large pot, add about three inches of water, cover, and boil for about twenty-five minutes. Or use a special bottle sterilizer.
3. Turn off the heat and let the bottles stand, still covered, for about one hour.
4. Remove the bottles from the pot, tightly screw on the nipple rings, and store at room temperature. These bottles of sterile water keep for about three days.
5. At feeding time, add the prescribed amount of formula mix and shake well. Use immediately.

NOTE: Be sure to rinse out a bottle as soon as your baby finishes it. Dried formula or milk can be difficult to wash out and can support the growth of harmful bacteria.

NOTE: It's a good idea to sterilize the water that you add to formula concentrate or powder, since the water in your particular area may not be pure. Boil for five minutes, and let cool before adding to the formula mix.

NOTE: Once bottles are made up, they should be used within forty-eight hours.

TO HEAT BOTTLES

Warm a bottle by placing it in a pan of hot—not boiling—water for a few minutes, or by holding it under the running hot-water tap. Test by shaking a few drops on the underside of your wrist. Formula should be lukewarm. If it is too hot, hold under the running cold-water tap for a minute and test again. Do *not* heat in the microwave oven. The formula can turn to steam, causing the bottle to explode when you remove it.

How long can you let a bottle warm up naturally outside the refrigerator? It's impossible to say, since the temperature of your home (or car or outside air if you're on an outing) can affect bacterial growth. Ask your baby's doctor. It's safest not to leave a bottle out overnight, in preparation for the first feeding of the morning.

Heating tip for when you're on the go: Take along a thermos of hot water. When it's time for a feeding, pour some hot water into the thermos cup and put the bottle in this for heating.

NOTE: You may not need to heat a bottle to lukewarm. Some babies like their formula at about room temperature.

BOTTLE HINTS

1. Until your baby is able to hold her own bottle, do not prop up a bottle for self-feeding. She could choke on the formula.
2. Some—but not all—pediatricians recommend discarding leftover formula after a feeding, since your baby's saliva can start to break it down and spoil it. Ask your baby's doctor for his or her advice.
3. Use small bottles or disposable bag inserts when your baby is young, particularly if she is preterm. These require less sucking for your baby to get her formula, and can reduce the amount of air she swallows.

FORMULA AMOUNTS

How much formula your baby requires each day depends on her age, weight, rate of growth, metabolism, and activity level. Her doctor is the most reliable source of information, since only he or she knows *your* baby's individual needs. The following chart shows the average daily amounts for the first six months (after that, a baby's nutritional needs are also supplied by solid food). These amounts are based on a baby's birth weight and percentile. Your baby's doctor will weigh her at each checkup, and tell you in which percentile your baby falls.

Baby's Age		*Percentile*	
	10th	50th	90th
1 month	14 oz.	20 oz.	28 oz.
2 months	23 oz.	28 oz.	34 oz.
3 months	25 oz.	31 oz.	40 oz.
4 months	27 oz.	31 oz.	39 oz.
5 months	27 oz.	34 oz.	45 oz.
6 months	30 oz.	37 oz.	50 oz.

10th percentile = about 5½ pounds at birth
50th percentile = about 7 pounds at birth
90th percentile = about 9 pounds at birth

Remember that babies often lose weight the first few days after they're born, as their bodies expel excess fluid present at birth, and as they settle into an early feeding pattern. Soon they start to gain;

by three weeks your baby will again be at her birth weight. If she seems to be continuing to lose weight, or if she seems to be having any problems feeding, be sure to discuss these with her doctor.

Setting the Schedule

Who should determine how often your baby gets fed? The current thinking supports demand feeding, which is feeding when *she* wants it, not every four hours or some other arbitrary schedule set up by you. During these first months, your baby may need to be fed every two or three hours; or maybe even at irregular intervals until she settles into a typical three- or four-hour schedule.

BURPING

Burp your baby frequently during feeding to help her expel any air she may have swallowed.

- Hold her to your shoulder and gently pat her back. Protect your shoulder with a diaper or cloth in case she spits up a bit.
- Lay your baby face down on your knees and pat or rub her back. Again, protect yourself with a diaper or cloth.
- Hold her in a sitting position with one hand wrapped around her chest and chin to support her body. Use the other hand to pat or rub her back.

Breastfeeding

Like bottlefed babies, breastfed babies also lose weight the first few days following birth. Again, this is because they naturally expel excess fluid and because the first few feedings contain colostrum (a yellowish fluid) rather than pure breastmilk. (Colostrum and early breastmilk are high in zinc and certain proteins that give a baby immunity from various bacteria and viruses that can enter through the intestine.) This weight loss is natural, and your baby will be back at her birth weight within about three weeks or so.

You might feel anxious about your breastfed baby getting enough milk, particularly because, in contrast to bottlefeeding, you can't see the amount your baby consumes. Chances are she is, as long as she appears satisfied after a feeding, is obviously thriving, and is wetting about six to ten diapers a day. A baby typically empties a breast after about twenty minutes of nursing. However, she builds up to this. At first the newborn might nurse just five minutes per breast, then ten minutes per breast the second day, and fifteen minutes the third day. Also, a very young baby typically spends more time on the first breast and drains it more completely. In the early weeks, your baby may spend about twenty minutes on the first breast offered, but only ten to fifteen minutes on the other. For this reason it's good to alternate breasts at successive feedings, for example, offering the left breast first at one feeding and the right breast first at the next. A safety pin worn on the bra can remind a mother which breast to start with at the next feeding.

COMMON CONCERNS

Adequate Supply. In the early weeks, a mother may need to increase her milk supply to satisfy her baby's demand. The best way is to expand the number and length of nursings; usually, the more a baby sucks, the more milk a mother will produce. As with bottlefeeding, let your baby set the pace: Feed her whenever she wants to nurse rather than impose a schedule. A mother might also try offering the breast between regular feeding times. Even if your baby is not actually hungry, she might want to suck, which will increase milk flow. A nursing mother should eat a healthy diet and drink lots of fluids. Tenseness can inhibit milk production, so a nursing mother should try her best to relax and do whatever is necessary to get plenty of rest. This is easier said than done, of course!

If a nursing mother has questions about adequate supply, she should talk to her baby's doctor. He or she will monitor how well the baby is growing, and will advise on whether she needs supplementary bottles.

Engorgement. Engorged breasts are hard and tight, yet tender because they are uncomfortably full. Engorgement can occur when a baby nurses infrequently or does not empty the mother's breasts while nursing, such as during her first few days when she is just settling into how to nurse. The mother can relieve the soreness by massaging her breasts before feeding, or by applying warmth to her breasts via a hot shower, a heating pad, or a hot-water bottle wrapped in a towel to guard against burning. Also, if breasts are over-full, it can be hard for a baby to take the nipple. Express a little milk before feeding to relieve the pressure.

Clogged Duct.   Occasionally a milk duct in a nursing mother's breast may become clogged, resulting in a tender spot, redness, or a small, sore lump. This can be caused by tight clothing that restricts the breasts or by infrequent nursing. Also, if a baby is held in the same position each time she breastfeeds, she may not adequately empty all the milk ducts, causing some to clog. Vary the positions, sometimes cradling her in both arms in front of you, other times holding her like a football, to the side in one arm. Be sure to nurse the baby frequently on the affected breast, to keep the milk flowing. Warmth via a hot shower, heating pad, or hot-water bottle wrapped in a towel can relieve some of the tenderness, too.

Mastitis.   Mastitis is a breast infection or inflammation, accompanied by fever, headaches, and a general flu-like feeling. It results from a clogged duct or a general infection. If a nursing mother has mastitis, she should discuss this with her baby's doctor—he or she will determine the severity of the infection and recommend a treatment, which may include nursing more often, to clear the duct; applying warm, moist packs to the affected breast; getting plenty of bed rest; and drinking fluids.

Sore Nipples.   This can be caused by many different things:

- Improper positioning of the baby at the breast, especially in terms of "latching on."
- Improperly breaking the suction at the end of a feeding.
- A baby who sucks unusually vigorously.
- Some mothers, especially those with fair hair, have naturally sensitive skin.

Possible remedies include the following:

- Before nursing, express a little milk by hand or with a pump. This can help stimulate the "let-down" reflex, so the baby won't need to work so hard to start the milk flowing.
- Help the baby "latch on" correctly. Some babies, especially newborns, have trouble finding and taking the nipple. If yours does, breastfeeding mother, hold her in one arm and

support your breast with your free hand, thumb on top and fingers underneath. Take care not to touch the areola (the darkish circle surrounding the nipple itself), because this is the part that goes into your baby's mouth. Stroke your nipple against her mouth or cheek to activate the rooting reflex. When she opens her mouth, center the nipple and areola slightly inside. If she takes just the nipple, start the procedure over. When properly nursing, your baby takes both the nipple and all or part of the areola. Sucking on just the nipple does not bring milk as readily, and can make your nipples sore.

- Help the baby break the suction when nursing is over by inserting a finger into the corner of her mouth. If you try to pull her off the nipple, she'll probably just clamp down harder, which can lead to sore nipples.
- Vary positions, so that the baby is sucking on a slightly different area at each successive feeding.
- A nursing mother should wash her nipples with water only, and air-dry or use a hair dryer on a cool setting. Soap and alcohol can cause nipples to dry and crack.
- Wear soft, clean pads inside the bra between feedings.
- If soreness persists or is so severe that nursing is painful, the nursing mother express milk by hand or pump and offer it to her baby in a bottle.

Mother's Diet.   Naturally, the breastfeeding mother's diet is very important regarding how successfully she nurses and what nutrients she passes along to her baby. First and foremost, she should eat a well-balanced, healthful diet that particularly includes foods rich in protein, calcium, phosphorus, and vitamins A and C. She should also drink plenty of liquids. A glass of water or juice before each feeding helps assure adequate fluid intake and helps trigger the let-down reflex, which allows the milk to flow. She should also discuss with her doctor or the baby's pediatrician whether she should take vitamin supplements. Many doctors recommend continuing with the supplements taken during pregnancy.

Certain foods in the mother's diet—milk, peanut butter, broccoli, garlic, chocolate, and highly spiced foods, to name a few—can cause a baby to be fussy. A breastfeeding mother should pay attention to which particular foods in her diet affect her baby.

Remember: Traces of almost anything a breastfeeding mother eats or drinks can potentially enter her milk.

There are also other things besides diet about which a breastfeeding mother should be concerned. These include the following:

- *Medications.* A breastfeeding mother should talk to her doctor or the baby's pediatrician before taking any medications. These include over-the-counter drugs, cold medicines, prescriptions, and oral contraceptives.
- *Alcohol.* Alcohol can be passed along through breastmilk, and no one can state unequivocally how much alcohol is safe for the mother to consume.
- *Drugs.* Cocaine can be passed through breastmilk, and has resulted in infant deaths, Heroin, amphetamines, and other illicit drugs may also be transferred to a baby via breastmilk.
- *Caffeine.* Babies can be made jittery from the caffeine passed along through breastmilk. Many pediatricians agree, however, that a baby is usually unaffected if the mother drinks no more than two cups of coffee a day. Remember that there is also caffeine in tea and many soft drinks, particularly colas.
- *Smoking.* The nicotine from cigarette smoke can be passed to a baby through breastmilk, even if the mother smokes as few as four cigarettes a day. The long-term effect of this is not known. However, smoke in the environment is definitely harmful, so it's best if neither parent smokes if there is a baby in the house.

EXPRESSING BREASTMILK

A nursing mother will need to express milk if she produces more milk than her baby needs, if she has very sore nipples, or if she wishes to save milk for a bottlefeeding when she can't be with her baby for every nursing (such as if she is employed outside the home). Milk can be expressed manually or with a breast pump.

By Hand

1. Thoroughly clean a wide-mouthed cup or jar. You might sterilize it by boiling in a covered pot for about twenty-five minutes, and letting it cool with the pot still covered.
2. Thoroughly wash your hands.

3. Massage your breasts gently to help stimulate the let-down reflex. Stroke from the outside of your breast toward the nipple, applying gentle pressure with the palms of your hands. Move your hands around, sometimes stroking from the shoulder down, from the waist up, from the sides in.

4. Hold the cup or jar under your breast with one hand.

5. Hold your breast in the other hand, with your thumb on top and two fingers below. Your thumb and fingers should be about one and one-half inches behind the nipple; for most women, this is on the approximate edge of the areola.

6. Gently press your thumb and fingers together while simultaneously pushing them back toward your chest. Also roll your thumb and fingers gently to empty the milk sacs.

7. Continue with the press-push-roll sequence until your breast is emptied. At first the milk will be ejected in small spurts, but soon it will flow freely.

A mother may have trouble expressing milk the first few times. That's natural—don't get discouraged! Also, at the beginning she will likely just express for about three to five minutes. Gradually work up to ten to fifteen minutes per breast.

By Pump. Ask other breastfeeding mothers or the baby's doctor for the type of pump they recommend. Some mothers find the syringe-type the easiest to use; others favor an electric pump that can be converted to manual if there's no convenient power supply. Follow the instructions. And be sure your hands, all parts of the pump that touch the milk, and the container into which you ultimately pour the milk are thoroughly clean. Again, at the beginning you'll likely just express for about three to five minutes per breast. Gradually work up to ten to fifteen minutes.

Good Book

We don't have the room to include every issue related to breastfeeding. So if you seek more information, we recommend the following book:

The Complete Book of Breastfeeding, by Marvin S. Eiger and Sally W. Olds. New York: Workman Publishing Company, 1987.

Vitamin and Mineral Supplements

Most babies do not need to take additional supplements; both breastmilk and commercial formula contain about the right amounts of vitamins and minerals (as well as proteins, carbohydrates, and fats). However, breastfed babies may require supplements of vitamin D and fluoride, and preterm babies might need other supplements as well, such as iron. Ask your baby's doctor for his or her advice. And follow it exactly; too many vitamins can be harmful.

Changing Diapers

Changing diapers—this is something you'll be doing for your baby's first few years. It will take up a lot of your day, too, particularly in the early months. It's not unusual for a newborn to go through fifteen or more diapers a day! Whenever possible, change diapers as soon as they become wet or soiled; this helps prevent rashes and possible infections.

CHANGING WET DIAPERS

If you use disposable diapers, you'll need to feel down inside to see whether the diaper is wet. The plastic outside coating stays dry.

1. Remove the diaper. Wash baby gently with a soft, moistened cloth or a baby wipe. Dry thoroughly, particularly in folds and creases.
2. Ask your baby's doctor for advice regarding ointments and/ or other preparations. Always shake powder into the palm of your hand and gently rub it on your baby. Never shake it on your baby directly. You could cause a cloud of fine particles you or she might inhale.

CHANGING SOILED DIAPERS

1. Use the dirty diaper to wipe away most of the stool. If there is any caked-on residue, wipe it away with a moistened soft cloth; or a baby wipe; or a thick tissue dampened with water or baby oil.

   NOTE: Clean a baby girl front to back, to prevent getting any stool in the vagina or urinary tract.

2. Clean the diaper area again with another dampened cloth or baby wipe, *remembering to wash all the folds and creases.*
3. You may want to wash the diaper area one more time with a soft cloth moistened with warm water.

   HINT: Cut up an old cloth diaper to make your own soft baby washcloths. You can launder these along with her diapers.
4. Dry your baby thoroughly in all the folds and creases.
5. Again, ask your baby's doctor regarding ointments and/or other preparations. Remember to shake powder into your hand and then rub it on your baby.

BOWEL MOVEMENTS

Most newborns have several bowel movements a day. These will decrease over time to about one or two movements daily. However, some newborns have just one or two movements from the start. These early stools will be especially runny, particularly if your baby is breastfed. If you use cloth diapers, cover them with rubber pants. If you use disposable diapers, choose the form-fitting kind, or make tucks in the legs of regular disposables and secure with masking tape. Be careful not to make the fit too tight, and keep the tape off your baby's tender skin. Always clean baby well at diaper changes.

Breastfed babies often have fewer bowel movements than babies who are bottlefed because breastmilk is more fully digested. After the first month or so, it is not unusual for a breastfed baby to have one large, yellowish bowel movement every other day or two. However, if your baby—breastfed or bottlefed—has no bowel movement for three days, she may be constipated. Other symptoms of constipation include pain or discomfort when your baby tries to move her bowels, or abnormally hard stools. Contact her doctor. DO NOT treat this yourself with enemas or laxatives unless instructed by the pediatrician. For infants under four months, typical treatment includes increased water in a baby's diet, maybe with a sweetener added, or the use of an infant glycerine suppository. For older infants, usually the diet is temporarily changed to add more bulk in the form of fruits and fruit juices (if the baby has started solids). Also, milk and dairy products may be reduced, again only under doctor's orders.

DIAPER RASH

Diaper rash is primarily caused by a combination of moisture, friction, and warmth. The longer your baby wears a wet diaper, the more chance that her skin will become irritated. Also, if you use airtight disposables or rubber pants, infrequent changing can lead to fungal skin infections. Diaper rash can also be caused by food sensitivities, particularly once your baby starts solids. The best prevention is keeping your baby clean and dry—which means frequent changing and thorough washing and drying at diaper changes. You can treat simple rashes at home:

- Exposing the rash to air. Let your baby go without diapers for periods throughout the day. Always keep a close eye on her, though, and make sure she is kept off rugs or other surfaces that would stain if she were to urinate or defecate diaperless.
- If you use disposable diapers, switch to cloth ones for a few days. And leave off the rubber pants.
- Ask your baby's doctor about using ointments and other preparations when your baby has a rash.
- Contact your baby's doctor if the rash hasn't healed within three days, or if there are red patches beyond the diaper area, or if the rash becomes infected.

THE SPONGE BATH

As long as you clean the diaper area well at changing time, a newborn usually does not need a real bath for the first several weeks. Instead, you can give her a sponge bath every few days. Lay her on an absorbent towel or other cloth and wipe her gently with a soft washcloth moistened with warm water. Many pediatricians recommend that a baby not have a tub bath until the navel and circumcision are completely healed, usually around fourteen days.

CARING FOR THE NAVEL

The remains of the umbilical cord will fall off naturally after about ten to fourteen days. However, sometimes the cord may stay for about three weeks. It may also hang by just a few strands of tissue for a few days before falling off completely. Be patient; don't try to remove it before it is ready.

To care for the navel, clean the base of the cord twice a day with a cotton ball dampened with rubbing alcohol. It also helps to keep the diaper folded below the navel until the cord falls off. If you use disposable diapers, cut a wedge in the diaper with scissors so that the cord remains uncovered.

It's natural for the cord to ooze a few drops of blood at the point where it attaches to your baby's skin. This stops by itself, or can be stopped by covering the area with a sterile pad and pressing very gently. Call your baby's doctor if bleeding doesn't stop after ten minutes, or if the tie has come undone and the cord is bleeding, or if the cord oozes pus (a sign of infection).

CARING FOR THE CIRCUMCISION

The circumcision area will be red and tender for the first few days. Soon it forms a scab at the incision line. This falls off naturally by about seven to ten days. Some doctors use a Plastibel ring over the circumcision. This will naturally fall off by about fourteen days. Do not pull it off; you might cause unnecessary bleeding. Like the umbilical area, it's normal for the circumcision to ooze a few drops of blood. Contact the doctor if:

· Real bleeding starts
· The head of the penis becomes black or blue
· The normal skin of the penis becomes red or tender
· You notice any pus (a sign of infection)

If the doctor used a Plastibel ring, gently cleanse the circumcision area with a water-moistened cotton ball about three times a day or whenever it becomes soiled. Your doctor might recommend applying petroleum jelly or an ointment to speed healing and keep the area soft. If the doctor applied a dressing (usually gauze with some petroleum jelly), remove it about two days after the circumcision. Ask the doctor how to do this; one way is to apply warm compresses that naturally loosen the dressing. Then continue treating as described above.

Baths

INTRODUCING THE TUB BATH

Your baby's doctor will advise you when to introduce a tub bath, and how often your baby needs to be bathed. Remember: A young baby doesn't need a daily bath because she doesn't have much opportunity to get dirty. You may want to wash her every day or every other day in hot weather. In any case, you should wash baby's face daily, and clean the diaper area thoroughly every time you change a soiled diaper.

It's normal to be nervous the first time you bathe your baby. You might find it easier to have your spouse or another adult around, to help you and hand you anything you might have forgotten to put close by. Or invite a seasoned parent to bathe your baby the first time, so you can watch.

You can bathe your baby either directly in the sink, or in a baby-sized plastic bathtub. If you use the sink, you might want to pad the bottom with a towel. Also, swing the faucet out of the way to minimize possible accidents. If you can't, wrap it in a cloth. Always run a bit of cold water last, so that the faucet won't be hot should your baby accidentally brush against it.

Here's one method for bathing. It uses a baby bathtub placed on a table so that you have plenty of room. You can adapt it to the changing table if the one you have is large enough, or to the sink and counter area.

1. Assemble all the necessary paraphernalia: soap, shampoo (if needed), two washcloths (one for the diaper area, one for the rest of your baby's body), towels, cotton balls and/ or swabs, and a clean diaper and other clothing in which you'll dress your baby after the bath.
2. Cover the table with two towels, one under the tub to catch any splashes and one on which you'll place your baby.
3. Fill the baby bathtub with a few inches of warm water, test the temperature with your wrist (it should be lukewarm), and carry it to the table.
4. Undress your baby down to her diaper and lay her on the towel.
5. First wash her face with one washcloth (or cotton ball) dampened with water only. Be sure to wash behind her ears. Cleanse around her ears and nostrils with water-dampened cotton swabs. Do *not* put the swab inside the nose or the ear canal. Pat her face, ears, and nose dry.
6. Remove your baby's diaper and clean her as you do at every diaper change, omitting the pat dry step.
7. Slip one hand under your baby's shoulders and grasp the upper arm that's away from you. Your own arm should now

be supporting her neck and head. Then slip your other hand under her bottom and pick her up carefully. Place her into the bathtub feet-first.

8. Continue to support her head and neck with one arm, and use your free hand to wash her with a soft washcloth. Be sure to cleanse inside all skin folds. If your baby's doctor suggests using soap, you might find it easier to lay your baby on a sculpted foam bath form that supports her head. That frees both hands for bathing. Or you may need to lay her flat. Always be sure to rinse off the soap completely to prevent drying out your baby's skin. HINT: A washing mitt can be easier to manage than a loose washcloth.

9. If you shampoo your baby, wet her hair with a washcloth. Put a little shampoo into your hand, rub it on gently, and rinse with a dripping washcloth. Or use your hand as a cup to bring water to her hair.

   NOTE: The fontanel is the soft spot on the top front of your baby's skull. It normally closes with bone by about nine to twelve months. When your baby is young, it might pulsate slightly with her heartbeat; this is nothing to worry about. However, if the fontanel should bulge, contact the baby's doctor. Otherwise, the fontanel needs no special care besides your being vigilant not to poke it accidentally. Don't be afraid to wash and shampoo this area as you do the rest of your baby's head.

10. After you've washed your baby's front (and hair, if needed), sit her up. Lean her against one arm, and use your free hand to wash her back and the back of her neck. Rinse well.

11. Grasp your baby firmly with the same grip used to place her in the tub, or else under her arms. Remove her from the tub and lay her on the towel. Pat her completely dry— including folds and creases. Diaper and dress her.

    SAFETY NOTE: If you must answer a ringing telephone or doorbell, wrap your baby in a towel and take her with you. *Never* leave her in the tub unsupervised. If you have a telephone answering machine, turn it on so that you won't be disturbed.

Crying: What It Means, What to Do

Crying is your baby's vivid and very effective way to communicate with you. All healthy babies cry; some babies cry more than others, and some are harder to soothe than others. Most crying is a natural reaction to discomfort; your baby is telling you that she needs help to become comfortable again. As you come to know her better, you'll discover that her cries sound different, depending on what she needs. Learning these distinctions helps you know how to answer these calls for help.

Some crying is a reflexive response to other sounds in the environment—especially vocal sounds. Studies have found that babies sometimes cry when they hear a recording of their own crying or another baby's crying, or will cry in empathy in the presence of another squalling baby. In fact, one outburst in a hospital nursery can set off a chain reaction in the other junior inhabitants.

Any crying is a form of communication. Figuring out and responding to these calls helps build a close, trusting relationship.

NOTE: Some babies—maybe as many as one in five—have a condition known as *colic*. They cry unrelentingly for long periods, usually in the early evening, and can be nearly impossible to soothe. A separate discussion of colic can be found on page 50.

THE FIRST LANGUAGE

Each baby cries in a variety of ways to express many feelings and sensations. But nearly every infant has a few distinct cries that form a first language.

"I'm Hurting." A baby in pain cries in an unmistakable way. It may begin as a shrill scream, followed by a silent period and a series of short gasps; then the cycle is repeated. Perhaps she has bumped her head, or maybe you've accidentally brushed her against something hot. And if your baby ever takes a spill, you'll hear this cry— her way of saying that she urgently needs you. A hurting cry may wind up a baby so much that she needs lots of help calming down again. Of course, if there is any question that she has really been injured, be sure to call her pediatrician.

"I'm Hungry." Cries that start slowly and build to a loud, demanding rhythm usually signal a need to eat. Many babies take a while to settle into a regular feeding schedule; they get hungry at various

times during the day. Food is usually the first thing to think of when you hear the hunger cry; even if your baby has nursed recently, she might just want a snack. Or maybe she wants company. Besides food, a baby "hungers" for attention and stimulation. When your newborn gives a hunger cry but refuses food, she may be saying "I want to be with you." Sometimes, too, she'll drink just a bit, but when you try to put her down will continue the hunger cry. Nursing, whether on bottle or breast, involves cuddling and feeling close, which your baby also thrives on.

"I'm Upset." Your baby may cry in a mild, fussy way when tired or in a bad mood. The longer this fussing is ignored, the louder it may become, but it usually sounds more forced than the hunger cry. Babies also cry to express discomfort, anger, and other physical and emotional states.

The quality of your baby's cry will help you determine what she needs, but you should also look for other clues, such as the way she moves or what's happening around her. For example, if she repeatedly draws up her legs and straightens them again, she's probably telling you that her stomach hurts. Burping can help.

NO FEAR OF SPOILING

Since crying signals a need, we suggest that you go to your baby when she cries. This will *not* spoil her, despite what you may have heard. At this age, she's too young to understand intention and consequence. But she will realize that when you help her become comfortable again, she can depend on you. In a study at The Johns Hopkins University, Silvia Bell of Johns Hopkins and Mary Ainsworth of the University of Virginia compared two groups of babies: those whose mothers had usually responded quickly and consistently to cries, and those whose mothers had often let them "cry it out." At twelve months, the babies in the first group cried less. They also had a greater variety of ways to express their needs, and tended to have more secure attachments to their mothers than babies in the second group. Some other studies have found these same results too. However, other factors besides maternal responsiveness could be the reason. It may be that responsive mothers in general have less fretful babies.

When you promptly and consistently answer your baby's cries, she can learn to trust you and, by extension, the world. Answering these early cries does *not* mean that your baby won't cry at all when she's older. But maybe she will cry less. Also, you shouldn't feel pressured to answer every cry immediately. Sometimes you'll be delayed by realities like food on the stove or an insistent doorbell; other times you'll just be too tired or distracted to comfort her right away. Such delays won't harm your baby if you try to keep them to a minimum. Consistency doesn't mean responding immediately to each and every outburst.

HINTS FOR SOOTHING

When feeding, cuddling, rocking, and your other regular techniques fail to quiet your crier, try some of these.

· Keep her in motion in a windup swing or cradle. Take her for a stroll in the carriage. Or carry her in a front-pack infant carrier while you take a walk or do household chores.

NOTE: Some babies resist being held close or confined, both during a crying spell and in general. The swing, cradle, and carriage often work well for them. Also, when your baby is particularly hard to soothe, you'll likely become tense; she senses this when you're holding her, which may add to rather than lessen her distress. Again, motion without contact may be the answer.

· Give her a pacifier. Many young babies have a real need to suck even when they're not hungry.

· Play any kind of music you think will be soothing. Some experts discovered that sounds approximating those a baby hears in the womb are especially good at calming newborns. This finding has been worked into records, toys, and other equipment for the crib. You can make your own audiocassette that simulates such sounds: Tape a running washing machine or dishwasher, or any other rhythmic, churning, low sound.

· Sometimes confining a baby fairly snugly comforts her. Wrap her tightly in your arms and hug her to your body. Or swaddle her in a small, square blanket.

1. Lay her on the blanket so that one corner is above her head.
2. Bring the opposite corner up over her feet to her chest.
3. Bring in each of the other corners across her chest, snugly wrapping her arms close to her body. Now hug her gently to your body.

WHEN NOTHING WORKS

When nothing seems to work, you're bound to get frustrated and upset—and feel like a failure as a parent. Don't blame yourself, or your baby. Some babies are especially vulnerable to the sounds that others take in their stride. A ringing telephone, a slammed door, a car horn in the street—almost anything sets them off. They frequently take longer than other babies to calm down, too. Then again, there _are_ occasions when a baby seems to need to "cry it out." If you've exhausted your soothing techniques repertoire (and yourself), it's time to put your baby to bed and get away from the noise. Check her every twenty minutes or so to make sure nothing is wrong physically. If you need to get away from her cries, call in a baby-sitter, friend, or spouse and leave the house for a while. The separation will help calm you down, and the alternate caregiver may be better at calming your baby at a time like this. If you can't get out, just keep telling yourself that it _will_ stop. It will, too.

Sometimes, prolonged, unsoothable crying in a baby who doesn't have colic can be a sign that she's ill with something, like an ear infection, whose other signs aren't apparent. If crying persists undiminished, especially if it sounds like a pain cry, you should call the pediatrician.

Colic

Colic is one of the mysteries of infancy and the bane of every parent whose baby suffers from it. The piercing, prolonged cyclical crying comes about the same time each day, usually early evening. By some estimate, as many as 20 percent of babies have this condition, and you'll know—all too well—if yours is among them.

Colic frazzles parents and baffles professionals. It occurs in both breast- and formula-fed babies. Some experts believe it's biological, and caused by some sort of intestinal discomfort. This is variously blamed on an immature digestive system; assorted allergies, especially to cow milk; maternal hormones passed to the baby through breast milk; a baby's eating too much or too little. Other experts think it's psychological, and blame it on tension in the family. Still others feel that colic is simply a _label_ given to any baby who cries a lot, routinely at about the same time each day, and

is particularly difficult to soothe. No one really knows the cause—
or the cure.

SPECIAL SUGGESTIONS FOR COLICKY BABIES

If your baby is colicky, you might try these soothing techniques.
Since the digestive system may be the culprit:

· If you breast feed, our consulting pediatrician, Bill Waldman, suggests you watch your own diet. He says that many of
 the colicky infants in his practice respond well when their
 breastfeeding mothers drink less milk, particularly mothers
 who drink more than sixteen ounces a day. Other foods in a
 breastfeeding mother's diet may cause her baby problems.
 These include peanut butter, fish, eggs, berries, gas-pro-
 ducing vegetables, an excess of fruit, carbonated beverages,
 and drinks containing caffeine.
· Try smaller, more frequent feedings.
· Recently, pediatricians have been looking more carefully at
 the connection between colicky spells and a baby's formula.
 Many babies have a condition called *formula intolerance*.
 Signs of this include excessive crying and gas; your baby may
 repeatedly straighten her legs, then pull them up to her
 chest after feeding. If you are using formula, consult your
 baby's doctor about switching to another brand. He or she
 may want to try using a soy-based formula, or a formula that
 contains digestive enzymes.
· Burp your baby with special care, especially after a crying
 spell, because she's likely to have swallowed air.

Some babies are unusually irritable because they're very sensitive to outside stimuli. Such babies may be helped by these
techniques.

· Swaddling her during a crying spell.
· Feeding her in a quiet, darkened place when possible.
· Keeping household sounds to a minimum.
· Laying her on a lukewarm hot water bottle, or giving her a
 warm bath, to help her relax.

Other babies fuss so much because they're unusually sensitive to
internal stimuli. Dr. Waldman suggests that they may be helped
with outside distractions like these.

- Fairly loud, steady sounds can paradoxically calm such babies. Try playing music, or running the vacuum cleaner.
- Place your baby in her infant seat on top of a running washing machine or dryer. The sound and vibration can calm her. Be sure to stay there *at all times* to make sure she doesn't topple her seat with her activity.
- Motion often helps, especially if it's fairly active. Rock your baby in a cradle or your arms. Push her back and forth across the floor in the carriage. Carry her around in a fabric front- or backpack while you dance around the room or walk swiftly around the neighborhood. Take a seat, lay her stomach-down across your knees, and thump your heels on the floor as you pat or rub her back.
- Many parents and pediatricians report that a car ride is the most effective way to soothe a colicky baby. Clever inventors have capitalized on this information, so on the market as of this writing are devices that attach to the crib and simulate a car going about fifty-five miles per hour, through vibrations and sounds. Some studies have found such devices effective in soothing a colicky baby's crying. However, we don't know the long-term effects of such devices. You might discuss them with your baby's doctor.

HELP YOURSELF

Advice for you, too: Relax as much as possible (it won't be easy, but try) and stop blaming yourself. Parents of colicky babies often have *major* feelings of helplessness and frustration since their babies don't respond to normal soothing. These can lead to *anger,* which makes such parents feel guilty. You can also help yourself by taking breaks from the constant stress. Have friends, neighbors, or a sitter look after your baby periodically so you can get away. Make sure both parents share the soothing duties. Talk to other parents of colicky babies—they'll have suggestions, too. And look toward the rainbow. Colic almost always stops by the third or fourth month, when your baby will likely, as one of our writers described her own infant, "evolve into one enormous smile."

Growing through Play

EARLY BODY POSTURES

A newborn tends to curl up when she's quiet, whether lying on her back or stomach. On her stomach she may briefly lift her head from the surface. Whichever position your baby seems to prefer—her stomach or back—change it occasionally to provide more varied experience.

SOOTHING MASSAGE

Touching is a form of loving communication. A gentle, relaxing massage can help your baby feel secure and close to you. After bath time or a diaper change, rhythmically pet or massage your baby's back, stomach, and limbs. Always watch her reaction to see whether she's enjoying these sensations.

HOLD ON TIGHT

A newborn automatically grasps an object that's pressed against the palm of her hand. This is a reflex that gives way to voluntary grasping over the next few months.

When your young baby holds an object by herself, she usually pays it so little notice that she moves it around as if it were a part of her hand. In fact, some infant behavior experts believe that at this young age, your baby can't tell the difference between what is part of her own body and what is a separate object. That comes with time and the experience of grasping things. You can start now by giving her light toys—and fingers!—to hold.

Turn this simple play into an exercise game. While your baby holds one part of a toy, you take the other and gently play tug-of-war. When she relaxes her arm, slowly move the toy from side to side or around in a small circle. Add a simple song like, "Round and round and round we go—and where we stop, nobody knows!"

TREATS FOR THE EYES

It's not too early to start looking at books with your baby. Select those with simple pictures and faces. Magazines can be an excellent source of big, bright pictures. Your baby might enjoy looking at pictures on her changing table. Cut some from magazines and tape them to the wall beside the changing surface. Make sure that she can't reach them and accidentally pull them down. Or stand up a large book on the changing table for her to look at during diapering.

You can also sit your baby in your lap, facing you, so that she can see the colors and patterns of the shirt or dress you're wearing. Support her back and head! And fathers—patterned neckties are special treats.

LISTENING TO THE WORLD

A baby can hear before she's born. The mother's heartbeat, intestinal sounds, and the rush of blood through vessels all reach her through the fluid in which she lives. It's generally agreed that babies can hear voices and music in utero, too. A newborn reacts to sounds in many ways: becoming more active if quiet, calming down if active, blinking, and waving her limbs. When nursing, she may pause or suck harder.

Newborns especially like voices. Your baby will often stare at your eyes as you speak. Talking to her also helps her feel close to you—and you close to her. Likewise, she enjoys the sounds her toys can make: rattles, music boxes, and the like. Keep the sounds gentle!

A daily outing exposes your baby to all kinds of new and exciting environmental sounds. And it's a great way to meet other people who will love talking to her!

Research Update: Looking Again at Bonding

The theory of *bonding*, as first suggested by Drs. Marshall Klaus and John Kennell, states that there is a period shortly after birth during which infants become significantly attached to parents, especially the mother. Many experts have since disagreed, citing flaws in the original study. Psychiatrists and child development experts Stella Chess and Alexander Thomas acknowledge that the bonding theory has certainly improved American birth procedures; often fathers are allowed in the delivery room, for example, and both parents are encouraged to talk to and handle the newborn. But as these researchers asked in "Infant Bonding: Mystique and Reality," an article in the *American Journal of Orthopsychiatry*, "What about the mothers who are unavoidably unable to have immediate skin contact with their newborns, either because of illness in the baby or mother, or because of inflexible hospital routines? Are these babies doomed to less than 'optimal development'?" After reviewing scores of studies, Chess and Thomas conclude that these babies, of course, aren't doomed. Bonding is an ongoing process, not a one-shot deal.

Now Drs. Klaus and Kennel have altered their premise to say that the primary beneficiary is the *parent* rather than the baby. This can ease the worries of parents who, for a variety of reasons (including Cesarians and adoption), could not or will not be able to attend to their babies immediately after delivery.

3

YOUR
ONE-MONTH-OLD

Overview

Now that you and your baby are settling into your life together, the confusion of the first month has likely diminished. You're probably noticing that his own temperament and personal style are emerging, and that you, too, are developing a style of relating to him that's yours alone. How you care for your baby certainly affects his style, but parents aren't the only influ-

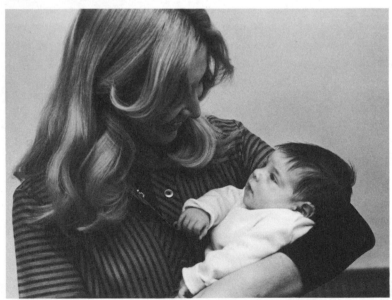

ence—even at this very young age. Babies are born with a temperament of their own. Parents with more than one child see this
clearly.

During this month, your baby settles into more predictable
patterns of behavior. That is, what he does on Monday—how much
he eats, why he cries, how he likes to be held and soothed—is a
pretty good indication of what you can expect on Tuesday. This is
such a contrast to his first week, when each day brought a whole
new set of trials (and errors)! Although most one-month-olds have
developed a fairly regular feeding schedule, sleep patterns still
often defy any sort of regularity. We can say with some confidence
that your one-month-old will sleep less each twenty-four hour
period than he did as a newborn; but he may sleep far more or far
less than another baby his very same age—and each pattern can be
normal. On average, many babies this age nap about four or five
times daily unlike newborns, who generally nap seven or eight
times a day.

Now you're quite aware that the transition from adult to parent
isn't always smooth. Your personal freedom and time for yourself as
an individual are dramatically curtailed. You must continually put
your baby's needs ahead of your own. A baby almost always affects
his parents' personal relationship, too. If you've ever neared that
dreadful point of thinking "Why did we ever *have* this baby?" (and
then felt horrendous for entertaining such a thought), remember
that you're not alone. Every parent we've worked with has desper-
ate moments and real bouts with self-doubt that are quite justified.
A baby *can* make you feel inadequate. But experience brings
confidence. It might make you feel better to know that second-
time parents have only a tiny fraction of the fears and inadequacy
feelings that first timers do.

Your one-month-old enjoys more and longer periods of alertness.
Since he's less sleepy than before, his crib is becoming an important first playground. He's still little able to control his limbs, so he
waves and kicks in random, jerky motions. Simple baby exercises
help him experience smooth, more coordinated large muscle movements. Many parents we know have developed their own set of
routines, and each is as individual as the baby-parent pair. Remember always to keep your movements gentle and smooth—take care
not to jerk your baby into position or strain his body. Let him set
the pace, too, by watching his cues and reactions. Some babies
prefer quiet exercising, others a more rigorous routine. For exercise
ideas, you might join or talk to someone from a baby exercise class.

Classes are a fun way to meet other parents and babies, too. For information on classes in your area, contact your local YWCA or YWHA, public library, community college, Red Cross, or groups like Lamaze that sponsor childbirth education.

Chances are you and your one-month-old delight in eye-to-eye play. Talk to him while he looks at you, and you'll probably be rewarded with a short "ah." Babies this age generally call out this sound only when they see a face—even a face on a doll or stuffed animal—and hear a pleasant sound at the same time. At this age your baby is increasingly eager to explore with his eyes and welcomes help in exploring the world. He also is attuned to sounds and turns to see where a sound comes from, as we discuss at the end of the chapter in "Growing through Play." Now, on to a closer look at some aspects of this second month of life.

Your Baby's Personal Style

Every young baby, like every adult, is a unique individual. Although how you raise your baby most assuredly affects his overall development and personality, experts believe that babies have clear tendencies toward certain behavioral styles right from the beginning.

In one of the most influential studies, psychiatrists Stella Chess and Alexander Thomas at New York University School of Medicine, with pediatrician Herbert Birch at Emory University interviewed a large sample of parents regarding their infants' reactions to routine activities such as sleeping, eating, dressing, eliminating, and moving about. These researchers found that babies showed substantial differences in their general *mood, activity level,* and in their *adaptability* to changes in routine. Large differences also existed in the *intensity* of these babies' responses; in their tendency to *approach or withdraw from* new experiences; in *persistence* (even though it sounds strange to talk about persistence in a young infant, it's certainly there in some babies); and in their *distractibility.* The infants also varied in the *regularity* of their natural eating and sleeping cycles and in their *sensitivity* (as their parents know only too well, some babies awake or cry at the slightest sound). A baby's way of typically reacting in all these nine categories is what Dr. Chess and her colleagues call temperament, or basic style of behavior. We might think of it as "personality."

Dr. Chess found that, on the basis of their reactions, many babies have one of three basic styles, and that many aspects of this style are retained throughout childhood. If you think about the way your baby usually reacts to regular experiences (eating, bathing, sleeping, how easy he is to soothe when crying), you can identify his basic style for yourself. You'll probably find, too, that life with any baby goes more smoothly when you take this basic style into account.

NOTE: Not every baby fits easily into one of the following categories; in Dr. Chess's study, 35 percent of the subjects couldn't be readily classified. Babies often mix characteristics from two groups; sometimes, for instance, a baby can be "easy" in some aspects, "slow-to-warm-up" in others. Still, these basic categorizations can be helpful in understanding *your* baby's behavior.

Easy. Easy babies are generally regular in their habits. They have a positive mood and show mild reactions to hunger and other discomforts. They usually accept new experiences easily. As these researchers express it, "In infancy, these children quickly establish regular schedules, are generally cheerful, and adapt quickly to new routines, new foods, and new people."

Slow-to-Warm-Up. These babies are thought of as shy. They share much of the style of easy babies but they need more time to adjust to new experiences. Dr. Chess and her colleagues say that slow-to-warm-up babies "typically have a low activity level, tend to withdraw on their first exposure to new stimuli, are slow to adapt, are somewhat negative in mood, and respond to situations with a low intensity of reaction."

Difficult. Difficult babies are unusually demonstrative. They react negatively to new experiences and even minor changes in routine, and tend to withdraw in the face of new stimuli. As Chess describes them: "As infants they are often irregular in feeding and sleeping, are slow to accept new foods, take a long time to adjust to new routines or activities, and tend to cry a great deal. Their crying and laughter are characteristically loud." Parents often find a difficult baby's crying unusually annoying, and in reality, it may be. Mary Lounsbury and John Bates at Indiana University had mothers listen to the cries of other babies. These listeners rated as particularly irritating the cries of babies whose own mothers considered them difficult. And when the acoustical properties of all the babies' cries were compared electronically, the cries of the difficult babies were determined to be especially demanding.

ACCOMMODATING YOUR BABY'S STYLE

If you have an easy baby, chances are your parenting job will run fairly smoothly, even if you have trouble adjusting to being a parent. He weathers your occasional tensions and short temper with aplomb. He's likely to make fewer demands on you than a more difficult infant. Some parents describe an easy baby as "So good I hardly know that he's there." Remember, though, that he still thrives on and benefits from your attention. If your baby is easy, don't let his equanimity allow you to ignore his real need for love and stimulation. A slow-to-warm-up baby likewise is fairly accommodating. He may not be so cheerful and adaptable as an easy infant, but he'll come to accept most new things in time if you are calm and tolerant.

It's usually the last category of temperament that puts the greatest stress on the new family. Difficult babies require considerable tolerance and patience. They can drive the sturdiest parents to distraction. Frequently, parents say that the worst part is feeling frustrated that they can't do anything to help their baby. But, of course, they can—and do. If your baby seems difficult, you can help by maintaining your patience, by being flexible in how you respond to his needs, and by keeping the stress he feels to the lowest levels possible. These things help him adjust to life at a pace that doesn't overwhelm him. Try your best, too, not to get discouraged. As he grows, he'll likely respond more easily and consistently, except at times of unusual stress. And his basic style may even change a bit over time, especially by year's end.

CHANGES OVER TIME

One reason a baby's style "changes" is because each baby is unique. Even if your baby can be generally identified as easy, slow-to-warm-up, or difficult, he has his own *individual* style which assimilates aspects of all three basic styles. Then again, babies do change over time, partly because they "grow out of" difficult aspects of their personalities and partly because of how their parents accept and accommodate the basic style. Follow-ups on the infants who participated in the Chess, Thomas, and Birch study found that babies designated one way at birth did not necessarily retain the characteristics of that category at a later age. Thus, if your baby might be considered difficult now, it doesn't mean that life will always be especially demanding. As Dr. Robert McCall of the University of Pittsburgh points out, "These descriptions (easy, slow-to-warm-up, difficult) provide a useful way to think about early personality, and they emphasize that some children are born with pronounced temperaments of one sort or another. But parents should not jump to the conclusion that a fussy eater, for example, will be 'difficult' in every respect now and forever more."

Nonetheless, the fact that babies seem to be born with an individual temperament certainly does make a difference. For one thing, you needn't blame yourself if your infant seems especially irritable. For another, this individual style, combined with the way you react to him, has an important influence on your infant's developing personality. And this personality—quirky or sublime as it may be—is one thing that makes him so very special.

Difficult Baby, Difficult Parents

Parents, too, have personal styles. Those who are comparatively easygoing themselves can usually cope well with a difficult baby. But when a difficult baby is born to parents who are less patient, the unfolding parent-baby relationship will be subjected to special stress. Such personality clashes aren't insurmountable, but they do require special tolerance. Remember that your baby isn't being "bad" or demanding on purpose. Try your best to accommodate his needs. If one parent is better able to cope, perhaps that one should assume the lion's share of caretaking. And should you have great difficulty relating to your baby, talk to his pediatrician or your own doctor.

Developmental Overview:
Large Muscle Skills

Many parents mark the stages of their baby's large muscle skill development (also called *gross motor development*) by four important firsts: the first time he (1) sits without help, (2) crawls, (3) stands, and (4) walks. Less dramatic than these milestones, but equally important, are other signs that your baby's body is slowly becoming responsive to his intentions—like lifting his head from the surface when lying on his stomach, and reaching purposefully toward a nearby object.

THE DIRECTION OF DEVELOPMENT

In general, physical development proceeds from the top down. Babies gain good control over head movements and neck muscles before the arms and hands, body, legs and feet. Similarly, they develop skilled arm movements before those of the fingers. Gross motor development likewise follows a general plan for all babies. Sitting precedes crawling, crawling comes before standing alone and walking. But babies differ greatly both in the ages they mark these achievements and in the ways they make these movements.

Throughout his first year, your baby works hard to get his body to move as he wants it to. You've already seen your newborn strive to raise his head from a flat surface. This may seem a tiny achievement, but once he can hold up his head reliably, he can more fully explore his surroundings with his eyes. Each time he achieves a modicum of motor control, he enjoys practicing it again and again. Practice leads to mastery, and mastery leads to good feelings about himself. Gaining control over his large muscles builds his confidence and motivation to explore, and exploring is the primary way he learns.

Parents can enjoy and enhance their baby's unfolding abilities. For instance, you can encourage your baby's self-confidence. An old-fashioned pep talk—"Come on, you can do it"—can boost his morale, and praise at success can add to his feelings of accomplishment. You can also sympathize with his momentary failures in ways that avoid adding to his embarrassment. "You almost did it. Good for you!" is far more positive than remaining silent, or worse, smiling or laughing at his failed attempts—even though he will produce some comical sights.

Parents can help in other ways, as we suggest in the "Growing through Play" sections throughout this book. But they can some-times give too much help, especially when a new skill is just emerging. You might be tempted to step in when your baby seems slow or especially clumsy. But try to be patient. Let him do as much as he can do—and wants to do—on his own. Offer help only when he indicates he really wants it. You'll get better at reading your baby's "Help me" signals as he develops. If you take your cues from him, you won't go wrong.

Pacifiers—Yea or Nay?

Most parents have questions about pacifiers. Do they harm a baby's teeth? Probably not. The best evidence suggests that a pacifier causes no problems if discontinued after teeth start erupting; those that are "orthodontically correct" (the package will say so) are not likely to lead to tooth deformity even when used after this age. Is a pacifier a fake substitute for what a baby really needs? Maybe yes, maybe no.

Most infants have a real need to suck even when they're not hungry. In a study at Simon Fraser University, British Columbia, Canada, Jean Koepke and Pat Barnes (currently at the University of Manitoba, Winnipeg) monitored newborns for two hours before each feeding and one hour afterward over several days. These babies spent nearly half the observed time sucking—a pacifier, their fingers—whether or not milk was forthcoming. It was clearly not related to nourishment. A pacifier also can calm a baby's crying, especially when he's tired. It can help relax a baby to sleep and even protect his sleep somewhat. Studies show that noises and distur-bances that would otherwise wake a baby and lead to crying just make a baby with a pacifier suck more vigorously. These babies may not need a pacifier *per se,* but it seems they do like—and benefit from—something to suck on.

On the other hand, not all babies are candidates for a pacifier. Some reject it in favor of sucking on a thumb, finger, or even clothing. Others show little interest in sucking whatsoever unless it's related to eating. If you like the idea, try a pacifier and let your baby cast the deciding vote.

The safest pacifiers are one-piece, with holes in the mouth guard to ensure that your baby can breathe easily. There are many dif-ferent pacifiers on the market, so you may want to test different types to see which your baby prefers. Babies often have very definite opinions of what type of pacifier—especially which shape of nipple—they prefer. Newborns generally like small, soft pacifiers.

A pacifier can have a purpose, but we recommend it as a last option rather than an immediate answer to every fuss. That fretful whimper could mean your baby is bored or lonely and wants some company and playtime. Remember, too, that you—with your soothing voice and comforting arms—are usually the most welcome solace when your baby cries.

SAFETY REMINDER: Make sure a pacifier is sturdily constructed; there should be no small part that might dislodge—and that your baby might swallow. Also, never hang a pacifier on a ribbon or string around your baby's neck. The ribbon could get caught on something and your baby could become entangled.

Early Crib Toys

Your baby's crib is by far his most vital and versatile piece of equipment. Beyond a secure place to sleep, it's also a gymnasium where he practices large motor skills that unfold over this year, like sitting, pulling up, and even cruising a few steps. When you add appropriate play materials, it's the arena for perfecting all kinds of physical and intellectual skills. And just as important, he can do all these marvelous things all by himself.

THE EARLY MONTHS

A very young baby has little control over his head position; he lies on his back or stomach with his head turned to the side. He also focuses best on objects about eight to twelve inches away.

You should prop toys against the crib side for him to look at. Choose things with bright colors; bold, simple patterns; and (the special favorite) faces. Good candidates are simple pictures printed on safe-to-handle vinyl, stuffed dolls and animals with prominent faces, and colorful toys he'll later handle. Babies like variety, so switch the toys every few days with ones he enjoys in other locations. Make sure everything is safe just in case your baby should get his hands on it.

- no sharp edges
- no long, slender parts that could fit down his throat
- no small parts—bows, eyes, buttons—he might remove and put into his mouth (printed faces on stuffed toys are safest)
- no trailing strings, cords, or ribbons he might get tangled in

Try mounting a large plastic *unbreakable* mirror on the crib side or end. Your baby loves to look at faces, and this "picture" always has some movement—even if only a changing expression. A mirror also probably helps build self-concept. Make sure it's sturdily attached so it can't topple over on your baby. And make sure the mirror is positioned so that it *cannot* reflect sunlight in your baby's eyes.

Add a colorful mobile. Features to look for:

- A music box that plays at least ten minutes if a windup.
- Visual elements that face down, toward your baby. (He'll especially enjoy watching them after about six weeks, when he prefers looking up rather than off to the side.) These should be fairly large with bright colors, bold patterns, and, again, faces. If these hanging eye-catchers are reversible for added variety, that's a plus, too.
- A display arm running from the clamp to the hanging visuals that pivots sideways, so you can swing the mobile out of the way when you change sheets, or want unobstructed access to your baby.

You must remove the mobile when your baby can push up on hands and knees, or pull himself to standing position (usually around five or six months). A mobile that also attaches to the wall will have a longer life. For example, you can hang it over the changing table.

DON'T OVERDO IT

The crib is a splendid playground, but it's still a place to sleep. Don't overdo it. Also, make sure your baby isn't confined to it too often or for too long a time. He needs to explore other environments, and he needs plenty of social contact. Pay attention to your child. He'll let you know when he wants to play elsewhere.

Growing through Play

HELP ME LOOK

Your young baby welcomes help in exploring the world around him. One way is to hold toys near his eyes. Another is to handle him in ways that increase visual alertness. Probably the most effective way is holding him up against your shoulder. A recent study by two researchers at Georgia State University found that in this position a newborn was three times more likely to stare at and follow an object than when lying down or sitting up. Even a crying baby often quiets, opens his eye wide, and looks around when held to your shoulder.

SOUND SEARCHES

From early in life your baby turns to see where a sound comes from. He might not look in the right direction at first, but his accuracy improves with age and experience. When he's lying on his back, facing to one side, try gently shaking a rattle on the opposite side of his head. Once he prefers looking up when on his back (usually around six weeks or so), try shaking a soundmaker way off to the side, or down over his feet, or even up beyond his head.

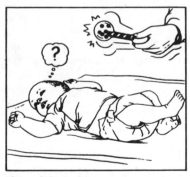

Sound Searches

Research Update:
Early Imitation — Yes or No?

One vital way babies learn is by observing and imitating other people. Thus, many researchers are looking at the age at which this begins. It's not a simple question. Sometimes it's unclear what constitutes true, intentional imitation. Then again, the particular experimenter can bias the baby's behavior positively or negatively. Here's a little insight into some current thinking.

One frequently cited study by Andrew Meltzoff (then at Oxford University, currently at the University of Washington, Seattle) and Keith Moore (University of Washington, Seattle) found that twelve- to twenty-one-day-old infants can imitate specific hand gestures, including moving their fingers sequentially, and facial gestures like opening their mouths and sticking out their tongues. Other researchers are a bit skeptical of this study's findings. In scrutinizing the Meltzoff-Moore data, Moshe Anisfeld of Albert Einstein Medical College found, as he said, "Serious defects in this research beyond the possibility of experimenter bias acknowledged by the authors." Jerome Kagan of Harvard University and Sandra Jacobson of Wayne State University, among other experts, also question both the methodology and the data interpretation. Meltzoff and Moore disagree, citing some convincing flaws in these detractors' own interpretations, and reinforce their original findings with other evidence of imitation found in additional studies they and others conducted.

Louise Hayes and John Watson of the University of California, Berkeley, were unsuccessful when they attempted to replicate the Meltzoff-Moore study. Eugene Abravanel and Ann Sigafoos of George Washington University, in similar experiments with older infants, found some babies partially imitate simple hand gestures, and babies under six weeks—but not older—may imitate an adult sticking out his tongue. So data on early imitation appears inconclusive. Yet, as we said, this is a complicated issue. For fun, you might look for evidence in your own baby.

4

YOUR TWO-MONTH-OLD

Overview

Your two-month-old seems more a baby and much less a newborn. In terms of skills development:

- She has far more control over her body; she can easily raise her head when lying on her stomach and hold it steady when sitting supported in your lap.

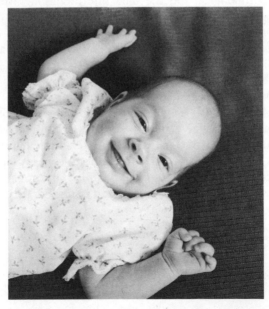

- Her limbs are much more relaxed and she can better control their movements; for instance, she can bat—albeit clumsily at first—at toys that you hold near her fists.
- She is quickly alert when you bring a toy into view, and looks at nearby objects with great concentration.
- She has many more ways of expressing herself vocally: coos and gurgles when you smile at and talk to her; pops, hums, and buzzes when she's excited; dismayed sounding noises when she's temporarily unhappy or frustrated. Thus, she now verbally expresses a wide range of feelings.

All these show that she's more eager and able to explore the world, and more responsive to the objects in her immediate environment.

Your two-month-old is also more responsive to you. She enjoys long periods of eye contact. When you talk to her, she often moves her entire body in synchrony to the rhythms of your language. This is also usually the age when babies start flashing that big, beautiful social smile. Such signs help her express her affection for you—although at this age, they aren't reserved for parents alone. Not incidentally, her smiles and other signs of closeness help reinforce the love you feel for her.

By this age, your baby has begun to make some sense out of all those images that bombard her daily. She might recognize a familiar object—like her bottle—and become especially eager when it comes into view. Studies also show that two-month-olds understand some rudiments about cause and effect, and will work hard to make things happen. In fact, a baby needs to know that she *can* influence her environment. She thrives on response. That's why her favorite toys will soon be those that respond with sound or movement to her now limited ways of handling them. She also loves having parents respond to her—to her cries, to her invitations to play, to her often subtle but never unimportant ways of expressing herself.

Some books for parents assure that by this age most babies establish a routine eating and feeding schedule. This is largely true in terms of eating, but quite often misleading regarding sleep. Many two-month-olds continue to have irregular sleeping patterns. True, they tend to sleep about the same number of hours out of each twenty-four-hour day; but when daytime naps typically occur, and how long each single nap—and the nighttime sleep—lasts can fluctuate greatly from day to day. You can depend on your baby to sleep for about a six-hour stretch at night, but when that stretch occurs is up to her. However, you can manipulate it somewhat. For example, suppose she sleeps from about 7:00 P.M. until about 1:00 A.M., when she awakens for a feeding. Try waking her a little early—say, about midnight—for the middle-of-the-night meal. She might then sleep until morning.

This month, your baby's pediatrician will most likely begin a series of immunizations that he will administer periodically over the next several years. At the two-month checkup, the following are typically given:

- A dose of oral polio vaccine (OPV), to which your baby will have no reaction.
- The first DTP shot (also called a DPT shot). This protects a baby from diphtheria, tetanus, and pertussis (whooping cough). The typical reaction is fussiness and a low-grade fever within four hours, and maybe a sore leg within twelve hours (if the shot was given in the buttock or thigh). According to our pediatric consultant, Dr. Bill Waldman, most reactions to DTP shots are lessened if the child is given acetaminophen, such as children's Tylenol, two hours after the vaccination is administered. Because this injection will likely make your baby uncomfortable for several hours, you should avoid scheduling anything important (hosting a major dinner party, for instance) the day of her checkup. And be sure to inform the pediatrician if your baby's reactions are more severe.

Early Learning: Cause & Effect

Researchers have long been fascinated by *contingency learning*, known more popularly as cause and effect. The eminent developmental psychologist Jean Piaget, writing earlier in this century, believed that babies can't learn even the most elemental cause and effect until at least three months. Piaget relied primarily on observations of how babies typically interact with objects. But more recent researchers argue that babies are able to learn contingencies at earlier ages *if the conditions are right*. To make the conditions right, the experimenter needs to create a situation that a young baby—with her very limited physical abilities—can control.

NEW EXPERIMENTAL METHODS

In two different sets of experiments, the toy used was a mobile redesigned so that a very young baby could make it move. John Watson and his colleagues at the University of California, Berkeley, attached a mobile to a pressure-sensitive pillow that could be placed under the baby's head. When a baby turned her head, the mobile moved. Then the researchers tested two groups of infants. One group was given this special mobile. The other group was tested with conventional mobiles they could look at but not control. Babies as young as two months learned to activate the mobile; that is, when the mobile stopped, the baby deliberately turned her head to start it again. In a similar experiment using another specially designed mobile, Eleanor Linde and Carolyn Rovee-Collier (Rutgers University) and Barbara Morrongiello (University of Western Ontario), also found that two-month-olds deliberately controlled the toy's motion. Such learning wasn't limited to the initial experiment, either. These babies remembered how to activate the special mobile when retested up to two weeks later.

Watson and his colleagues learned something else, too. The babies they tested cooed and smiled more often at this special mobile than the other babies did at their conventional mobile. Merely being familiar with the toy wasn't the reason, because both groups were equally familiar with their respective mobiles. Rather, being able to control the mobile inspired these added signals of pleasure. It appears that very young babies not only can *learn* the contingency relationship built into this special mobile, but they also *enjoy* this feeling of controlling their own environment.

MORE EVIDENCE

There's other evidence that young babies can learn very simple cause-and-effect relationships. For examples, different sets of studies confirm that a six-week-old whose pacifier is connected to a focus control will suck hard to bring a blurry picture into clear focus. She increases her sucking when the picture begins to fade, suggesting that she realizes a connection between sucking and picture quality.

In another study, two- and three-month-olds learned to illuminate a light by turning their heads to the left. After several trials, the infants tired of this particular contingency and ceased turning their heads. But when a new cause-and-effect relationship was

introduced—turning the head to the right to illuminate the light—
the head turnings increased.

JUST THE BEGINNING

Such experiments show that a very young baby can learn how to
cause an event. But she still has a lot to learn about cause and effect.
One important step is truly understanding that she is causing the
effect.

Most experts believe that the two-month-old probably doesn't
realize that *she* is controlling the mobile's movement in the studies
described earlier. There's supporting evidence in Watson's experiment. The researchers wondered whether the babies who learned
to control the mobile would be perplexed or frustrated if they no
longer had such power, so in some trials the sensor was turned off.
What happened? The babies showed no surprise or sense of defeat.
It appears that they were motivated by the pleasure of watching the
mobile turn as well as by the act of learning how to make it move,
not by the expectation of a reward (movement) for their behavior
(head turning). Had they truly understood cause and effect, they
would have been plenty surprised! According to Piaget, a baby
begins realizing that she herself controls the event at around four or
five months.

Even so, a young baby obviously enjoys learning and playing.
Toys that *respond* when she handles them—by making sounds and
moving in interesting ways—will be favorites for several months
yet. Batting games are especially appropriate for the two-month-
old, as we suggest later in this chapter.

THE MORE WE LEARN

This brief overview can't touch on all the details of learning
contingency relationships. Even if it did, chances are it would soon
be obsolete. Through new experiments, often involving up-to-the-
minute technology, we're discovering more and more surprising
facets of early learning. Suffice it to say, learning is ongoing at
birth, and babies truly are a lot smarter than we generally give them
credit for being.

The Social Smile

Parents usually look for any sign that their baby not only recognizes
them, but also that she really *likes* them. In their eyes, nothing

demonstrates this affection so vividly as a smile. But early smiles may be deceptive.

FIRST SMILES VS SOCIAL SMILES

Researchers in infant behavior agree that first smiles are not signals of loving affection. A newborn often smiles at anything—or nothing. You probably noticed early smiles most often when your baby was drowsy or sleeping fitfully. These are thought to be spontaneous reactions of her young nervous system, and not the result of "gas," as many people believe. In our own work, we've also found that very young babies sometimes smile during play when they're very relaxed. Such smiles can be prompted by any caregiver, not just parents. Newborns also smile when the room is quiet and no one is handling them. Even deaf and blind babies smile.

Between about six and about eight weeks, though, these first smiles are replaced by another, more social sign of responsiveness. At some point when you and your baby are staring into one another's eyes, she breaks into a big, beautiful, toothless grin. This new smile is quite different—it's broader, it comes when she's awake and alert, and it's clearly directed at you. This social smile, however, is still not an unmistakable sign of special love for parents, even though you might wish to interpret it as such. The two-month-old also smiles at strangers who look into her eyes. She may even smile at large black dots on a light background, or at a drawing of a face showing only eyes and the facial outline. But the first social smiles are a beginning, and soon your baby smiles most readily, and most broadly, at the people she loves best.

A REAL RELATIONSHIP

Even if social smiles aren't reserved just for parents, they do play a large role in the parent-baby relationship. Eye contact and smiling are part of any meaningful love affair. Many parents feel that a real two-way relationship with their baby begins when she responds in these ways. Contrary to the popular cliché, not all parents love their baby at birth. In one study of fifty-four first-time mothers, only half had positive feelings about the baby right away, and only seven described these feelings as love. Many had initial feelings of "distance" and unfamiliarity, which lasted a month or two. Interestingly, it was the baby's ability to "see" her mother and respond by smiling that most often triggered her feelings of love—feelings that seemed to have something to do with being recognized and appreciated in a highly personal and intimate way. Even if these mothers might have misinterpreted the sign, there's no question of its power. Your baby's smiles do prompt smiles of your own, too, and this back and forth affection strengthens the unfolding parent-baby bond.

So go ahead and enjoy these social smiles, even if they aren't reserved just for you. They make you feel good, and your response makes your baby feel good. They will soon become special. In fact, smiles will light up her whole face the moment your eyes meet— and these will be signs of her special affection. Remember, though, that some babies naturally smile more easily and readily than others. If your baby rarely smiles, it assuredly doesn't mean that she doesn't love you.

SMILE-PRODUCING HINTS

· When your baby is comfortable and relaxed, but alert, look into one another's eyes, talk to her gently in a high-pitched voice, and smile.

· Try making an exaggerated "surprise" face: Open your eyes wide, raise your eyebrows, and say "oooohhh" in a high-pitched voice. You might also bob your head.

· When you and your baby play together, you'll notice that she builds toward little peaks of excitement, after which she relaxes slightly and pauses to study you. Often she releases that final burst of energy in a smile. If you pause while she reaches the crescendo, rather than continue to talk and stimulate her, chances are you'll see that smile.

Be Sensitive to Signals

Anytime you and your baby play together, whether you're trying to prompt a smile or to interest her in a toy you're holding, it's possible to try too hard. You should always be sensitive to the signals she gives that she's had enough for the moment. For instance, here's a common scene. You and your baby are giggling and "talking" to one another, both delighting in this pleasant game. She smiles and gurgles and waves her arms as she stares into your eyes. Suddenly, her behavior changes. She yawns and turns away. Her sounds subside. She may look serious or grimace. She twists her body away as you try to reengage her in play. When this happens, you shouldn't feel put off. This is your baby's way of letting you know she needs a break from the pleasures of play.

No one can be absolutely certain why babies need to take frequent "time-outs" this way, but experts present some theories. One is that your baby needs this quiet time to absorb some new experience or information. Another is that your baby has reached a peak of excitement, and uses this hiatus to calm herself down before entering another upward-surging play episode. One thing's for sure: In a pleasant play setting, turning away is rarely a form of rejection. It's much more likely a temporary rest period. Such breaks are a signal that you, too, should take it easy for a moment. Rather than trying to restart play yourself, pause and wait for your baby to establish contact once again.

You should also be sensitive to her behavior when she plays with toys. If she refuses to look at or twists her head away from that object you wave so enticingly in front of her eyes, continued waving won't make her like it any better. In fact, it could upset her. On the other hand, if she does appear to enjoy something, don't remove it in your haste to present another one for her enjoyment. Rather, let her explore it—now mostly with her eyes, but later with hands as well—as long as she demonstrates the desire.

It all comes down to being sensitive to your baby's signals. They're the way she tells you what she likes, what she wants to do, and when she wants to stop. Your sensitivity prevents turning fun into frustration.

Growing through Play

DEVELOPING HEAD CONTROL

A young baby's head is too heavy for her neck and back muscles to support, so you, too, should support it when you lift and hold her. This prevents sudden or extreme stretching and twisting of the neck muscles. But you needn't treat her too delicately; she's really pretty tough even at the earliest ages. She likewise needs less help as she gains control over her head position. When carried, for example, a six-week-old can usually hold her head clear of your shoulder for a few minutes. Still, it's best to avoid sudden movements that might cause her to lose her balance. By eight or so weeks, a baby can hold her head steady when sitting supported in your lap. A three-month-old lifts her head quite well when lying on her stomach, supporting her weight on her forearms and later her outstretched hands.

Developing this head control lets your baby better look at things that interest her, and it prepares the way for sitting up. Help your two-month-old build her strength with these activities:

- Frequently hold her up to your shoulder so she can look around.
- Place her on her stomach in different settings—the living room floor, your bed—so she has new and interesting things to look at. Always stay close by if she's on a raised surface.
- When she's lying on her stomach, dangle a favorite toy a few inches in front of her. Then raise it slowly while encouraging her to push up, up on her arms to keep the toy in view.

BATTING PRACTICE

Your two-month-old delights in batting at simple objects that dangle near her fists. It's good eye-hand coordination practice, and an important step toward reaching and grasping with accuracy, which will develop over the next several months. Good batting toys include anything that is colorful (to attract your baby's attention), is fairly light, is large enough to be an easy target, and that makes sounds when hit.

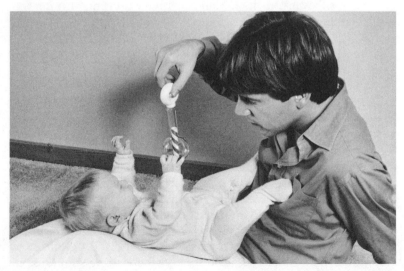

Batting Practice

· Lie your baby on her back, dangle a toy just a few inches above her hands, and encourage her to hit it. If she has trouble getting started, tap it against her fists a few times.
· When she's more skillful, hold the toy further away. She might also like to bat toys when sitting in your lap, with a toy out in front of rather than over her.

SAFETY NOTE: If you dangle the batting toy from a piece of string or similar material, make sure the string is no longer than six inches. Also, remove the string before handing your baby the toy to play with by herself. Otherwise, she might get tangled in it.

CLOSER LOOKS

Your two- or three-month-old looks at objects with great concentration, often for long periods of time, so hold up colorful, fascinating things for her to explore visually. Notice how she quickly becomes alert when you bring a toy into view; she might even squirm or change position or raise her hands—all ways that she spells out interest. Chances are she'll be especially delighted when spotting a favorite object, like her feeding bottle, because she is now beginning to recognize familiar things.

SOUND REACTION

Most babies react differently to different sounds. An infant usually changes her facial expression or activity (such as quieting down if she was moving) when she hears a sudden loud sound. A tea kettle's whistle or similar high-pitched sound may make her freeze or cry. High-pitched sounds like a police or fire engine siren make *us* freeze, too. For many mammals, these piercing-type sounds are warning calls that cause an instinctive alarm reaction. (If you think your baby isn't hearing loud and high-pitched sounds, discuss this with her pediatrician.) Just as you give your baby treats for her eyes, offer some for her ears. Research suggests that vocal and musical sounds are favorites. Your baby loves listening to musical toys like a stuffed animal or mobile with a music box—and especially to your singing.

ADDED VOCAL EXPRESSION

During this month, your baby adds lots of new sounds to her vocal repertoire. She's likely to coo and gurgle when you smile at and talk to her; make little pops, hums, and buzzes when she's excited; and even offer dismayed sounding noises when, for instance, you take away a favorite toy. Now she expresses a wide range of feelings: interest, amusement, excitement, surprise, and affection. Those coos and gurgles will make you feel even closer to her. And when you touch and talk to her, she'll "talk" to you even more.

Research Update:
Adoption and Attachment

With all the attention given to the importance of bonding at or near birth, nonbiological parents often understandably worry about their relationship with their adopted baby. A study by Leslie Singer, David Brodzinsky, Douglas Ramsay (Rutgers University), Mary Steir (University of North Carolina, Chapel Hill), and Everett Waters (State University of New York at Stony Brook) might put them at ease. They observed fifty-four mother-toddler pairs when the child was between thirteen and eighteen months of age. Half the subjects were not adopted, the other half had been adopted within a few months of birth. These researchers found no difference in mother-toddler attachment between the two groups.

5

YOUR THREE-MONTH-OLD

Overview

Babies in general have an inborn curiosity and drive to learn about the world surrounding them. Their unfolding skills let them act upon this drive, and during this month you'll see big steps in your baby's learning through play. Most likely:

· He visually examines tiny objects and parts of toys, such as beads within a transparent rattle.
· He begins to grasp things voluntarily rather than by reflex, and reaches out to secure things that are nearby.
· He explores parts of his own body, especially hands and feet.

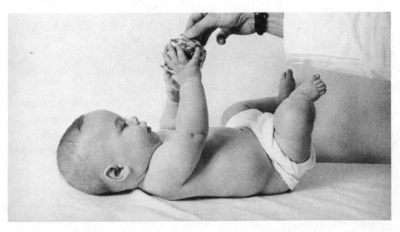

As with his arms, your baby is gaining better control over his leg movements, and soon delights in kicking. You can enjoy and enhance these arm and leg skills with the games included in "Growing through Play."

Toys now become an increasingly vital part of your baby's learning; they're the tools that let him practice emerging skills, and they set foundations for discovering the properties of objects in the world and how objects "work." Physical skills open up opportunities that can be hazardous as well, so you need to be increasingly vigilant about potentially dangerous objects that are within your baby's reach.

Many experts believe that by this age, if not before, your baby can see many of the same colors you can, and naturally differentiates among the main colors—red, blue, green, and yellow, and probably many other colors. He also favors bright shades over duller ones, and seems particularly drawn to red and blue. So make sure his toys are colorful.

Your three-month-old is more expressive in his enjoyment of the world and more responsive to the people around him. He makes many more sounds than before—chuckles and laughs as well as coos and gurgles. He also begins talking longer and longer when looking at interesting things, or when you two play together. You'll likely hear "ah," "ya," and other vowel sounds, which are made with the throat.

He is also better at differentiating among basic speech sounds others make when talking to him; this discrimination is a step toward making such sounds himself. These new communication abilities allow you and him to enjoy simple two-way "conversations." He also shows his growing attachment to you by becoming much more relaxed and confident in your company than when he is with less familiar people, and by babbling and cooing much more readily toward you than at less familiar people.

One more thing. . . . If your baby was that one out of every five babies who has colic, this is probably the month when, almost by magic, that cyclical late afternoon/early evening wailing will most likely stop. Happy day!

Big Steps in Reaching & Grasping

Your newborn can barely explore manually. His hands are often curled or fisted; he automatically grasps any object you press against his palm. A three-month-old's hands, though, are usually open, and that early reflex grasp is giving way to a voluntary one. During this transition period, he holds objects less securely and for shorter periods than in his earliest months. Don't worry. This is a step forward, not backward. With this voluntary grasp—which is clumsy at first but improves steadily throughout the remainder of this year—he now can hold on to things that he wants, not merely those placed in his hands. This is a leap forward in his ability to explore his world actively. Voluntary grasping gives him great pleasure, so make sure your baby has appropriate objects on which to practice.

BEGINNING TO REACH WITH ACCURACY

At first you'll still have to hand your baby toys to grasp. But at some point during this month, he makes another great stride: He begins to reach for nearby objects by himself.

The forerunners of this *eye-hand coordination* skill lie in the simple batting games he enjoyed last month. The big difference now is that he reaches with open hands rather than fists, and that he grasps the toy you hold out so enticingly. To reach and grasp is actually quite a complicated process, involving skills and computations that adults, with their well-developed eye-hand coordination, take for granted. To be successful, your baby must:

- understand that his hands are tools for acquiring and exploring objects;
- be able to orient his hands so that they can take hold of the object he's reaching for; and
- judge whether or not the object he wants is actually within his reach.

He has been developing these first two skills with all the practice he has had holding objects. The final one grows out of his increasing control over his arm muscles and his growing ability to judge distance. A study by Albert Yonas, at the University of Minnesota, found that three-month-olds are more likely to try for objects that are actually within their reach rather than those too far away. Apparently, they are able to judge distance and discriminate between what is and what is not possible to reach.

The ability to reach for and grasp things develops slowly. Many of your baby's early reaching efforts will be clumsy, as he miscalculates the distance between himself and the toy. Sometimes, too, his fingers won't do exactly what he wants them to. He'll refine his skills with lots of practice—practice that you can give him through reaching games.

- Choose toys that catch his eye with bright colors or shiny coatings that reflect light. Make sure they have parts small or slender enough to fit easily into his hand, but no separate parts small enough for him to put entirely into his mouth.
- At this age, your baby reaches with both arms simultaneously, and has greatest success when lying on his back. So hold toys directly above his chest, close enough to ensure easy grasping. As his skill grows, he'll also enjoy reaching games when sitting on your lap or in his infant seat. Within a month or two, he'll start reaching with one hand only.

Developing eye-hand coordination is one of your baby's major accomplishments. Not only does it enable him to explore actively; it's also fundamental to thousands of other skills he'll need throughout life, from being able to turn on a light switch to hitting a tennis ball with a racquet. It's not surprising that he begins early—he has a lot to learn. And with your help, he'll particularly enjoy the process.

Why Babies Need Toys

Objects play an impressive role in your baby's development, whether they're toys designed specifically for young children or kitchen gadgets that double as playthings. For one thing, they occupy a lot of his time—and will continue to do so increasingly throughout his early years. For another, toys offer a rich source of stimulation that helps develop skills.

It's obvious that toys aid a baby's skills such as batting, reaching, grasping (several different ways), shaking, pulling, stretching, squeezing, and throwing. Mastering these and other physical abilities requires *practice*, and practice requires *objects* that a baby can handle safely and easily. Less apparent is the role toys play in developing a baby's social skills. As play specialist Catherine Garvey of the University of Maine points out, toys provide opportunities for babies to play with other people. Babies often extend toys as invitations for interaction—to other babies as well as to adults. The rich social exchanges that follow these invitations enhance many areas of development.

It also appears that toys can encourage language and communication. Many researchers have noted that babies tend to coo and babble at toys even when parents aren't around. In a more formal study, Roger Bakeman and Lauren Adamson at Georgia State University observed twenty-eight parent-child pairs over a series of several months, noting among other things the ways a baby engaged and conversed with his mother. As expected, a baby used more gestures and words when his mother was attentive rather than inattentive. But unexpectedly, these toddlers used words and gestures most often when mother and child were playing with a toy, particularly when the child was around fifteen months.

TOYS AND INTELLECTUAL SKILLS

Children learn primarily by direct physical experience of the world around them. They are much more likely to figure things out with their hands than in their heads alone. And the younger the child, the more this is true. Toys are the tools that lead to learning. By handling objects—shaking them, fitting them together, counting them, stacking them on top of one another, hiding and finding them—a baby comes to understand concepts like cause and effect, shape, spatial relationship, number, and object permanence.

Many researchers have examined which factors in the home environment appear to benefit cognitive development. In reviewing five important studies, Allen Gottfried (California State University, Fullerton) and Adele Gottfried (California State University, Northridge) found that whatever the child's age—be it three months or two years—the factors that correlated most highly with superior intellectual "test" scores were _maternal involvement_ and _play materials._ The _play materials_ scale meant that the home had several toys that encouraged pulling, pushing, eye-hand coordination, fitting, building, and other skills; and that the child had ready and easy access to these toys. In other words, babies living in homes where there was a variety of highly responsive play materials, and who had plenty of opportunities to play with these toys, tended to score higher on developmental tests than babies living in less stimulating environments.

All your baby's environments are filled with objects, and probably each object has at least some teaching potential. But researchers are finding that some objects have much more built-in value than others. Drs. Leon Yarrow, Judith Rubenstein, and Frank Pedersen at the National Institute of Health found that, in addition to a stimulating environment, a child also benefits from playing with individual toys that are complex enough to provide lots of information and challenge in and of themselves. A complex toy incorporates:

- a variety of colors
- many different visual patterns
- opportunities for different tactile sensations
- a number of shapes and contours
- responsiveness

Indeed, highly responsive toys—toys that make sounds, change shape, and move in interesting ways when a baby handles them—are especially valuable. Responsiveness is self-reinforcing. When a toy responds to a baby's play, it encourages him to continue playing. This repeated practice leads, over time, to mastering skills. Mastery builds confidence, so the baby is encouraged to practice other skills. And the cycle goes on. In other words:

Cycle of Play

MATCHING TOYS TO SKILLS

Having a variety of highly responsive toys certainly holds a baby in good stead, but too much isn't necessarily a good thing. Toys should ideally be matched to a baby's skill level. They should offer him at least one bit of immediate success, so that he's encouraged to continue playing. Yet they should challenge his newly unfolding skills, so that he doesn't tire of them quickly. If a toy is too advanced for your baby right now, he's less likely to play with it; if he does, he's apt to become frustrated. You need to be aware of your baby's developmental level, so that you can help match playthings to his skills stage. We give you guidelines throughout this book. You also should keep an eye toward not overdoing it. Too many toys at once will confuse your baby. Give him only a few at a time. And make sure that his crib or playpen isn't so overloaded that he seems bewildered by the choice of what to do next.

YOUR ROLE

Studies like those mentioned here suggest that a baby benefits substantially from playing with objects that let him practice emerging skills and that respond to his ways of playing. Naturally, he needs you, too, as a toy provider, teacher, friend, and playmate.

You'll always be a favorite "toy" as well, since parents are by far the most responsive objects in a baby's new world—as well as the most loving ones.

Babies and Toy Safety

Good rules to remember!

1. Toys must be safe for mouthing. Make sure each one is nontoxic, has a durable finish, and is too big to fit completely into your baby's mouth. Also, every part of a toy should be so large that it can't fit down your baby's throat to block his air passage.

2. Toys must be free of sharp points and edges, small holes that can entrap a finger, trailing strings and ribbons a baby might get tangled in, and any potential pinch points.

3. Beware of small parts that your baby might pry off a toy and try to swallow. The soundmaker in a squeak toy should be internal or so strongly attached that *you* cannot possibly pick it out. Make sure soft toys are free of buttons, bows, or eyes your baby might pull off. For this age, embroidered or printed faces are safest.

4. To prevent possible entanglement injury, remove any hanging toy from the crib when your baby begins to push up on hands and knees—usually around five months. Also remove mobiles at this age. Most have hanging elements that are not safe for a baby to handle, and he might get caught in the suspension arm.

5. Never hang toys (or even a pacifier) on a string or ribbon around your baby's neck. He might become entangled in the string or get it caught on something and suffocate.

6. Remember that toys designed for older children may be unsafe for your baby!

New Safety Needs

You might reasonably have assumed up until now that your baby would stay wherever you put him if you had to leave the room for a minute. That's no longer true. Your three-month-old's developmental strides, especially with regard to mobility and eye-hand coordination, place him in a newly vulnerable position. His neck, back, and limbs are becoming stronger. He may now be able to arch out of his infant seat—or topple it and himself in an attempt. He may soon be able to move forward by pushing up on arms and "dragging" himself along. Any day he might surprise you by rolling over. You need to pay particular heed to his safety.

- Always keep the crib sides locked into the upright position. You might also lower the mattress a notch.
- Be sure you strap him into his infant seat. Be careful never to place his seat near the edge of the kitchen counter or table top or other off-the-floor surface. With all his wiggling, he could easily topple his seat. And *never* leave him in his seat on a raised surface if you leave the room.
- *Never* leave your baby alone on a sofa, changing table, or other fairly narrow raised surface, whatever his age. He just might scoot around—and over the edge. Ignore the ringing telephone or buzzing doorbell; or take your baby *with* you to answer these calls. (It almost goes without saying that you must *never ever* leave him alone when he's in his bath, either.)
- Make sure you always strap your baby securely into his stroller (and, of course, car seat).

Now that your baby is beginning to reach for objects, you have to be doubly careful of things that are nearby. For example:

- If he's sitting on your lap near a table, make sure there are no hot beverages he might suddenly reach for and spill, and no unsafe objects he might grab and pop into his mouth. Sharp things could cut him; small ones might make him choke.
- When you place your baby on the floor, likewise make sure his immediate surroundings are free of small or otherwise dangerous objects.
- Hinges and other hardware on his equipment (stroller, infant seat, etc.) must be free of pinch-points and sharp edges.

In general, never underestimate your baby's skills, particularly when safety is an issue. If you stay one step ahead of his developmental strides, you'll be in a good position to anticipate situations that might prove threatening.

Growing through Play

KICKING FUN

As with his arms, your baby is gaining better control over his leg movements, and soon delights in kicking. Add some fun with these two games.

1. Hold your hands against the bottom of his feet and let him kick against them. He'll like this gentle resistance.

2. Hold over his feet toys that rattle or jingle, so that his kicks produce exciting sound and movement. Some ideas:

· Good-sized rattles. Dangle these from your fingers.
· A small stuffed animal that has a bell inside. Hold it by the tail or an ear.
· You can make a big kicker target by dropping a rattle into an empty cardboard container, like a cereal or cracker box. Hold the box by one of the top flaps so that it swings freely when your baby makes contact. Be sure the box has no crumbs!

SAFETY NOTE: Some books suggest stringing a kicking toy across the crib. We don't like this idea; it's possible that your baby could get tangled in the toy.

PLAYING WITH HANDS AND FEET

Babies are constant explorers. They want to look at, touch, and handle all the interesting things near them. So hands and feet naturally become favorite objects for exploration; after all, they're always close by and they move about in the most fascinating ways!

When a baby first begins to explore these body parts, he probably regards them as just another group of objects. He doesn't seem to understand that they are attached to him. When hands and feet leave his view, he makes no effort to see where they have gone and doesn't try to bring them back into view. Over time, though, he begins to understand that he can control the comings and goings of his hands and feet. He drops them out of view, brings them back, makes them disappear again, and even looks for an arm that has moved out of sight. You can help him understand what these mysterious objects are by talking about them as he plays—"That's your hand, Stephen."

PLAY NOTE: Some books recommend giving your baby brightly colored mittens or socks to wear, saying that these attract his attention to his hands and feet. The idea might be nice, but there's no proof that they increase a baby's interest in those body parts. Some toy companies make rattle- or bell-type toys that strap onto wrist or ankle. If you use them, be sure to pay careful attention to your baby's reaction. After a while, he might no longer enjoy having such toys fastened to his limbs, yet he can't voluntarily get rid of them.

MORE TO LOOK AT

Now that your baby has better visual acuity, he likely enjoys looking at tiny objects, such as beads inside a clear rattle. Hold things close for him to explore.

SAFETY NOTE: To prevent possible choking, never leave within your baby's reach objects that are small enough to fit into his mouth.

HOUSE TOURS

You might also take your baby on simple tours around your house. As you carry him from room to room, hold him so he can look at pictures, hangings, and photographs on the wall; a carving on top of the banister; plants; knickknacks on dresser and bookcase; candlesticks on the mantelpiece; clocks; and the like. Again, talk about these eye-catchers. And be sure to stop at every mirror.

IDEA! Make a house tour a part of some other ritual. For instance, it could be a lovely lead-up to bath time.

SOUND GAMES

At about three months, your baby begins talking longer and longer when looking at interesting things, or when you two play together. He'll likely make "ah," "ya," and other vowel sounds. This cooing-type talking will be used differently with objects and people. He often talks to his toys without pausing, as if he knows not to expect a response. Yet, when he "talks" with you, your baby frequently pauses to watch your movements and facial expressions, and to listen to your response. It's a sign of his increasing understanding! So be sure to take time for face-to-face talking play. When your baby makes a sound, repeat it (as best you can) right back to him. Soon he'll start answering back, and you can keep this conversation going for long periods.

Research Update:
More on Early Attachment

As we reported in earlier chapters, very young babies are able to discern their mothers from other women, and usually smile most readily and for longer periods at parents than at strangers. There's more evidence of parental preference at this age. By the end of this month a baby will babble and coo much more readily toward his parents than at less familiar people. In a study at The Johns Hopkins University, Donelda Stayton (Johns Hopkins), Mary Ainsworth (University of Virginia), and Mary Main (University of California, Berkeley) observed that babies this age also appeared unusually free and confident when sitting on their mothers' laps. They likewise eagerly explored their mothers' faces, clothing, and hair. On unfamiliar laps, babies were much more restrained, often barely touching the stranger.

Since you most likely add to your baby's confidence, be sure to stay close when he's introduced to a new person or potentially troubling situation. Also, since he can now reach with some accuracy, remove your glasses so that he can explore your face freely.

HINT: Many mothers we know switch from pierced earrings to clip-ons for the next several months. A baby can give a nasty yank!

6

YOUR FOUR-MONTH-OLD

Overview

Your four-month-old is generally much more active and alert than when younger. She sleeps less and at somewhat routine times. She probably has settled into two naps—one in the morning and a longer one in the afternoon. If she's like the sixteen babies whose parents we surveyed, she's awake an average of eleven hours out of twenty-four every day. (Remember, though, this is

truly an average; one mother of a four-month-old told us that her baby is awake only about seven hours a day, another with a baby the same age says hers is awake sixteen to eighteen hours.) It's not unusual for your baby to begin the day crowing enthusiastically; and once she's up, she's considerably more tuned in to her environment. Professionals who work with infants have also noticed this new ebullience. "Four and five months are a kind of golden age for researchers in infant perception and cognition," explains Marc Bornstein, Head of Child and Family Research at the National Institute of Child Health and Human Development. "By this time, babies are able to sit in an infant seat on their own, they're alert and easily attracted to new sights and sounds, and they don't yet mind being left by themselves the way older babies do."

The typical four-month-old is well equipped for all sorts of exploration. She sees many colors. She's alert to sounds, and searches rapidly and correctly for sounds made out of her sight. When placed on her stomach, she can easily lift her torso to a forty-five degree angle, supporting herself on her arms, and survey her surroundings. She can focus fairly well at a variety of distances, and enjoys watching action in all parts of the room. She can reach easily for nearby toys with one hand, rather than both, if she chooses, and can just as easily bring them to her mouth to explore them more thoroughly. Soon she'll begin to roll from her back over onto her stomach—or stomach to back. This ability lets her better control her own opportunities for exploring—she can get herself into a better position for examining her environment, and she can roll to get closer to things she wants to see or handle.

Your four-month-old is also quite a sociable being. She has a larger repertoire of sounds that express her needs and feelings: squeals, gasps, and gurgles of delight. Sometimes she screeches just to hear herself—delighting in her ability to be so demonstrative. Likewise, her face is more animated, and it gives undeniable clues to her mood. She is better at reading your facial expressions as well. The four-month-old makes great strides in her language development. She engages in lengthier conversations than before, and pulls her own weight when the two of you talk together.

What about intellectual strides? Child development expert Jean Piaget, observed that during this month your baby is more aware of how she influences the world, and eagerly repeats actions that produce an effect on the environment. The four-month-old who, sitting in your lap at a table, hits a rattle against the tabletop, will notice the resulting noise, and will reproduce it again, and again, and again. She links some sounds correctly with the objects that make them. She knows the sound her favorite rattle makes; in fact, she'd be rather surprised if it were suddenly to ring like a bell. She is getting better at attaching voices to the appropriate people, too.

At this month's checkup, your baby will most likely receive her second series of immunizations. These are the same as she received during her two-month checkup:

- A dose of oral polio vaccine (OPV); this causes no reaction.
- The second DTP (diptheria-tetanus-pertussis) shot. As before, you can expect fussiness and a low-grade fever within four hours. If the shot was given in the thigh, your baby may have a sore leg within twelve hours. These reactions are lessened if your baby is given acetaminophen like children's Tylenol two hours after the vaccination is administered.

NOTE: A few babies may have more severe reactions to the DTP shot. Be sure to inform the pediatrician if your baby does.

All these developments bring both new excitement and new challenges for parents. You have to be even more mindful of her safety—remember that she'll put almost every object she grasps into her mouth. She can now roll closer to possible danger. Our interviews with parents reveal that, since their baby is so active, this is the age they often consider joining a swimming class or giving their baby a workout in a community pool. Baby swims aren't without risk, however; see the "Research Update."

Starting Solids

There's no magic "day" when you should start solids. Your baby's doctor will advise you, since he or she knows your baby best. However, this is the month when many doctors and parents start thinking about solids—if not actually introducing them.

THE PHASES OF FEEDING

A baby's feeding development in this first year has three overlapping phases.

First is the nursing period, which starts at birth and continues through about four to six months. During this phase, your baby's nutritional needs are met exclusively by formula or breastmilk (and any supplements your baby's doctor prescribes). Developmentally, she isn't ready for solids. She usually gags on non-liquids because of an extrusion reflex she is born with; this reflex helps prevent her choking should an object get too far into her mouth. She also is unable to move solid foods from the front to the rear of her mouth for swallowing. In addition, her kidneys and intestinal tract are best equipped to digest the proportions of fat, protein, and carbohydrates found in formula or breastmilk.

Between four and six months, a baby enters a transitional period of feeding, during which nursing is supplemented by solids. Your baby can now handle solids because:

- She is losing the extrusion reflex.
- Her more mature digestive system can better handle solids.
- She's becoming able to swallow solids by moving them from the front to the rear of her mouth with her tongue.
- She's beginning to drool; this excess saliva aids in swallowing.

Many doctors and the American Academy of Pediatrics recommend waiting until about five or even six months before introducing solids. It's not until this age that a baby becomes able to indicate when she wants more food and when she has had enough. She exhibits desire by leaning forward and opening her mouth to take another bite. She lets you know she has had enough by leaning away or turning her head. Until a baby has these self-regulating skills, feeding her solid foods may represent a type of force-feeding.

The final phase of feeding takes place during the last quarter of this year. At that age your baby learns to chew—first by moving her jaws up and down, later by rotating her mouth somewhat. This is the time when a majority of her nutritional needs are met by solid food, and when you can introduce food that hasn't been completely pureed. But ask the pediatrician's advice before introducing food that has lumps, since every baby develops at an individual rate.

During toddlerhood, your child will eat what is essentially an "adult" diet. However, you'll need to cut foods into small bite-sized portions so that she doesn't choke. Also, food should be seasoned more mildly than adults usually prefer.

Some parents try to rush introducing solids because they have heard that this helps a baby sleep through the night. There is no strong evidence of a correlation between solids and longer sleeping. A baby sleeps through the night only when her stomach can hold enough to reduce the pressing need for more frequent feedings. This happens naturally as she matures, whether or not she is on solids. And coincidentally, this usually occurs around six months.

INTRODUCING SOLIDS

Begin by offering one new single-ingredient food (rather than a mixed dinner) each week or so. This method lets you check to see whether your baby has a reaction to a particular food. Skin rash, vomiting, diarrhea, cramps, excessive gas, and irritability are common symptoms of a food intolerance or allergy. Don't be angry or discouraged if your baby rejects solids at first. Some babies take longer than others to accept new experiences—including new foods. Also, your baby may dislike a certain food, so try another one instead. If she continues rejecting all solids, maybe she's not quite ready to start them. Try again in a few weeks. However, if she continues rejecting solids after six months or so, you should discuss this with her doctor, since formula or breastmilk alone probably doesn't supply all the nutrients she needs at this age.

Some special tips:

- Use a small spoon at first, and hold it a little inside your baby's lips so that she can suck in the food. If you place the food on her tongue initially, she probably won't know that she's supposed to swallow it—and may just let it dribble back out of her mouth. If your baby has trouble managing the spoon, let her suck the food off your otherwise clean finger the first few times.
- When your baby is ravenous, such as at the first meal of the day, she likely won't want to take the time with spoons and solids. Nurse or bottlefeed her first to reduce the most pressing hunger pangs, then introduce a spoon of solids.
- For the first few "solids" meals, try an alternating approach. Start off with breast or bottle, switch to some solids, go back to breast or bottle, then more solids. Remember that at this age, most of her nutrition still comes from breast milk or formula.
- Since your baby's saliva causes food to break down, do not feed her directly from a jar, because if she doesn't finish the entire portion you will have to discard the remainder (her saliva would be transferred to the jar via the feeding spoon).

Rather, put food into a bowl. Always discard the uneaten portion left in the bowl, too.

FIRST FOODS

The typical first solid food is an iron-fortified single-grain cereal (usually rice) mixed with formula or breast milk. You should experiment with the proportion of liquid to solid to see which consistency your baby prefers. Many pediatricians suggest trying pureed fruits and vegetables next. Favorites include peaches, applesauce, peas, sweet potatoes, and squash. Again, always wait about a week between each new food to determine your baby's possible intolerance. Pureed meats are probably best introduced between seven and ten months, when your baby is better able to handle their high protein content. Chicken and turkey are usually offered first, since they have less fat than beef and pork (and thus are easier for baby to digest). If the doctor agrees your baby should have meat, but your baby shuns it, mix the pureed meat with another food your baby loves. Foods to avoid because many babies are allergic to them or don't tolerate them well at this age include tomatoes, citrus (including orange juice), fish, berries, egg whites, and spinach. Check with the pediatrician regarding when to add dairy products such as yogurt and cottage cheese, because these can cause allergic reactions, and because of the high protein content. Starting around eight or nine months, you might add crackers and foods with small lumps instead of totally pureed ones, so that your baby can practice chewing. However, to minimize the chance of choking, be sure that all solids introduced before twelve months require only minimal chewing, and that lumps are easily crushed between her gums.

Remember, though, that these are merely guidelines. Always discuss your baby's diet with her doctor. Also, once your baby starts solids, you'll need to reduce her intake of breastmilk or formula to guard against overfeeding her. Again, ask her doctor's advice.

Helping Language Grow: The Early Months

The ability to speak is one of the greatest gifts and most powerful tools of humankind. Most things we do, alone and with others, involve words. Your baby will say *her* first words sometime after her first birthday, but the process of learning to talk begins much earlier. In fact, you've been actively involved in teaching your baby from her very first days. Here is a capsulized overview of how you aid your baby's language development.

RESPONDING TO HER INVITATIONS

You set the stage for two-way communication by responding regularly to your baby's attempts to signal you, first with her cries, and later with her gestures, facial expressions, and coos and other sounds. Your response helps her learn that she can be effective in communicating her needs and wants.

HELPING HER UNDERSTAND CONVERSATION STRUCTURE

Conversations have a structure—one person alternately speaks and pauses so the other person has a chance to participate. You can build on turn-taking by pausing often when you talk to your baby, and by frequently asking questions that beg a response. Most parents do this almost spontaneously. How many times do you say things like "Hi, sweetie, how are you today?" Both greetings and questions encourage interaction and allow you to treat any response from your baby as an "answer." A smile, squirm, glance, or gesture is enough to keep the conversation going.

Research has shown that babies this age are remarkably skilled in this important aspect of conversation. Conversation, like a song, has its own lyric, rhythm, and melody. You may have noticed that when you talk to your baby, she frequently moves in synchrony to your speech, and is most active when you pause. It seems she senses that it's her turn to "talk," even before she can say a word. Dr. Beatrice Beebe, of Columbia and Yeshiva universities in New York, studies the conversational exchanges between infants and their mothers. She has found that by four months, long before they have mastered the "lyrics" of conversation, babies understand its tempo and rhythm. They make a series of sounds, varying the pitch of their voices; they pause and listen while their mothers respond; and they begin making sounds again when their mothers have finished. This turn-taking has been noted by other researchers, but it has usually been attributed to mothers' behavior. It was thought that the parent waited for a pause in her baby's vocalizations, filled the silence with her own voice, and stopped talking again when her baby started. Dr. Beebe's studies credit the baby as well with these conversational skills.

SYNCHRONIZED VOICES

The impact of your four-month-old's conversational skills on your relationship with her can be better understood if we look at adult interactions. Studies have shown that when two strangers are put into a room and asked to talk to one another, their conversation most often develops a pattern of turn-taking with regard to talking and listening. After being observed in conversation, the participants were asked, in private, to comment on each other. It turns out that the closer the match between the lengths of the two people's conversational bursts and pauses, the more positively they responded to each other.

This doesn't mean that you should measure your conversational bursts and pauses when talking to your baby. "It would be a great tragedy," Dr. Beebe explains, "if this research were used to make parents self-conscious. We are simply quantifying the things that mothers have known for centuries and all do naturally." We *are* suggesting, though, that you should definitely pay attention to your baby when you talk together, and not feel that you must dominate the conversation. It seems that she is able and eager to hold up her side as well.

TALKING TO HER IN SPECIAL WAYS

Unquestionably, the best way to lay good language foundations is to talk to your baby. This doesn't mean becoming a chatterbox; too much talk is boring. But neither should you refrain from speaking to her even though she can't respond in kind. Describe things when you play together. Label the parts of her body when you change and bathe her. The specific words may be meaningless now, but over time—and no one can say exactly when—your baby will begin comprehending their meaning.

How you talk is important as well, and researchers have found that parents fall naturally into speaking patterns that attract a baby's attention and simplify comprehension. Adults throughout the world speak to babies in a special way that some language experts call "motherese" or "parentese." This refers more to the way parents speak their words than the specific words they say. When talking to a baby, parents generally:

· raise the pitch of their voices
· use short utterances, liberally sprinkled with one-syllable words

- pause longer between utterances than when speaking to an adult
- slow the rate of speech
- elongate vowels, thereby emphasizing the melodic quality of speech
- repeat key words in a variety of similar short sentences

Such special language is also often termed "baby talk," since it is directed almost exclusively at babies and is so very different from normal conversation. Baby talk has a negative connotation in some circles. After all, some experts theorize, how can babies learn language if the language they hear is distorted? Yet, most linguists agree that this baby talk is just as beneficial as it is natural. In a study at the University of Oregon, Anne Fernald found that four-month-olds generally prefer baby talk to adult speech. Her detailed analysis found that babies pay closer attention to wide variations in pitch, to monosyllabic utterances, to a slower rate of speech, and to more rhythmic sounds. In other words, the characteristics of baby talk are well matched to the preferences of babies. Of course, which came first is an open question. Did parents start speaking this way *because* they noticed babies liked it? Or did parents speak this way anyway, and babies began to prefer it just because they (the babies) heard it so often?

This match between parental speech and baby comprehension is not just a matter of serendipity. In many ways, human adults—like adults of many species—are innately predisposed to tend to their young. Baby talk is just one example of such instinctive behavior. In fact, even adults who make an effort to use "proper" language when talking to a young baby usually shift unconsciously into baby talk, regardless of whether they call dogs "dogs" or "bowwows." Practically all parents reduce the amount of this baby talk as their child grows; before the end of the first year, they lower their pitch, introduce more complex vocabulary, and establish themselves as good language models.

WHAT COMES NATURALLY

The natural character of baby talk (or motherese) can't be over-emphasized. This almost spontaneous attempt to communicate with your baby in a special, simplified way is probably your greatest contribution to her early language learning. As Roger Brown, a leading language researcher at Harvard University, points out,

"There is no set of rules on how to talk to a child that can even approach what you unconsciously know. If you concentrate on communicating, everything else will follow."

Hand to Mouth

Our consulting pediatrician, Bill Waldman, told us: "Very often when parents come in for a baby's four-month checkup, they'll say something like 'My baby's impossible. She grabs everything in sight and chews on it. I guess she's teething.'"

Chances are, though, such parents are misinterpreting their baby's behavior. With very rare exception, four-month-olds are not yet cutting teeth. Nor is this activity usually related to feeding; babies have other ways to let parents know they're hungry. What is happening is that the baby is *exploring things with her mouth.*

Mouthing is a very important facet of her early explorations. By mouthing an object, your baby learns about its size, shape, texture, and sometimes even sound. With its rich network of nerve endings, a young baby's mouth is well developed for these purposes. One study clearly illustrates how accurately infants perceive with their mouths. Researchers Andrew Meltzoff and Richard Borton designed two pacifiers—one with nubs, the other smooth—and gave infants either one or the other to suck without letting the baby see it. After a baby had sucked one pacifier for a while, the researchers showed her both pacifiers. In most cases, the babies preferred to look at the pacifier they had been sucking. The researchers concluded that even though these babies had seen neither pacifier with their eyes, they had "seen" with their mouths.

Most babies begin mouthing objects before four months. Yet it's during this month that mouthing takes off, because now your baby can reach accurately for nearby objects that interest her, and can easily bring them to her mouth for further examination. Mouthing continues to be a favorite way babies explore for the next several months. It drops off significantly toward the end of the year, mostly because the older baby has developed more sophisticated handling skills for exploring and learning about toys. Nevertheless, a one-year-old will still occasionally pop things into her mouth.

NEW BEHAVIOR FOR YOU, TOO

These oral explorations can create problems for parents. Since mouthing is a vital part of learning, you shouldn't try to discourage it. You probably couldn't even if you tried. Yet, as Dr. Waldman goes on to say, "There's a good reason for parents to have some negative feelings about all this gumming and mouthing. Many things shouldn't be put into the mouth. And it takes time and energy to keep track of your baby at every moment. But it's important for parents to understand the value of this exploration—and later of climbing and ripping and banging as well as mouthing—and to provide a rich variety of these experiences." You can help:

- See that your baby has a range of toys—different sizes and shapes and surface textures—to mouth.
- Make sure the objects your baby mouths are safe and clean.
- Keep unsafe and unsuitable objects well out of her reach.

The Father Factor

Most of the studies we quote throughout this book look at mothers—rather than fathers—and their young children. There are some very practical reasons for this maternal emphasis.

Even today, the mother is almost always primarily responsible for the baby's care. If one parent stays at home, it's overwhelmingly the mother; when both parents are employed outside the home, the mother is still far more likely to shoulder most of the child-rearing responsibility. Therefore, mothers tend to know their babies better, and are more accurate reporters of a child's behavior patterns and developmental abilities. Then again, mothers are far more available to participate in studies, interviews, and such. They often choose to be participants even if the father is just as available. We maintain a family network of over twenty-five hundred families with whom we conduct research. Even when we hold nighttime discussion groups to which either parent is invited, it's usually the mother who attends unless we specifically ask for fathers. This bias has, by and large, led to a self-fulfilling prophecy. For years the father's main consequence in his baby's life was believed to be family breadwinner or mother's aide-de-camp.

Yet a father is unquestionably important in his own right. Some researchers have explored the father's unique role in his infant's life. To cite just some of the recent findings:

- An informal study by Henry Biller (University of Rhode Island) found that mothers are more likely to inhibit exploration, while fathers encourage their babies' curiosity and urge them to solve cognitive and physical skills challenges.

· Michael Lamb's (University of Utah) observational study of eight-month-olds found that mothers engage in more conventional and toy-related types of play, fathers initiate more physical (rough and tumble) and more varied types of play.

· Studies suggest that infants with two parents who actively care for them tend to show separation anxiety later and terminate it earlier than do children with a maternal caregiver alone.

Research can certainly look at aspects of a father's importance. Some studies, like those mentioned above, show that variety is beneficial, and two parents offer more variety than one—particularly since fathers are prone to encouraging active exploration. Other studies stress the father's significance in sex role development and gender identity, although this seems more consequential when the child is beyond infancy. All this research is valuable. It has helped professionals and parents alike take a new look at what a father can contribute. It makes us aware of the factors that can help a baby thrive. And it can prompt parents to look more closely at the way they interact with their baby.

However, this is a case where we especially caution parents not to read too much into research, because such "defining" of the father's importance carries an innate limitation. Research can rarely pinpoint what each individual father—or mother, for that matter—offers his baby that's so dramatically unique. Parents do serve particular functions: food provider, caregiver, play partner, and more. But the special significance that a particular father has in his own baby's life is unquantifiable. It springs from the special relationship the two of them share. And that's influenced by the father's style and personality, the individual way he relates to his baby, the child care and child rearing tasks he performs, and the time he and his baby share together. A father's active participation in every aspect of his baby's life will benefit every member of this close and developing relationship.

Growing through Play

BEGINNING TO SIT

Babies go through several stages in learning to sit up. At about three or four months, when they easily control the muscles supporting the head, most babies enjoy sitting in a swing or other seat, or while supported in a parent's lap. They also enjoy being pulled to the sitting position, in team sit-up games.

1. Lay your baby on her back on a smooth, soft surface (the crib mattress, changing table, your bed, your lap, etc.).
2. Grasp her hands and s-l-o-w-l-y pull her to the sitting position. Hold tight so that she doesn't accidentally fall.
3. Gently lower her again.

At first her back may sag and her head may lag behind her shoulders. But as her muscles strengthen, she sags less and less. In fact, a month or so from now, she may grab your extended hands and pull *herself* up.

THE ROLLOVER

Most babies begin rolling from back onto stomach around four or five months. At first, your baby will rock up onto her side and slip onto her back again. Let her know how pleased you are with her efforts! She'll be amazed and pleased by her new skill, and will practice tirelessly until she's successful. Then she'll practice tirelessly until she can roll over with ease. You can help her along by rolling her gently onto her side, so that she gets the feeling of this new movement. When she seems eager to attempt this motion alone, make sure her clothing isn't getting in the way and that she has a firm surface on which to practice. You might give added encouragement by waving a toy and giving her a pep talk.

SAFETY NOTE: Now you need to make doubly certain that she's never left on a raised surface.

NOTE: Some babies first roll from stomach to back; some do both at about the same point. It's a matter of individual difference.

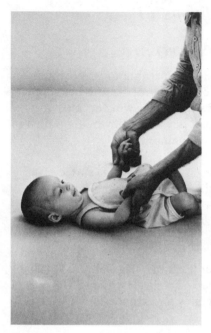
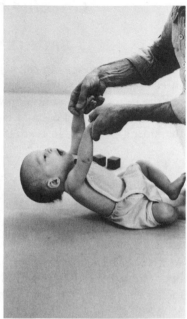

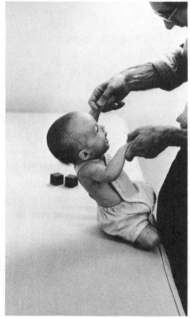

Sit-up Games

ONE-HANDED REACH

Soon your baby shifts from using both hands to just one hand when reaching for objects. This signals both increasing eye-hand coordination and greater dexterity with her fingers. Give her lots of practice with reaching games! In addition to reaching when on her back, your baby may like to reach for things while sitting in your lap. Be sure you keep a protective arm around her so that she doesn't accidentally fall.

TOUCH TOURS

You'll also notice that your baby is now more dexterous when she holds an object. Before, she tended to grasp a slender toy part between her thumb and all four fingers, with her fingers moving as one—as if she were wearing tiny mittens. Now she moves fingers independently and may hold a toy with thumb and two or three fingers. She uses her fingertips more often, too, to explore an object's surface. Make sure her toy collection contains a variety of different textures.

Remember the "House Tours" suggested last month? Your four-month-old might enjoy touching as well as looking. As you carry her around your house, pause to let her feel the softness of your bed-spread, the texture of a wall hanging, the different fabrics of the curtains, water rushing over her hand in the sink, the bristliness of your hairbrush. You may want to hold her hand and stroke her fingers against objects that would be unsafe for her to grab—and yank off the wall. In nice weather, try a yard tour, so that she can feel the textures of leaves and grass and the rough tree trunks. These touch tours are excellent opportunities for beginning to teach your baby about the names and textures of different objects.

FACE VALUE

Remember that faces are still a baby's favorite sights, so take your baby out into the world so that she can see plenty of them. A backpack-type carrier brings her up to face level. She might even enjoy looking at faces (and other pictures) in a local art museum.

SOUNDING OFF

Between four and five months, your baby engages in lots of experimentation with sounds: squealing, gasping, gurgling, blowing bubbles with saliva. Many babies settle on a favorite "sound of the moment" and stay with it for a while. These increased sounds set the stage for more baby-parent imitation. When your baby makes a sound and you repeat it, she may stop and stare as if you've done something surprising. Soon, though, she'll enjoy this imitation and will repeat the sound back to you. So do it again!

Research Update: Baby Swimming—A Caution

Since a four-month-old seems so active, many parents start thinking about enrolling in parent-baby classes like exercise and swim programs. On the whole, these can be great experiences. You get to meet other parents, your baby meets other babies, and both of you can share in a social but still personal, one-on-one atmosphere. Yet swimming classes have recently come under close scrutiny. The *California Medical Association Journal* has urged parents to "Refrain from enrolling their infants in swimming programs that include water submersion." And Marjorie Murphy, aquatic director of the YMCA of the United States, has urged that children under the age of three not be placed under water.

The source of this concern is *infant water intoxication.* This problem can arise only when babies are completely submerged under water—not when their heads are kept above the surface. When a person swallows enough water to lower the concentration of salt in the blood, tissues swell, consciousness is decreased, and seizures may occur. Symptoms of water intoxication range from restlessness, weakness, and nausea to muscle-twitching, convulsions, and coma. Infants are particularly vulnerable to water intoxication for two main reasons:

· Infants' body weight and blood volume is significantly lower than adults'.
· Although an infant may reflexively hold her breath when submerged, she often opens her mouth under water. Once she resurfaces, she swallows whatever is in her mouth.

Babies who suffer water intoxication often don't appear to have a problem when they're in the water. They don't necessarily sputter or choke. In fact, evidence of intoxication might not appear until several hours later, leading many parents to assume that she is just tired or cranky from so much exercise.

Infant swimming, in classes or in a community pool, can be lots of fun and great exercise. But remember the possible risk. To be safe, keep your baby's head above water.

7

YOUR FIVE-MONTH-OLD

Overview

Now your baby is well on his active way. He rolls easily from back to front, or front to back, so that he brings himself closer to things he wants. He reaches accurately for things nearby, and positions his arm and hand correctly to accommodate an object's size, shape, position, and apparent hardness or softness. He uses his fingers with increasing skill to examine things. He can

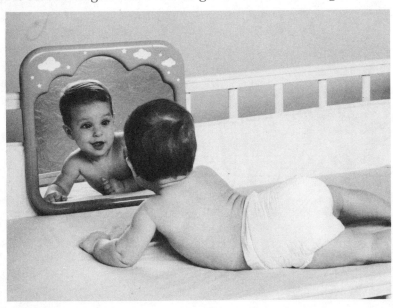

use both hands, too, and now holds a toy in one hand while he explores its details with the other. This helps your baby learn how many parts a toy has and whether the parts are similar.

In fact, you can almost see him learning every minute—so this is frequently the age when parents become concerned about the "best" way to teach a baby, and the pros and cons of formal baby "teaching" programs. We discuss these topics in "Helping Your Baby Learn" (page 110).

Your five-month-old is probably very attentive to sounds, and continues searching quickly and correctly for sounds that are out of his sight. He even turns to find softer sounds, like a whisper or the rustle of paper. Music and rhythm are favorites now, too, if they haven't been before. You'll hear him add some vocal rhythms, too. He may well "talk" more now than last month, spouting long and melodic coos. Interspersed with these musical offerings are short nonsense sounds. Surprisingly, he might vocalize most when he has something in his mouth—his fingers, a toy. He likes to experiment with the ways objects can alter the sounds he's making. He might start making some consonant-and-vowel sounds, like *ma* or *ba*, but these more commonly appear during the next month. He also vocalizes when looking into a mirror, and makes all kinds of sociable overtures to his reflected image. But does he know whom he's looking at? Probably not at this age. Nevertheless, mirrors are usually favorites, and mirror games are fun ways to support his developing self-identity.

Your baby is getting stronger and more coordinated almost daily. Many five-month-olds can sit with minimal support—say, while holding a parent's outstretched arm for the little bit of balance they need. They might sit alone for a few moments, too, before tumbling over. When on his stomach, he may lift his head and all four limbs off the surface, like he's "flying"; indeed, he may even rock a bit in this position. Over the coming months, he'll rock as well with limbs on the ground, and start moving his limbs while he rocks—a sure sign he's preparing himself for crawling. But he's not thinking this far ahead; he rocks and waves and kicks purely for pleasure, exulting in the exercise he can give himself. He also likes exercising with you. All this physical activity and practice are setting the stage for some dramatic behavior advancements you'll likely see when he turns six months.

Helping Your Baby Learn

One of the most influential findings in infant development research conducted in recent decades is that babies are learners at birth. Such information has been passed along to the general public through various sources, so that a primary topic of concern among parents today is just how—and how much—they should teach their babies. The issue is immensely complicated. No answer holds true for every family because each baby, and each parent, is unique. Most opinions on this matter are just that—opinions. Because there's little hard fact, we offer our opinion in the hope that it helps you make up your own mind.

HOW BABIES LEARN

Experts whom we especially admire agree on a few basics.

1. Babies are naturally curious and eager to learn. This has been well documented by hundreds of studies.
2. Babies have a tremendous appetite for new experiences. Again, research has shown that even newborns, because they're eager to learn, bore of exploring the same things in the same ways. Once they have "learned" all they can from a toy or experience, they want novelty. Now, the same object may appear "new" a few hours later, but at any one sitting they do like variety.
3. This curiosity and appetite for new experiences drives a baby to explore his environment. And he learns best through all this experimenting, trial and error, and hands-on experience. In simple terms, babies learn through play.

Watch your own five-month-old when he's given a new toy. He uses every skill in his repertoire to learn about it. He looks at it intently. He brings it to his mouth and fingers it to examine its size, shape, and texture. He shakes it to see how it moves, and whether it makes any sounds. When he's more skillful, he'll pull and twist and squeeze it to see whether it's rigid or elastic. He'll hit it against the floor or throw it, to explore both the sounds it makes and how it changes shape. Later still, he'll try to fit it inside another container to explore relative size. The more responsive a toy is to his handling, the more he'll continue these explorations. All these play activities help him learn. Quite understandably, he learns plenty from all his interactions with you and other people.

BABY READING PROGRAMS

You've probably seen those eye-catching advertisements stating that you can teach even a baby to read. The claims are equally seductive: Improve Your Baby's IQ! Babies Learn Best! Simple, Proven, Fun! Are such claims proven or puffery? Are baby reading programs themselves beneficial or benign; can they even be harmful?

Glenn Doman, the developer of the most famous program, claims that his flash card system does indeed teach early reading, and that he has plenty of proof: the thousands of satisfied parents and book-wise babies who have graduated. He also claims that babies learn faster than older children (which in many ways is true) and that parents can indeed influence a child's IQ.

Yet many experts in language development and reading claim that a program like Doman's doesn't really teach reading. It may aid in word recognition, but reading is a far more complex process, and one that the brain is incapable of handling well until sometime between three or four and eight years of age, depending on the child. A program might hasten the early steps, but it does not measurably influence the true age at which an individual child would begin reading through the "old method." Moreover, experts fear that the time a baby spends staring at those flash cards might cut into time that he could spend freely exploring toys or the environment, activities that are vital for all kinds of physical and cognitive development. Other experts feel that a rigid program might put so much pressure on a baby that it destroys a love of reading.

Many educators agree that you *can* prepare a baby for reading. In our opinion, the best, time-honored way is through all kinds of language games and book play. Most parents concur that it's the most enjoyable way as well.

Is it really more fun to sit opposite your baby, flashing printed words and pictures on cards, than to hold him in your lap while you look at books together? Are letter drills more inviting than cuddling close while you point out words in a book's text and talk about pictures? Are didactic approaches more effective than you and your baby imitating each other's sounds or singing nursery rhymes together or talking about real objects in the environment—or all the scores of ways you build language skills through play? We don't think so.

Yes, you can teach a baby to read—or more accurately, you can lay the strong foundation for later reading skills. But you don't need impersonal programs. Many widely available parenting publications offer learning and play ideas that are not only effective, they're fun for both you and your baby. And many of the materials you need are free.

TO SUM UP

No doubt early learning is vital. It should be joyous as well. This isn't a time for rules and structure; in fact, such didactic approaches may even be counterproductive. There's a catchy phrase that's been circulating in the early education profession for years: "learning to learn." That can sum up the first few years of life. This is the time children learn about people and objects and the way things work. Through all this play they learn how to learn: how to be creative and flexible in solving problems, how to enjoy the very act of learning. Early enjoyment and success make them eager to learn more. And it sets the stage for the more formal learning that's offered through schooling. We think that the above guidelines help you encourage—not stifle—this natural inquisitiveness.

Who's in That Mirror?

Your baby spends countless hours exploring things, and one of those favorite "things" is himself. This process of self-discovery, or self-recognition as it is sometimes known, begins right at birth. There are many ways you'll help your child develop a strong and positive image of himself throughout his life. During his first year, this means providing a solid sense of security, so that he'll feel the world is a safe, supportive place. It also means helping him learn the names for different parts of his body, how these parts function; indeed, even what he looks like.

Mirrors can support this process of self-discovery, and we don't need to convince you how much they fascinate your baby. But while he looks at, touches, pats, and talks to his image . . . *whom* does he see in that mirror?

A RESEARCH PERSPECTIVE

Researchers have devised various experiments to determine at what age a baby realizes that he's seeing himself—rather than just another baby—in the mirror. In one study with three-month-olds, each baby was placed face-to-face with a mirror, then with another baby the same age. (Or the order was reversed.) The experimenter, Tiffany Field of the University of Miami Medical School, found that babies looked longer at the mirror, but they smiled, vocalized, and squirmed more at the other infants. These findings suggest that the babies tested could at least tell the difference between a reflected image and another baby, but it doesn't necessarily mean that the babies knew they were looking at *themselves* in the mirror.

Psychologists Bennett Bertenthal (University of Virginia) and Kurt Fischer (Harvard University) tried other experiments. In one study, parents dressed their babies in a special vest that, unbeknownst to the baby, held a hat about six inches above his head. Then the baby was placed in front of a mirror, his parent drew his attention to the mirror and asked him to find the hat. The researchers felt that if the baby looked up or tried to grab the real hat, then he must realize it is he—not another baby—in the mirror. On the average, babies searched successfully for the hat at about ten months. But did this mean that the baby truly recognized himself? Or did it mean that he knew the difference between a real and a reflected image?

SPOT TEST

A more specific test was tried by Michael Lewis (Rutgers University) and Jeanne Brooks-Gunn (Educational Testing Service). Mothers and babies (six to twenty-four months old) were brought into a laboratory for play sessions, one couple at a time. During the session, the mother casually dabbed a spot of rouge on her baby's nose without his realizing it. Then the baby was placed in front of the mirror and his reactions were observed. If he pointed to or touched the spot on his own nose rather than the reflected image, the researchers reasoned, then he must realize that he's looking at himself. (If he thought he was looking at another baby, he would touch the spot in the mirror.) Lewis and Brooks-Gunn found that:

- Babies between six and fourteen months smiled at, touched, and talked to their reflected images, but none tried to touch the spot on his own nose.
- About one-quarter of the fifteen- to eighteen-month olds, and one-half of the eighteen- to twenty-month-olds, touched their own spot, suggesting that they realized they were looking at themselves.
- Nearly two-thirds of the twenty-one- to twenty-four-month-olds recognized themselves (touched the spot).

ENJOYING THE "OTHER" BABY

The fact remains that babies take great pleasure in mirrors long before they are able to recognize themselves. As some of the studies here found, and as you have undoubtedly noticed, your five-month-old reacts to his reflection as he might to another baby: smiling, cooing, and reaching out to touch it. Some babies a bit older than this have also been observed to look *behind* the mirror for the "other" baby. So part of this fascination with mirrors probably stems from a baby's impulse to be sociable. This is a sign that your baby might enjoy playing with other infants his age. If you do arrange some get-togethers, keep in mind that your baby will reach for his age-mate the way he does for a mirror image. He'll try to grab the other baby's eyes, mouth, ears, and hair. Fun can come to a noisy end if babies this age aren't closely supervised.

MIRROR FUN

Sociability is just one part of the story. Mirrors are also fun because the picture they show is ever changing—your baby never sees exactly the same thing twice. So add mirror fun to his playtimes.

- Lay a nonbreakable mirror on the carpet for your baby to peer into when he's lying on his stomach.
- Hold your baby on your lap and look into a mirror together. Point to and talk about the different parts of his face and body. Encourage him to talk to and kiss his pictured pal.
- Get the entire family to sit or stand in front of a full-length mirror mounted on a wall or door. Let your baby see, respond to, and learn about everyone.

- Hold your baby in your arms and dance in front of a wall or door mirror. He'll like watching as well as feeling the action.
- When you take your baby shopping with you, sit him in front of a three-way dressing mirror. Instant triplets!
- Fasten a nonbreakable mirror to the side of the crib. (There are a few products on the market such as Johnson & Johnson's Baby's First Mirror, designed specifically for this purpose.) Then your baby can enjoy mirror play when you're not around. Position the mirror so that it cannot reflect sunlight in your baby's eyes.

SAFETY REMINDER: *Always* supervise play that involves a glass mirror, even one attached to a wall or door. Your baby could accidentally break it with a toy or other hard object. And *never* place a glass mirror in the crib.

Growing through Play

HELP WITH SITTING

Young babies enjoy sitting while supported in an infant seat or swing, or when held on your lap. By five months, many are ready to sit without so much support—for instance, while you hold only one of their hands. Or if you set your baby in a sitting position on the floor, he may lean forward, supporting himself on his arms. Some babies grasp their feet for a few moments before tumbling off to one side. But they usually enjoy the experience of sitting, even if it only lasts a short time.

MORE EXERCISES

Now your baby's greater strength permits some more strenuous exercise. Be careful not to overtax him or jerk him into position. And always pay attention to make sure he's enjoying the routine.

First Push-ups. With your baby lying stomach-down on the floor, supporting his torso on outstretched arms, lift his legs a few inches from the surface. Encourage him to push up on his arms.

Beach Ball Roll.   Hold your baby securely by his waist and "roll" him backward and forward across a large inflated beach ball or a round bolster cushion.

Super Sit-ups.   Sit-ups are more fun than ever because your baby's back rarely sags, and his head lags less behind his shoulders, when you pull him to a sitting position. Up . . . down . . . up . . . down. On the downward journey, sometimes relax your arms a bit so that he "falls" slightly before your secure grasp restrains him from hitting the surface. He'll like this element of surprise. Good position: You sit in a comfortable chair, your baby lies on his back on your lap, facing you.

Sit-and-Stand-ups.   Lay your baby on his back on the floor. Grasp his hands and slowly pull him to a sitting position, then on up to a standing position.

Big Bouncers.   Hold your baby around the waist or under his arms so that he stands upright. Now help him bounce about— maybe to a bouncy song on the stereo or radio.

NURSERY RHYME GAMES

In case you haven't started already . . . Now is the time to add nursery rhymes to your playtime together. Babies like the rhythm and music inherent in such ditties, and especially enjoy being moved to the rhyme. A good edition of Mother Goose rhymes is a wise investment. For extra fun, add a dramatic finale to each rhyme. Babies love this bit of surprise, and soon look forward to it with mounting excitement. To get you started:

· Clap your baby's hands together while you sing the "Pat-a-Cake" song.

> Pat-a-cake, pat-a-cake, baker's man,
> Bake me a pie as fast as you can.
> Prick it and pat it and mark it with a "B,"
> And put it in the oven for (baby's name) and me.

Tap him on the tummy when you reach his name.

· Pull his arms back and forth in a chug-a-chug motion while you sing "Row, Row, Row Your Boat." Add a funny "Yeah!" or "Oh!" and clap his hands together at the end.

- Pull his toes in turn to each different "piggy" in "This Little Piggy Went to Market." On the "Wee, wee, wee, all the way home," squeeze his little toe, or run your fingers up and down his leg, ending with a tickle under the chin. The funnier your voice becomes, the more he likes it. (Pssst . . . Fingers can be "piggies," too.)
- Hold your baby in your lap, facing you, with your arms securely about his waist, for some spirited verses of "Rock-a-bye Baby." Rock him from side to side on the first three lines. But when you come to "the cradle will *fall*," let him fall backward slightly, then bring him back to sitting. If you repeat this rhyme several times at a sitting, slightly vary the distance he "falls."
- Hold your sitting baby under his arms and bounce him merrily as you sing:

> All around the cobbler's bench,
> The monkey chased the weasel.
> The monkey thought 'twas all in fun —
> *Pop* goes the weasel.

On "pop," lift him up!

Research Update: Microwave Warning

Many babies start on solid foods at around five and six months, and in today's kitchens, the microwave oven has often taken over as a quick and clean way of heating food. In fact, some books and magazine articles suggest heating jarred baby food in the microwave. But a recent article in *Pediatrics*, a leading professional journal for pediatricians, warns against this appliance for heating both bottles and jarred baby food. In one incident, the disposable plastic liner of a "nursing bottle" exploded after it was removed from the microwave, scalding the baby. A baby food jar can feel cool to the touch when removed from the oven, but because a microwave heats from the inside out, parts of the contents can be boiling hot.

Remember that jarred food heated on top of a stove doesn't necessarily heat evenly either. Always stir and test the food before giving it to your baby.

8

YOUR
SIX-MONTH-OLD

Overview

Your six-month-old enters into an "Age of Exploration" as all those skills she has been practicing since birth come together to make her seem far more grown-up. A number of behavioral advances make this such a rich era:

- Your baby has very good eye-hand coordination, and reaches for objects swiftly and surely.
- Her grasping skills are vastly improved, so that she uses fingers (as well as mouth) to explore the intricacies of playthings.
- Her arm skills, too, are advanced. Now she can deliberately wave and shake objects to see what happens, or stretch an elastic toy with both hands, or pound a favorite rattle against the floor to make as much noise as possible. All these arm and hand skills enable her to learn even more about the properties of objects.
- And maybe most importantly, now (or soon) she can sit all by herself. Among other things, this frees her hands and arms for play. And since she probably can't yet crawl, she's content to stay in one place, handling everything within reach.

These new skills mean new potential dangers, so this is the time to think about baby proofing. And now that your baby is probably able to hold her bottle, she'll take a bigger role in feeding herself. This, too, can be a source of problems, as we discuss in "Beware Nursing Bottle Mouth!" (page 121).

When she's prone rather than sitting (or trying to sit), your six-month-old may alternately lift her chest, then stomach, from the floor while supporting her weight on arms and legs. If she lifted both together, she might start to crawl—at least a little bit. Not many six-month-olds do raise chest and abdomen simultaneously; and most of those who master this step don't figure out how to move arms and legs alternately to propel themselves forward. Nonetheless, this lifting and lowering while on all fours is a precursor to crawling as well as a simple exercise that many babies enjoy.

You'll see advancements in your baby's social and emotional development as well. This is the age when most babies begin making consonant-vowel sounds like *ma, ba, pa,* and *da;* different types of sounds are used for different situations, as we discuss later in this chapter. Soon your baby strings a number of these syllables together in delighted babble. These babbles also incorporate rising and falling pitches and tones, so that it sounds almost as if she's carrying on elaborate conversations. Listen closely, though, and you'll realize it's just gibberish. Yet it's a vital step in language development, for out of these babbles true words will emerge.

Your baby has new ways of showing how close she has become to both her parents, too, and probably relates to each parent in a different way: seeking comfort and solace from Mom, excitement and playful stimulation from Dad. These are typical and understandable, as we point out on the following pages. A favorite game, peekaboo, works right into this love for parents. Your baby thrills in the surprise of seeing you appear, even if you've left her sight just for a second.

At the six-month checkup, a baby typically receives her third DTP (diphtheria-tetanus-pertussis) vaccination. As when she was younger, your baby may become particularly fussy and have a low-grade fever (less than 101°) within about four hours, and may have a sore leg within twelve hours. Acetaminophen (such as children's Tylenol) given two hours after the injection can reduce the reactions. And if your baby's reactions are more severe, let the pediatrician know. (Sometimes pediatricians reduce the amount of pertussin administered in the vaccination to minimize the reaction if it caused much discomfort the previous time. Be sure to consult your doctor if that was the case.)

Sitting Alone: Quite an Achievement!

All that physical activity of the early months usually culminates in a major developmental milestone at around six months: Your baby begins to sit without support. Some babies, of course, start sitting earlier, others wait a month or two. Regardless of when a baby begins, though, sitting up is a major achievement.

MESHING WITH OTHER SKILLS

When your baby becomes confident about keeping her balance while sitting, she can use her arms and hands freely to reach, grasp, and manipulate a wide range of objects. Soon, she'll spot a nearby toy, lunge forward to grasp it, and return to sitting so that she can play with it. While sitting unencumbered by a lap or infant seat, she can turn her head for a much broader view of her environment. Babies this age are also more interested in conversations between two other people, and sitting allows her to pay better attention. Sit a baby between two adults engaged in conversation and she'll turn her head from speaker to speaker, as though she were watching a tennis match.

> NOTE: A baby who's just learning to sit may not be able to get out of the sitting position without help. A slumping back or an unhappy face might tell you that she's ready to return to lying on her stomach or back, or wants you to pick her up.

NEW PRECAUTIONS

Some parents make the mistake of thinking that once a baby can sit and manipulate toys so successfully, she'll spend long periods amusing herself. But even though your baby is so independent, she still welcomes your participation in play. When your baby starts to sit, you need to be even more alert to what's in her environment. Although a dangerous object may appear well out of reach, your baby will pitch forward; once on the floor, she can wriggle over to enticements like a dangling lamp cord or an unprotected electrical wall outlet. This is the time to begin baby proofing! We give suggestions later in this chapter. Remember also to remove mobiles and all toys that hang over or across your baby's crib or playpen when she is able to sit or push up on hands and knees. She could get entangled in them.

Beware Nursing Bottle Mouth!

Bottle feeding is one method of providing nourishment to an infant, but too often the nursing bottle containing sweetened liquids is misused as a pacifier for comforting the infant or controlling behavior. This habit can lead to a condition in which the two-, three-, or four-year-old's teeth are destroyed by dental caries (tooth decay).

—American Dental Association

Nursing bottle mouth is severe tooth decay caused by too much bottle nursing outside of normal feeding times. Naturally, regular bottle feeding doesn't lead to this condition; rather, it can result when a baby:

- nurses too frequently and for long stretches at a time, such as when the bottle is used as a pacifier or when a baby is put to bed with a bottle at night or nap time;

• nurses on bottles containing sweetened liquids like sugared water, soft drinks, even powdered drinks to which you add water (or that are already presweetened with sugar).

The treacherous thing about nursing bottle mouth is that the severe decay, as the American Dental Association points out, usually doesn't show up until several months or even years after a baby's teeth start coming in.

THE CAUSES

A baby's teeth, like anyone's, are susceptible to decay. Decay can happen when sugar mixes with *plaque* (a sticky, colorless film on the teeth); together they form an acid that can attack tooth enamel. Sweetened drinks are clearly potential acid-makers. However, even formula and milk and fruit juices contain sugar. The longer the liquid remains around a baby's teeth, the greater the chance for decay. That's why using a bottle as a pacifier can be so harmful. If your baby frequently sucks from a bottle for long stretches of time, as babies often do with a pacifier, her teeth are exposed to lots of acid.

Dental professionals are especially concerned when a baby is given a bottle to suck at nap time or bedtime, even if the bottle contains milk or formula. According to *Nursing Bottle Mouth*, a pamphlet from the American Dental Association,

During the day, saliva helps to wash some of the liquid out of the mouth. However, at bedtime or during naps, the saliva flow decreases, allowing the sugary liquid to pool around the teeth. When this pooled liquid remains in the mouth for prolonged periods, teeth are constantly attacked by acids.

STEPS TO PREVENTION

1. Avoid giving your baby soft drinks, powdered drinks, sugar water, diluted gelatin, or similar sweetened liquids. If she needs a bottle between regular feedings (as often happens on a hot day), fill it with plain water. Of course, if your baby's pediatrician has recommended other bottle feedings, you should follow his or her advice.
2. Never let your baby fall asleep with a bottle. Feed her in your arms until she's ready to sleep, then offer her a pacifier if she needs one.

3. Avoid using the bottle as a pacifier if possible. Find a substitute soother.
4. Once your baby's teeth start coming in, clean them regularly. We offer dental care hints in our next chapter.

Beginning Babbles

The babbling of a six-month-old is decidedly different from the crooning of a younger baby. The long, melodic vowel sounds—the *aaahs* and *eeees*—that were prevalent earlier are now replaced by a combination of consonants and vowels. First she usually makes these *ma, pa, da, ba, na, di* and similar sounds one at a time. Then she combines them together into long strings. These first babbles are usually a repetition of the same consonant-vowel in every syllable, such as *mamamama*. This is called *reduplicated babbling*. Later, maybe at around nine months, a baby mixes several consonant-vowel syllables in the same string, and babbles things like *babamamamadadamumu*. She also varies her voice pitch and volume.

According to speech specialist Rachel Stark at The Johns Hopkins Medical Institutions, a six-month-old often talks differently to toys and people. She makes her new *ba* and *da* and *pa* sounds most often when playing with toys, usually while waving, shaking, or banging them. With people, she usually makes more of the old crooning sounds, like a long *aaaah* to call for attention or to scold you for not coming sooner to feed her. She may use *ma* and *na* sounds when things go wrong and she starts to fuss.

WHY THESE SOUNDS FIRST

In studying the order in which babies articulate sounds, English psycholinguist Roman Jakobson found that the first consonants babies pronounce—such as *m, b,* and *p*—originate in the front of the mouth. These sounds are largely made with the lips. The second set of sounds, like *d* and *t*, originate midway along the upper palate. These require skillful tongue placement against the roof of the mouth. Later consonants such as *g* and *k* originate in the rear of the mouth and require partially closing the throat.

BABBLES AND WORDS FOR PARENTS

In many countries, the first sounds a baby babbles are often used as names for parents. Jakobson and other researchers theorize this is because languages themselves have adopted babies' typical first utterances as references to mother and father. This is reinforced by the babies themselves because of their emotional and physical closeness to their parents. This may be because, as we pointed out above:

- Babies often use *ma* and *na* sounds when they start to fuss. Mothers have traditionally been the ones who comfort babies and attend to their needs. So it follows logically that *mama* and *nana* are common "names" for mothers (and grandmothers).
- Babies often use *pa* sounds when playing. Fathers traditionally tend to be more playful than mothers (more about this in "New Expressions of Love" later in this chapter). Following the above reasoning, this may be why *papa* has entered so many vocabularies as a name for fathers.

This knowledge of first utterances can be of practical help to parents. If you anticipate and listen closely for the sounds your baby makes, you'll be better able to reinforce them with lots of repetition—and lots of enthusiasm. It's also helpful to point to yourself when your baby says *pa* and answer with, "Papa, I'm your papa" (or *mama* when you hear *ma* sounds).

These early *ma* and *pa* utterances aren't real words; true first words probably won't appear until some time around or after your baby's first birthday. But they are a sign that your baby is developing a larger repertoire of sounds, sounds that become the building blocks of true speaking. Have fun reinforcing her babbling.

New Expressions of Love

Your six-month-old has definite ways of expressing her love that she reserves for parents alone. Some are general. Many a baby this age greets her parents by clapping her hands or raising her arms to show that she wants to be picked up—and by snuggling close when she is held in your arms. There's no doubt now that parents are her favorite people, and all her wonderfully heartwarming signs of special love give you growing confidence in yourselves. This can be quite a change from the earliest months!

Other expressions of love reflect the different relationships your baby enjoys with each parent. In research at the University of Wisconsin, psychologist Michael Lamb (now at the University of

Utah) spent many hours in the homes of babies six to twelve months, observing how they and their parents spend time together. One thing he noted was the physical contact each parent had with his or her baby. As you might expect, mothers most often held their babies for feeding, changing, and other physical care, and for comforting. Fathers held their babies far less often and for shorter periods, and most of the father-baby contact involved active, highly stimulating play.

Dr. Lamb also looked at the different ways a baby related to each parent. When both parents were available, a baby usually stayed much closer to her mother, and spent more time inviting the mother to pick her up. A baby under stress—because she was tired or a stranger entered the room—almost always sought her mother's comfort. At other times, however, a baby tended to relate more closely to her father, especially when she was not in physical contact with either parent. Most of babies' looking, smiling, laughing, "talking," and other play-type behaviors were directed toward fathers.

Studies like this one show that a baby's attachments to her parents tend to differ in observable ways. This doesn't mean that such patterns are predetermined or unchangeable; they're thought to be based on the ways mothers and fathers typically relate to babies. Babies often look to mothers as a primary source of care and security, because in most families the mother has the greater responsibility for daily child rearing. The playful relationships most fathers have with their babies makes fathers an important source of pleasure and excitement. And the strength of babies' attachments to their fathers reflects the vitality of this intense, highly stimulating relationship.

Naturally, these observations don't hold true for every family. Patterns of responsibility for family income and child care are no longer so tightly drawn as they were in the past. Then again, each parent has his or her own personality—some fathers are naturally more emotionally caring than their spouses, just as some mothers are more ebullient and playful than their husbands. And either parent can provide both qualities of comfort and excitement. This especially happens in families where there is only one parent, or where one parent (almost always the father) has limited contact with his baby.

Nonetheless, in almost every two-parent family we have studied, each parent relates to his or her baby in distinctly different ways, and the baby recognizes and responds to these differences. Such patterns—and consequently, the young child's attachments—may change over time, as each parent adopts new roles of comfort and stimulation, sometimes based on circumstances, sometimes based on the preferences the child herself shows. What is clear, though, is that your baby does enjoy a very special relationship with each parent, and that she influences you just as much as you influence her.

Growing through Play

GETTING READY TO CRAWL

Many a six-month-old rocks on her belly as a forerunner of crawling. She lifts her chest, then drops it and lifts her bottom, drops it, then her chest again . . . Some babies love rocking in its own right. Others seem frustrated that they can't move forward. You can help your baby make some progress by holding your hands against the soles of her feet so that she pushes forward a bit.

THE TOY EXPLORER

Because your baby is now at the "Age of Exploration," make sure she has plenty of toys to explore. Here are some shopping guidelines.

· The best toys inspire and respond to several skills; waving, shaking, pulling, poking, and the like. Remember that interesting sounds and movement are still the most powerful rewards for this age. Especially look for toys that have a few parts attached to one another, so that as your baby plays, the toy flops about and changes shape. Transparent toys, with things that move inside, are often favorites, too.

· A toy should be easy for your baby to pick up once she drops it—because she will, repeatedly. Toys that lie perfectly flat on the floor will be hard for her to get hold of again. Look for those in which some portion serves as a handle that is raised off the floor.

· Toys should be fully washable—your baby still mouths anything she gets her hands on. Plastic is an excellent material for this age because it's comparatively light, strong, colorful, and easy to clean. Wood tends to be less successful because it's heavier and can splinter. Fabric toys are fine, too, provided they flop about, make sounds, and are completely machine washable.

PEEKABOO!

Starting about this age, and continuing for the next several months, peekaboo will probably be a favorite game. One reason is that your baby loves the surprise of seeing you reappear after you temporarily leave her sight. Another is that this game may help her deal with the separation anxiety many babies start undergoing during the second half of the first year (more on this in our next chapter). Perhaps by experiencing your brief comings and goings in a game atmosphere, she becomes better able to deal with the real ones.

Whatever the reason, peekaboo is immensely popular. The versions are endless, but the structure is the same: a person "disappears," then reappears accompanied by a jolly "Peekaboo, I see you!" cry. (Of course, when your baby is the one who disappears, you'll have to supply the vocal accompaniment.) Some ideas:

· When your baby is looking at you from her crib, duck down out of sight, then pop back up with "Peekaboo, I see you!"
· When your baby is lying on your lap, facing you, cover your eyes with your hands. "Where did Shelley go?" Then off come your hands with "There she is! Peekaboo!" (You might also hide your face behind a toy, a book, or other barrier.) For a twist, cover your eyes with *her* hands.

- Once your baby gets the hang of this game, cover her eyes with your hand. Or help her cover her eyes with her own hands.
- Cover your face with a diaper or small towel. After a few rounds, your baby might like to snatch away the covering.
- You might also try covering her head with a diaper. But be sure she's in a playful mood, and that she enjoys this version; being covered up frightens many younger babies. However, most babies enjoy this game by around nine months or so. And once they learn how to play, they'll soon begin covering themselves with the diaper and waiting for you to remove it.

Research Update:
High Chair Cautions

By the time a baby sits well alone (and is eating solids), most parents have moved her from an infant seat to a high chair for feeding. As well designed as most high chairs are nowadays, they still carry a risk. According to recent safety statistics, each year more than nine thousand babies are treated in emergency rooms for high chair–related injuries.

- Always strap your baby in her high chair, using both the waist strap and the crotch strap (so that she can't wriggle out the bottom).
- Even though she's strapped in, never leave your baby unattended in the high chair. Ignore the doorbell, as you should when she's on a changing table or in the tub, or take your baby with you to answer it.

Be especially vigilant when you take your baby to restaurants. A random survey of fifty-four restaurant high chairs conducted by safety specialists at Temple University found that 41 percent of the restaurant high chairs had no restraint straps. If a restaurant high chair lacks a suitable restraint system, you should feed your baby in your lap or bring the car seat (or an infant seat) in from the car. Remember: Your baby depends on *you* to keep her safe.

9

YOUR SEVEN-MONTH-OLD

Overview

Whaat's in store for this month? Regarding your baby's social and emotional development, you're likely to see a new expression of attachment to you: He may become quite anxious when you leave him. This seeming setback is actually a developmental advance, as the next section discusses.

Your seven-month-old likewise displays new physical and learning advancements.

- He probably begins standing with support, an exciting precursor to walking.
- He explores objects more skillfully, and may now use them as tools to make things happen.
- He expresses himself more understandably. He strings consonant sounds together into long babbles filled with tonal and vocal inflections. He's also better at using his voice to let you know exactly how he feels and what he wants. He may call to you, coaxing a conversation, or shout to be picked up. His hands and facial expressions, as well as his sounds, help convey the meanings of these demands.

All these skills give you new opportunities for play. In addition to your regular games, this is a good time to introduce books and music if you haven't earlier.

Most babies sprout a tooth or two at this age. Teething may involve some pain, and may be accompanied by some physical symptoms. Once your baby starts teething, you should begin good oral hygiene.

Separation Fears

Every baby enjoys a special relationship with his parents. Around seven or eight months he may express a new facet of that special closeness that may be more hectic than heartwarming.

When he was younger, your baby probably let you leave him without complaining. But now he may become anxious and upset when separated from you, even if only for a moment. In fact, he may cling desperately when you try to put him down, or cry when you leave the room. This phenomenon is so common that psychologists call it "separation anxiety."

WHAT IS SEPARATION ANXIETY?

Although sometimes frustrating for you (and your baby), this separation anxiety actually indicates a forward step in his development. He recognizes that you and he are quite distinct and separate people, and that you have a very special place in his life. The problem is, while he realizes how much he loves and needs and depends on you, he still has the elementary idea that once you leave his sight you may be gone forever. It will take time and experience to learn that things that disappear—even parents—usually reappear. But for now all he knows is that you're gone, and he feels abandoned.

ALL BABIES ARE DIFFERENT

We've found in our research with hundreds of families that different babies feel this anxiety to different extents. Some show slight concern about separations, others react vehemently to being left by their parents. Also, some babies suffer for just a few weeks while others are miserable, even panic-stricken, for months. However, most children fall between these two extremes. It seems that such differences are a factor of the child's general temperament and how frequently he has been left in the care of others during the early months.

SURVIVING THIS PERIOD

You're bound to feel quite a strain when your baby is upset by your leave-takings. It may help you to keep in mind that this period of separation anxiety is a normal state of behavior that your baby will soon outgrow. His budding awareness of how much he needs and loves you will blossom more positively in the emotional richness of the later years. Here are some ways you can help your baby, and yourself, through this phase. These suggestions may also hasten the day when he will happily let you leave.

First, take his anxiety seriously. It may seem unjustified or even silly to you—you *know* you'll be coming back. But your baby doesn't, and this fear is very real to him. If you can, keep separations to a minimum for a while. For example, carry your baby around in a backpack when doing light household chores, or keep him near you in his walker or playpen. Have friends over in the evening instead of going out. Take your baby on errands whenever feasible. If both parents work outside the home, make sure your baby is left with some familiar, loving person that he trusts.

Second, researchers are also finding that a baby tolerates household apartness best if he can still see you when you can't be in the same room together.

- A study by Mary Ainsworth and Silvia Bell found that in situations where the mother left the room *and shut the door behind her,* every baby cried and ceased playing.
- In another study, Carl Corter at the University of Toronto

found that crawling babies played contentedly in a strange laboratory playroom for several minutes before following the mother after she walked out an open door.
· And in another study, Dr. Corter found that when the mother was visible in another room, each baby was content to stay and play longer than when the mother was completely out of sight.

Third, when you must go out without your baby, always prepare him before you leave. Explain in simple terms that you must leave him and that you'll be back later. He won't understand your words, of course, but he will sense your concern. We recommend that you *do not* try to slip away unnoticed. This might seem easiest for you at the moment, but once your child discovers your unexplained absence, he'll be much more frightened than if you had discussed your departure. After such a betrayal, your baby's fear that he may suddenly find you gone could make him even more anxious and clinging than he normally would be.

Fourth, help your baby become involved in some enjoyable activity before you go. One reason your separations upset him is that you represent order and stability. He usually deals better with your leave-taking if you first set him up with some familiar toys, or involve him in a favorite game with the baby-sitter.

A RECURRING PHASE

This first period of separation anxiety will likely last only a month or two. Your sympathy and understanding will probably shorten the stage, and will make it easier to bear while you're in the midst of it. Nonetheless, babies and toddlers are prone to bouts of separation anxiety throughout the early years, even after they have learned that parents will come back again. This usually happens when the child is left by parents in an environment other than his home—say, at the sitter's or a day-care center. We'll pick up this story in later chapters.

Spotlight on Teething

The average baby cuts his first tooth at six-and-a-half months, but there's a lot of normal variation. As our consulting pediatrician, Bill Waldman, tells us, "I've heard of kids who were born with teeth, and I've had children in my practice who were fifteen months old before the first teeth came in." So don't worry for several months yet if your baby is toothless. Then if your baby's pediatrician feels there might be a problem, he or she will arrange for an X ray to assure that the teeth are really there, below the gum, waiting to pop through.

IS TEETHING PAINFUL?

Pediatricians don't agree on how much discomfort, if any, teething may cause. "Whatever pain there may be," Dr. Waldman says, "is probably caused either by gum tissue trauma as the tooth erupts or by small infections under a flap of gum tissue." Children also vary widely in their reactions to teething. Many babies exhibit little or no discomfort; others are quite fussy and irritable and drool profusely when each tooth comes in. And there are a few babies who may be uncomfortable for as long as a few weeks as each tooth erupts.

WHEN TEETH TYPICALLY ERUPT

UPPER TEETH	AGE IN MONTHS	
central incisor	8-12	
lateral incisor	9-13	
canine (cuspid)	16-22	
first molar	13-19	
second molar	25-33	

LOWER TEETH	AGE IN MONTHS	
second molar	23-31	
first molar	14-18	
canine (cuspid)	17-23	
lateral incisor	10-16	
central incisor	6-10	

TYPICAL TOOTH EMERGENCE

The first teeth to appear are the lower central incisors, or the two front teeth on the bottom. Next come the upper central incisors, which erupt about two months later. At around nine or ten months the lateral incisors on the top and bottom come in. These are the teeth that flank the front teeth. The first molars typically appear around twelve or thirteen months. Next come the canines, which fill the gap between the lateral incisors and the first molars. Canines erupt around eighteen months. Between two and three years, the second molars come in, completing the set of twenty primary (or baby) teeth. But this is merely a *typical* schedule of eruption, a fact we can't stress enough. Many babies don't sprout teeth right on schedule. Some also follow a different pattern of eruption; sometimes the upper teeth come in before their lower counterparts. Also, we know children who grew first molars well before lateral incisors.

TEETHING AND ILLNESS: IS THERE A LINK?

The other common question: Does teething cause fever, diarrhea, runny noses, and other symptoms? Dr. Michael Levi, assistant clinical professor of pediatrics at New York University, says that most probably there is no direct link, but notes that many children he sees definitely have a higher incidence of fever and diarrhea when they're teething. He gives one explanation: "Teething is an overall body stress, and like other stresses it lowers the child's resistance to infectious agents that under normal circumstances would not produce illness. The same germs that live in a child's intestines with no ill effects at other times could produce diarrhea or other low-grade infections when that child is teething."

Then again, the "link" between teething and colds or fever might just be a coincidence. Most babies begin teething soon after six months. At about the same age, many of the natural immunities passed from mother to baby, particularly during breastfeeding, start wearing off. Thus babies this age are naturally more often prone to slight illness.

Teething sometimes *does* cause loose stools. A teething baby may create and swallow enough saliva to dilute materials in his intestine. However, most pediatricians agree that teething itself does not cause diarrhea or gastrointestinal illness as was once thought. So if your baby has a fever or other illness when a tooth is coming in, don't assume it's a natural side effect of teething. He may be sick, and you should talk to his pediatrician about it.

RELIEVING DISCOMFORT

Even if teething doesn't cause illness, many babies seem to find it uncomfortable. Gnawing on a teether provides general relief; biting down creates a pressure form of anaesthesia. Teethers come in all sizes and shapes and materials. Whichever ones you select, make sure that each is:

- easy for your baby to grasp and hold, with one or both hands;
- light enough so that he doesn't tire of holding it (babies like to chew for a good long time!);
- easy for you to keep clean.

A favorite teething toy can offer psychological comfort as well as physical relief for sore gums. When a baby is fussy and irritable, a familiar toy can help him feel safe and comfortable, especially when you aren't available to soothe him. In this sense, a teether functions like a favorite pacifier—but with a sturdy, chewy difference.

Safety Notes

1. Make sure the teether is safe!
   - No sharp edges or points
   - No small openings that may trap a finger, lip, or tongue
   - No part that might fit into his mouth far enough to cut off his air passage or cause him to gag or choke
2. Never hang a teether on a piece of ribbon or string around your baby's neck, like a necklace. He might get the string caught on something—and possibly choke.

Some pediatricians also recommend a local anesthetic that numbs the gums on contact; this may help relieve teething pain. Others prefer to avoid any kind of medication—no matter what it is—that's not absolutely essential. Ask your baby's doctor before treating teething pain with over-the-counter preparations.

EARLY CARE AND CLEANING

"As soon as the first tooth comes in, clean it after feedings with a washcloth or gauze pad moistened with water," advises Dr. Stephen Levin, a pedodontist and representative of the American Academy of Pediatric Dentistry. (A pedodontist is a dentist with special training in dental care for children.) This helps remove plaque, a sticky, invisible film that harbors decay-causing bacteria. You should start brushing once a few teeth have come in. Dr. Levin recommends using a child's brush with soft, tufted bristles, and moistening it with water. Toothpaste is unnecessary at this age, and many young children don't like its taste. (However, you should definitely use a fluoridated toothpaste when your child is about two years or older; fluoride is an excellent cavity fighter.)

MORE TIPS

Good diet and good teeth go together. Be especially conscious of sugar intake—sugar can cause tooth decay. Avoid letting your baby fall asleep with a bottle or use the bottle as a pacifier (see "Beware Nursing Bottle Mouth!" on page 121). Plan regular dental visits. Dr. Levin and other pedodontists we consulted recommend making the first general dental visit around a child's second birthday. Naturally, though, you should take your baby to the dentist any time you suspect a dental problem.

This attention to care and diet certainly won't be wasted. As Dr. Levin adds, "Dentistry has come a long way in recent years. With proper oral hygiene, with fluoride, and with the use of sealants, your child may never have any cavities."

First Library

It's no secret that babies like books, and that books go far to build language skills (particularly vocabulary). But what books are best for babies? What features make them so successful? We took these questions to sixteen parents of babies from two to twelve months. Each was asked to select up to five of her baby's favorite books, then to talk about them one by one.

FAVORITE TITLES

Suppose you asked sixteen friends to select their five favorite books. Chances are, you'd find little overlap from person to person. The same thing happened in our study. Out of the sixty books that parents mentioned as favorites, there were fifty-one different titles! (Not every parent chose five books, so the total was sixty rather than eighty.) That's hardly a consensus. Much more revealing, though, are the themes that almost all babies and parents favored. So as you choose books for your baby, keep the following in mind.

Familiar Activities. The absolute favorite books illustrate things babies themselves do—playing simple games like peekaboo, eating, taking a bath, playing with toys, and going to bed. After all, babies are fairly egocentric. Their world is small. They relate most readily to familiar activities.

Familiar Objects. Especially other babies, and objects typically in a baby's world.

Animals. Particularly baby animals, and animals doing things that babies do. One reason that pictures of babies and animals are so popular is because they give parents so much to talk about: facial expressions, gestures, parts of the face and body, and so forth. Animals have another plus—they make funny sounds. Babies love parents to make these sounds, too (and older babies like to imitate meows and growls and quacks).

Rhymes and Poems. Babies enjoy the rhythms and cadence of language, and love nursery rhyme games.

FAVORITE FEATURES

Just as some themes are favorites, so are the following features.

Durability. Books must stand up to repeated readings—and babies aren't careful readers. Teachers as well as parents in our study favor cardboard and heavy vinyl books. Be sure all have smooth, rounded corners. Cloth books, on the whole, don't work. The pages are hard to turn and such books become limp over time.

Clear Pictures.   Books should have bright, colorful realistic pictures with uncluttered backgrounds. Many experts say that the best books for babies this age have a single, isolated object on each page. We've found that this is *not true*. Babies bore of such simple books. Pictures *should* be fairly uncomplicated, but the more that's going on, the more you have to talk about. For example, if it's just a ball, you're limited to saying its name and talking about its color, shape, and other immediate attributes. But if the picture shows a baby playing with a ball, you can talk about the baby as well, what he's wearing, and what he's doing with the ball.

Washability.   For any book that your child will handle by himself, the pages must be surface washable.

Brief Text (If Any).   At this age, you don't read a story, you talk about the pictures. Remember, these guidelines refer to books you and your baby look at, talk about, and handle together. Some babies also love being read to—from any book *you* might like. Reading aloud to your baby, perhaps just as he's dozing off at nap time or at night, also builds his language skills, and helps him enjoy the wonder and marvel that books can add to his life.

Growing through Play

STANDING WITH SUPPORT

Lift your baby to a standing position near the sofa, a chair, a low table, or other sturdy support. It's a nice, new way to view the world. Or hold him upright under his arms and let him bounce on your lap. Or maybe hold his outstretched arms and let him walk a few steps, or bounce and "dance" to music on the stereo. These are all important forerunners to later walking skills. And despite what you may have heard, they won't make your baby bowlegged.

BABIES AND MUSIC

Babies love music as much as they do books. And just as book play builds skills and a love of reading, music play builds skills and a love of music.

Babies appear to be quite receptive to musical stimulation. Sister Donna Kucenski, a researcher in early childhood music education, tested her specially designed Sequential Musical Sensory Learning Program with a group of forty babies, some starting as young as three months. These babies were first evaluated using established tests of musical achievement geared to each baby's age. Then, over months, they were periodically exposed to a curriculum of songs, musical games, and music-based physical exercises. Afterward they were evaluated again. Sister Kucenski found that the babies improved significantly on the three test scales used for evaluation. These babies also scored far above a group of same-aged babies who were not exposed to the musical curriculum.

This study doesn't mean that you should create a formal curriculum. Nor does it tell us the role of musical stimulation in child development. But it *does* lend strong evidence to the theory that musical appreciation and skills can begin in the first year of life.

- Let your baby listen to the whole range of musical styles and tastes that you enjoy.
- Bounce or rock your baby to music that has a definite beat. Or hug him to your body and dance together.
- Play music or chant as you exercise him.
- Sing to your baby, and play plenty of nursery rhyme games.

Be aware of how your baby responds to music you play on the radio or stereo. Some children become agitated when listening and bouncing to music that is loud or has an uneven rhythm. Then again, some babies have very definite tastes—even at this age. Always let your baby be the judge. After all, music is a personal joy.

Research Update: Inborn Knowledge

We often talk about the importance of experience and practice for teaching, but babies also appear to understand some things almost intuitively. For example, they may have an apparently inborn reflex to dodge approaching objects. In one set of studies, infants under eight months at the Harvard Center for Cognitive Studies were shown a cube that began to move slowly toward them. As the cube drew within apparent striking distance, the babies squirmed, turned aside, and otherwise tried to avoid being hit. Yet these babies had no previous experience with being struck by flying objects.

∞∞∞∞∞∞∞∞∞ **10** ∞∞∞∞∞∞∞∞∞

YOUR EIGHT-MONTH-OLD

Overview

F or the next several months, your baby shows some very definite signs that she's becoming more independent. For one, she is increasingly interested in her age-mates. For another, she's becoming better able to comfort herself rather than always depending on you. She shows this self-comfort skill most demonstrably by forming an attachment to an inanimate object.

Parent's we've interviewed often confide that they feel ambivalent about such signs of independence; they are pleased and excited about watching these new skills emerge, but a bit rueful about being less important in her life. It's true—you _are_ less important. But you are most definitely not being replaced. Think back to when your baby was born. The private close-knit love you and your spouse or partner shared stretched to include this delightful new family member. And just like yours, your baby's emotional world isn't finite.

One situation when she may especially need your comforting is when she awakes at night, which often happens this month or the next. We offer suggestions that let her know she can depend on you, but still help her develop the skills needed to get herself back to sleep again.

Another sign of independence is a desire to feed herself, which usually tumbles forth at this age if not before. Rudimentary self-feeding is possible because she has fairly good arm and hand skills, and you'll see unmistakable signs that she wants to take part in mealtimes: grabbing for the spoon as it approaches her face, or trying to pick up bits of food—even pureed things that slip through her fingers—from the high chair tray. If you can tolerate the added time a meal will take and the inevitable mess that arises from her clumsy attempts, it's a good idea to foster these early self-help skills. Your baby will appreciate her burgeoning independence, and will gain marvelous practice in grasping and eye-hand coordination.

Self-feeding is closely intertwined with manual dexterity. The better your child can grasp a small chunk of a foodstuff, the more likely she'll get it into her mouth. Right now she tends to grasp with thumb and two or so fingers, so she'll likely have the most success with crackers and biscuits and other fairly chunky items. During the last quarter of this year, she'll start using a _pincer_ grasp—thumb and forefinger alone in a highly dexterous and precise apposition—so she'll be able to pick up crumbs and other tiny bits.

Remember that your eight-month-old _can_ chew, as long as the foods are soft and crumbly. Not everything needs to be pureed. Also, remember that it's best to avoid berries, citrus fruits, fish, and egg whites at this age, as many babies do not tolerate them well. It's also best to discuss with the pediatrician every food you feed to your baby.

Your baby's forays into the social world will be full of ups and downs. Around eight or nine months, she is often shy around strangers. In one way, this is related to her separation anxiety discussed in Chapter 9. She'll likely snuggle into your safe arms—another sign you're the one she loves best. She also demonstrates her love by wanting to be near you during the day. Since you probably spend a lot of time in the kitchen, it makes sense to remove dangerous items from low drawers and cabinets, so that she can explore them without too much interference from you.

Soon your baby begins to crawl. This opens new play opportunities, but also means that she is likely to start getting into things. So this is the age to think about your approach to discipline. Remember: If you remove breakables from low tables and ledges, and do your best to make your home safer for your baby to explore, you'll have fewer problems that might call for disciplinary action.

There are other advancements, too. Earlier your baby tended to explore only one object at a time, but now she begins passing a toy from the preferred hand to the other, so that she can grasp a second toy. And when holding two objects, she'll soon compare them visually, touch or bang them together, and maybe try to fit one into the other. Soon you should add multipart toys to her collection.

At this age, your baby begins to make sounds like *s* and *ts* (as in "hats"). Unlike the *ma* and *pa* and *da* sounds made largely with the lips, these new sounds require her to make a narrow funnel in her mouth, between her upper teeth (if she has any) and lower lip, or between her tongue and the roof of her mouth. She must also keep this funnel open as she blows air through it. Studies have found that babies almost always make these more difficult sounds when carefully examining the details of a toy.

By eight or nine months, a baby begins to grasp the concept of *object permanence*—that an object that leaves her sight isn't necessarily gone forever. So now's the time to add some hide-and-seek games with toys.

Stranger Anxiety

Many an eight- or nine-month-old is fearful of unfamiliar people. This *stranger anxiety* draws from the same developmental wellspring as separation anxiety, discussed in our last chapter. Just as your baby now understands that she is an individual, separate from you, she also realizes that she's separate from these strangers—and she's not quite sure how to size them up. Are they friend or foe? Are they helpful or threatening?

This shyness with strangers, or even people she sees infrequently, is perfectly understandable. Think of how you might feel in her place. No matter how gregarious you are, you'd likely be taken aback, too, if an unfamiliar person started to hug or tickle you, or picked you up without warning.

INDIVIDUAL DIFFERENCES

Just as babies differ in intensity of separation fears, they show different levels of stranger anxiety. Some react dramatically to a new face—crying and twisting away, or clutching a parent in fear. Some have basically neutral reactions, such as a watchful stare. Others flirt a bit, looking at the stranger until he looks back, then glancing away and back, away and back. These babies usually warm up after a few minutes, though they may be most comfortable if the stranger keeps his distance. Then again, some babies rarely seem shy of strangers. But nearly all babies exhibit some wariness, even if the symptoms don't show. A study by Joseph Campos found that all the nine-month-olds he tested showed accelerated heartbeats—a sign of fear—in the presence of strangers.

What accounts for such differences? One factor is a baby's general temperament; some babies are just more easygoing than others. Another is how a child is reared. Babies who have generally been cared for by a number of consistent adults (including frequent babysitters) seem to be more comfortable with strangers. There may be gender-related differences as well. A study by Eleanor Maccoby (Stanford University) and Carol Jacklin (University of Southern California) found that, all other things like personal style being equal, boys tend to be a little more fearful of strangers than girls. The stranger's behavior affects the baby, too. Several separate studies, by Harriet Rheingold and Carol Eckerman, Inge Bretherton, and others, have found that initial wariness is greatly reduced when the unfamiliar person gears his behavior to the baby's signals and engages the baby in play with a toy.

EASING THE SITUATION

When your baby greets someone with wails instead of smiles— especially when that "stranger" is a grandparent or other relative she hasn't seen for a while—it can be pretty tense for all of you. According to the researchers above, you can defuse this tension with patience and guidance.

First, help your baby see that this person is a potential friend. Hold your baby in your arms as you talk to the stranger, maybe even in an exaggeratedly friendly way. This will help her feel secure and that this stranger is *your* friend. Also help the other person understand what you're doing, so he or she will give your baby a little room. This strategy has another benefit. When attention is diverted away from your baby, she has time to size things up for herself. Babies often need much more watching time before getting involved with new people or activities than many parents realize.

After a few minutes, show your baby that this new person can be *her* friend. Have her or him make a friendly gesture towards you, such as offering a toy or other object your baby likes. When you accept this "gift," your baby sees that this is someone she can trust. Now invite the stranger to offer her the same toy while speaking in a friendly manner. From this point on, they can continue making friends at whatever pace seems comfortable for your baby.

Unless your baby is tired or ill, your guidance and her natural curiosity will likely win out. Remember that even after she has warmed up, she may be more comfortable relating to this stranger from the security of your arms for a while longer. Chances are, though, she'll soon go to her newfound friend.

If your baby continues to shrink from this stranger, though, do not cajole or try to force her to hug or kiss the person. This can make her even more timid and fearful, and will *not* break her of her shyness. Respect your baby's feelings. She may have her own, very legitimate reasons for keeping her distance from this other person.

Stranger anxiety seems to ease up a bit within a month or two. As we discuss in Chapter 12, "Your Ten-Month-Old," babies near the end of the year often take the initiative to interact with strangers.

Cuddlies and Security Blankets

Most babies have a strong attachment to a special object. The most common is a pacifier; a survey of 690 children aged three to twenty-four months, conducted at the University of Wisconsin by Richard Passman and Roderick Adams, found that 66 percent were attached to pacifiers. Pacifiers offer sucking, which is among a young baby's strongest sources of comfort. But around eight or nine months, many babies become attached to a special blanket or soft toy. This offers warmth rather than sucking, which demonstrates a baby's growing ability to comfort herself. Even though this "dependency" is so common, some parents worry: Is it harmful? We've found no conclusive evidence that a lovey or cuddly, as these objects are usually called, has any negative effect on personality. On the contrary, in fact, many experts support such attachments. As the noted pediatrician T. Berry Brazelton writes in *Infants and Mothers*, "I am always gratified when children form attachments to objects. . . . It gives them one more advantage in coping with the rigors of growing up, with all its frustrations and necessary separations from mother."

An increasing body of evidence suggests that babies have a powerful psychological—even physical—need for what is called *contact comfort*. In his famous research with baby rhesus monkeys, Dr. Harry Harlow created two substitute "mothers." One was a cold wire structure holding a feeding bottle, the other a warm, padded construction offering physical comfort but no food. As expected, baby monkeys fed from the wire mother. But when they were tired or afraid, they went to the cloth substitute, suggesting that its warmth was more emotionally satisfying than sucking or feeding. Other researchers have noted that institutionally-reared infants who received the necessities of food, clothing, and shelter—but little cuddling—often failed to thrive. There's even evidence that emotional warmth and stroking can help premature babies develop better.

In our culture, parents can't carry and touch and play with their babies constantly. So babies benefit from warm, soft objects that provide contact comfort when parents aren't available. A cuddly or lovey, termed a "transitional comfort object" by pediatrician and child development expert D. W. Winnicott, can have further importance in a baby's life. A favorite toy can ease some of the eight-month-old's separation anxiety by offering substitute warmth and security when parents leave. One teacher we know reports that babies in her center often soothe themselves by rhythmically rubbing a soft toy against their skin. Passman and Adams found that babies were more likely to play in and explore strange environments when they had loveys with them than when they didn't. In fact, a "security blanket" was as effective as the baby's parent in making her feel comfortable in unknown settings. (The term "security blanket" is very apt; Passman and Adams found that 60 percent of the children they studied were, indeed, attached to a blanket.)

Soft toys have other strengths, too. They add a variety of textures to a baby's toy collection. Stuffed dolls and animals with faces often inspire babies to "talk" more frequently than do other toys. Teachers tell us that older babies tend to "humanize" soft toys, treating them with nurturing care, hugging and stroking them just as they themselves are cared for by their parents. As one teacher said, "Soft toys help babies to feel loved and to learn how to return love."

If your baby adopts a cuddly, it will likely be her most important possession. Keep it handy when you and your baby travel to new places, go on outings, visit the pediatrician, or whenever an upcoming situation might cause her some discomfort or uncertainty. Be sure the baby-sitter knows your child's cuddly, too!

Tips on Choosing Soft Toys

Parents and teachers we surveyed offer these guidelines for selecting soft toys.

1. Look for bright colors.
2. Make sure each toy is machine washable.
3. Make sure the fabric is colorfast; your baby will chew this toy a lot!
4. Choose toys that are durable and well-made; make sure the seams are securely sewn with tough thread.
5. Toys should be free of buttons, snaps, hooks, bows, and other small parts that could be pulled off—and swallowed.
6. Make sure plastic eyes and other facial features are so strongly attached that *you* can't pick them off. Embroidered or printed faces are the safest.
7. Toys that make sounds have a big advantage. Babies love to make sounds with toys.

A Cry in the Night

Parents expect an infant to cry for them during the night, usually because she needs to be fed. After a few months she starts sleeping through the night—or so parents think. Actually, these babies awaken several times a night (as do adults), but drift back to sleep without crying or calling out, so their parents never know. But this can change at around eight or nine months.

Don't be surprised if your baby who used to sleep soundly now starts crying for you at odd hours. A study of 160 London infants found that about 50 percent of the nine-month-olds started waking up again during the night. And Janet Younger, a nurse who has studied this subject extensively, found that night waking—or at least babies' calling out when they do awake at night—often begins again after the onset of separation anxiety and stranger anxiety. Night waking is common during toddlerhood, too. In analyzing data gathered as part of the New York Longitudinal Study of Temperament and Development, Antonio Beltramini and Margaret Hertzig report that 57 percent of the one-year-olds studied awaken and summon their parents at least once a week; 29 percent do this one or more times every night.

The reasons for these calls in the night are thought to be largely psychological. Separation anxiety is considered the leading culprit. As Jane Curtis, pediatric consultant at Montefiore Hospital's Sleep-Wake Disorders Center, explains, "Between eight and ten months, many babies begin to cry for their parents' attention. They wake up, realize that they are alone, and they are frightened. Awareness of being separated from their parents frightens them during the night, just as it does during the day."

The awake baby naturally wants reassurance that parents are nearby and will come when she needs them. Stressful or new situations—a hospital stay, mother's returning to work outside the home, starting in day care or a new play group—may cause a young child to call for reassurance over several nights until she gets used to the change. Occasional physical discomfort—teething pain or symptoms of a mild illness—is a possibility, too.

TO GO OR NOT TO GO?

Does responding to nighttime cries spoil your baby and encourage this to become a habit? Does ignoring her break the cycle? No one, expert or layman, can give the definitive answers. We recommend responding, just as we recommend responding when she cries or calls for you during the day. Night waking is a behavior, not a bad habit. Your baby doesn't wake herself on purpose, just so she can call for you. She cries or calls because she needs you. If she fears abandonment—as babies often do when going through separation anxiety—her worst fears will be realized when you don't respond.

When you hear a nighttime cry, listen to its tone before responding. If it's not urgent, give your baby a chance to comfort herself. But when she still complains after a few minutes, or begins to sound really upset, then it's time to help calm her down again. Try calling in so she can hear your voice. If that doesn't comfort her, go into her room and tell her you're there, in your own bed, right near her. Perhaps sit next to her crib for a while, and maybe rub her back soothingly. Or rock or carry her quietly around the room. Keep the room dim and quiet to give the message that this is still sleep time. Keep your voice to the matter at hand, which is sleep—not play, not songs, not games, and not food (unless she still has a regular nighttime feeding).

AN OUNCE OF PREVENTION

Although you can't prevent your baby from waking at night, you can help her develop the resources to get herself back to sleep.

The best way, according to Dr. Curtis, is to allow your baby to put herself to sleep at bedtime. Young babies almost always doze off in a parent's arms, then are placed in the crib. That's natural. But if you continue this practice after the half-year mark, you can actually prevent your baby from learning how to fall asleep by herself—and remember, you won't be available every night. Also, when she does cry for you at night, she'll have a tougher time drifting off again if she hasn't had the opportunity to develop some skills for getting herself to sleep.

A regular bedtime routine helps build these skills. As Dr. Curtis says, "The routine, of course, will vary from family to family, but the important thing is that it be consistent. It should begin at roughly the same time every night. A bath, some quiet play, perhaps a story or song may be included. But ultimately, parents should put infants into their cribs while their infants are awake, and allow them to find their own way to lull themselves to sleep. Some babies suck their fingers. Others rock or croon themselves to sleep." A cuddly can help, too.

TIPS FOR SITTERS

Be sure to teach each sitter your baby's bedtime routine and how to handle night waking. Also, try to have a sitter come over before your baby goes to bed, even if you don't need to leave that early. Explain to your child that you'll be going out later. This is far preferable to sneaking out after she falls asleep, hoping she won't awaken during your absence. If she does, and cries out for you, imagine her panic should a stranger walk into her room! When the sitter can't come over early, tell your baby that you will be going out later and that Angela (or Bill or Grandma or whomever) will be caring for her while you're gone. She won't fully understand this right now, but over time she'll begin to catch the meaning of this explanation.

THIS WILL PASS

Caring for a night-waker can be temporarily exhausting. Try to keep it in perspective. As you drag out of bed *again,* remind yourself that this phase will pass, and that your baby will feel safer and more secure because of your willingness to help her through the night.

Thinking about Discipline

Few child-care issues generate more concern than discipline, even when children are still babies. The debate usually starts with a basic question: What is meant by the word *discipline?* Is it punishment, as some parents view it? Is it teaching right from wrong?

We like to think of discipline as guiding your child's behavior—whatever her age. Throughout the early years, discipline has two goals:

1. Short-term: Stopping dangerous or obnoxious behavior on the spot.
2. Long-term: Teaching the child how to act so that eventually she'll be self-disciplined.

For babies, the short-term goals are the most realistic. But over time they'll evolve into the long-term goals as well.

SHORT-TERM GOALS

Why short-term goals? As you think about discipline for an eight-month-old, it's important to keep in mind her developmental needs and capacities. She's a bundle of curiosity, and she must explore new things as part of her development. She needs to touch and taste and feel in order to learn. But she's too young to realize potential dangers. She's likewise too young to understand directions; too young even to control her actions. So you must stop dangerous behavior as—or even before—it happens. We recommend three basic techniques.

1. Babyproofing. Since it isn't realistic to expect your baby to control herself or understand danger, you're better off guarding against trouble *before* it starts. Babyproofing is the best way. If potential dangers are out of your baby's reach, she'll have fewer opportunities for making the mistakes that might call for disciplinary action.

2. Distraction and Substitution. When you see your baby heading for trouble, distract her with some object or activity you know she likes. If she's already handling something she shouldn't be, substitute an acceptable plaything for the dangerous one.

3. Keep "NO" to a Minimum. Decide which behaviors are truly dangerous—these *must* be stopped—and which are merely annoying. For annoying ones, try distraction and substitution. Save *"No!"* for the others.

You can't make your home—or the world—completely safe for a baby's explorations. At times she unexpectedly gets near something that might harm her, such as a hot oven door or an unprotected electrical outlet at a friend's house. These are the times to say *"No!"* and remove her immediately from the source of danger. Also tell her briefly why you are doing so. To the word "No!" add a few others (such as "Hot—it burns," or "sharp," or "hurt") which communicate clearly and firmly the nature of the danger and your concern for her safety. This lesson is best delivered while you are holding your baby—or at least restraining her eager hand. Then help get her mind off the fascinating untouchable by offering something else to play with.

If you use this final technique only in situations where the danger is clear and present, your disapproving tone will get through to your baby even before she understands the words you say. Unfortunately, some parents fall into the habit of overdoing "No," using it almost without thinking anytime their baby reaches for something they wish she wouldn't. The problem is, a baby who hears "No" repeatedly may conclude that the word has very little meaning. If you use *"No!"* sparingly, your baby will gradually learn that you stop her only when real danger exists.

ALSO KEEP IN MIND . . .

As you think about discipline, remember that each baby is an individual. Some acquiesce willingly to distraction and substitution, and quickly learn that "No!" really does mean "No!" Others may put up a bit of resistance and need more patience and practice to incorporate your rules. Your method of discipline must be tailored to your baby's special strengths and sensitivities. Of course, parents are individuals, too. Your approach to discipline must fit into your personal values and style of living. Think of how to incorporate the basic techniques—babyproofing, substitution, and the sparing use of "No"—into your own plans. They will help guide your baby's behavior until she's old enough to understand how she *should* behave. Then she will start controlling herself.

Growing through Play

FIND THE HIDDEN TOY

When your baby was younger, she lost interest in a toy you covered up or removed from her view. At this age, or in the coming weeks, she begins to search for it. This advancement shows that she's beginning to understand the concept of *object permanence*— that something continues to exist even when she can temporarily no longer see it. Find-the-hidden-toy games are fun ways to help her learn. Let's look at a typical version.

While you and your baby are sitting on the floor together, offer her a toy, say, a rattle. When she reaches for it, quickly put it on the floor and cover it with a small towel or diaper. "Where did your rattle go? Can you find your rattle?" She might just look at you quizzically if she's new to the game. No matter. Pull the cloth away with "Here it is!" Then hide the rattle again, maybe this time

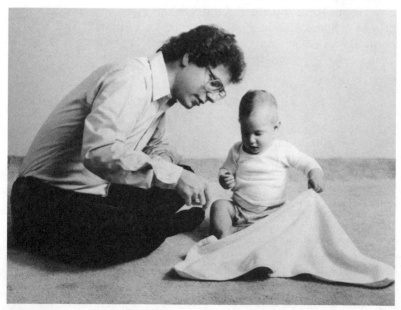

"Where's your rattle, Stephen?"

"You found it—good going!"

leaving a part exposed as a clue. With practice, she'll snatch the towel away—and smile delightedly at the discovery (and her own prowess). Some variations: Hide a toy inside a pot with a lid; hide it behind your back—your baby crawls around you to get it (good exercise for large muscles).

Research Update:
First Friends

Experts are confirming what many parents have told us over the years: Even a baby can begin forming friendships with children her own age. A study by Jacqueline Becker at the University of California, Berkeley, found that not only do babies interact with each other; the more time two babies spend together, the more sociable they become.

Dr. Becker looked at thirty-two pairs of nine-month-olds. The experimental group of sixteen baby pairs met alternately in one or the other's home for ten sessions over a twenty-day period. A control group of sixteen other baby pairs met just twice, and these sessions were on average twenty days apart. Each group had the same number of same-sex and mixed-sex pairs. In all the play sessions, the baby's mother in whose home the babies played was in the room. Some findings:

· The "experimental" babies spent a good deal of the playtime directing behavior to one another—more than to their mothers or to toys. Interactions included looking and smiling at one another, vocalizing, shaking or showing a toy for the other baby to see, touching, and imitating simple actions. These positive interactions far outweighed negative ones.

· The more familiar the babies became, the more they played together. As the sessions went on, the baby pairs dramatically increased the number of complex interactions. But when Dr. Becker placed an "experimental" baby with a new baby after the ten sessions were over, the social behaviors each "experimental" baby had shown when playing with her old friend declined significantly. As further evidence, the "control" babies who played together only twice showed no increase in social play from one session to the other.

Such findings don't suggest that your baby will play with her peers for long periods of time. But they do show that she will probably play in ways that exhibit increasing social interaction as the babies become more familiar with one another.

Remember that not every baby will automatically become a friend of every other baby. Each of us, babies included, has personal tastes. And when babies play together, stay close to make sure they don't accidentally harm one another. Keeping these cautions in mind, it's a good idea to help your baby form some early friendships.

11

YOUR NINE-MONTH-OLD

Overview

Big changes during this last quarter!

· Your baby makes great strides in terms of gross motor skills. He begins to crawl, pull himself to a standing position, walk while holding your hands or another support, and maybe take a few steps all by himself.

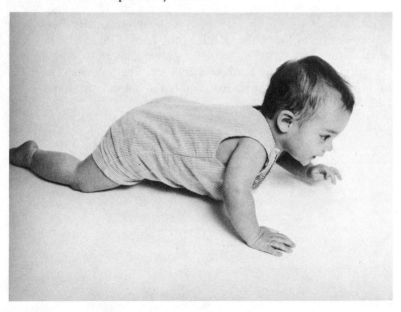

- He becomes fascinated with organization and connection—where things belong, what goes with what—and experiments with ways his toys can be arranged, stacked, nested, and so forth. This demonstrates a growth of both physical and intellectual skills, and opens a whole new avenue of learning.
- His language skills grow, too, and by the end of this year he might even say a few recognizable words.

Your baby understands many things said to him well before he says his first word. But even more than the actual words you use, your baby can comprehend your intentions. You can help him understand what you're saying through gestures and facial expressions. For instance, he'll easily guess what you want if you stretch out your arms while saying "Come here." Add lots of explanatory gestures to your conversations together. And as your baby hears the same words many times over in the same situations, he learns what the particular words mean as well.

Starting around nine months, you'll probably see new developments in self-feeding, too. As we said last month, your baby has probably already started to feed himself with his fingers. Between now and year's end, he tries drinking from a cup as well. At first you'll need to hold it for him, maybe with his "helping" you; by himself, he would tilt it too far and too quickly, because he lacks the necessary control over wrist movements. Soon, though, he'll take a bigger role in holding it himself, until he takes over the job completely.

NOTE: A two-handled cup with lid and spout helps prevent spillage, and makes it easier for you and your baby to hold it simultaneously. We suggest a lidded cup with spout for about the next year. According to research, most children aren't able to lift an unlidded cup or tumbler, drink from it without spilling, and replace it on the feeding tray or other surface until about twenty-one months.

Looking at Crawling

A typical six- or seven-month old alternately lifts his chest, then stomach, from the floor while supporting his weight on arms and legs. It looks like he's ready to move into the crawling position—but few babies that age do, because they don't lift chest and stomach together. A month or so later, many babies begin to move, usually pulling themselves forward with their arms while dragging legs and stomach across the floor. They know where they want to go, but it takes a while to discover the best way to get there.

Later, the arms begin reaching out in alternating movements like the strokes of a swimmer, the legs move more, chest and stomach come off the floor simultaneously, and true crawling begins. Between nine and twelve months, the crawling movements of earlier months become more rhythmic, and crawling becomes a well-coordinated and speedy way of moving.

IMPORTANT FOR MANY REASONS

Not every baby crawls in the familiar hands and knees position. Some creep along on hands and feet, others employ their arms more than their legs. A few seem almost to bypass this stage, preferring to go right ahead with learning to stand and walk. But whatever means of locomotion a baby chooses, crawling (or creeping or scooting or whatever method your baby employs) is a big developmental step because a mobile baby has more control over his world. He can help choose where he wants to go and what he wants to explore (at least, in your home). What freedom! Crawling is great exercise, builds coordination, and helps develop large muscles. It also appears to be vital for developing some other skills, too.

In an article published in the *Infant Mental Health Journal*, Joseph Campos (University of Denver) and Bennett Bertenthal (University of Virginia) reinforce the importance of crawling for developing a fear of heights. When noncrawling babies were placed on a sheet of glass over a well, they had no negative response. Yet when crawling babies the same age were likewise placed on this "visual cliff," they showed significant heart-rate accelerations. Campos and Bertenthal also point out that crawling helps a baby develop spatial orientation.

This last point finds further support in a study of twenty-six ten- and eleven-month-olds by Janette Benson (University of Denver) and Ina Uzgiris (Clark University). Each baby watched the experimenter place a toy into a clear plastic box with the back panel removed. The box was then covered. The baby could retrieve the toy only by going around to the box's rear, before or after he uncovered it. In some trials, the infant crawled around the box himself; in other trials his mother carried him around.

Benson and Uzgiris found that babies who crawled around the box themselves were far more successful at retrieving the hidden toy than those carried. And interestingly, infants who solved the problem on their own when crawling did not transfer this learning to later trials when they were carried by mothers. These results, according to the researchers, support Piaget's theory that babies need practical experienced-based knowledge to develop spatial understanding. The findings also suggest that by moving through space himself, a baby comes to understand better the spatial relationships between the toy and the box.

GAMES FOR THE CRAWLER

Your baby's curiosity encourages him to crawl, and the sheer joy of moving under his own power drives him to practice and practice and get better and speedier. . . . He doesn't need to be taught this skill. But you can make crawling more fun by giving him some enticing thing to crawl toward: a toy shaken just out of his reach, a favorite finger food, or your outstretched arms. When he's steady on hands and knees, you might try these games:

- Slowly pull a toy across the floor for your baby to chase.
- Roll a ball and encourage your baby to "Go get it!"
- Get down on your own hands and knees and "chase" your baby.
- Give your accomplished crawler a change of pace. Using firm couch cushions, build a series of broad steps and invite your baby to crawl to the top to get a prize (a favorite toy, an excited hug from Daddy or Mommy).

Beware of Small Objects!

You should definitely clear floors and low surfaces of small objects—buttons, coins, marbles, etc.—since your crawling baby can explore under his own power. There are some other choking hazards with which you might not be as familiar.

FOODS

Now that your baby is feeding himself finger foods, you need to pay special attention to food-related choking hazards.

A task force comprising pediatricians, otolaryngologists, pathologists, and other experts assembled by the American Academy of Pediatrics reports that children under four years of age are at the highest risk of choking and suffocating on foods, and that the peak incidence is around one year. They report greatest culprits are round, firm foods like pieces of hot dogs and other meats, round candies, and grapes. These are approximately the shape of the upper airway (pharynx) and if trapped in the throat can completely cut off air. The task force also warns that small, hard foods such as nuts, candies, and raw carrot sticks can be risky, since young children tend to swallow them without chewing. Such foodstuffs are inappropriate at eight or nine months, anyway. They can get trapped in the lower airways, again, cutting off air. These experts recommend that parents take special caution with the types of food mentioned above, and that they cut things into small bite-sized pieces when possible.

BUTTON BATTERIES

Dr. Toby Litovitz of Georgetown University Hospital reports increasing cases of children swallowing the button-type batteries commonly used in watches, cameras, calculators, and hearing aids. As he writes in a recent issue of *Pediatrics* and an earlier issue of the *Journal of the American Medical Association*, ingesting batteries is dangerous for two reasons. One, the round battery can become trapped in the throat and block off air. And two, a battery's contents can be released inside a child if it gets trapped in the gastrointestinal tract. Some fatalities have been reported.

BALLOONS

Young children have also been known to aspirate deflated balloons; the elastic material can clog the air passages. *Never* let your child play with a balloon unsupervised.

SMALL TOY PARTS

Most baby toys made by reputable American toy companies are designed to pass safety standards. One standard makes sure that any given part is too large for a baby to swallow. However, you should take care if you have an older child as well, or when your baby visits a home in which there is an older child. According to the *Home Safety Newsletter* published by the National Safety Council, swallowing toys is a leading cause of toy-related injuries. And the most common toys that babies swallow are pieces of toys intended for children three years and older.

New Toy Interests

The types of toys your baby enjoys and how he plays with them change dramatically over this first year. Around nine or so months, you'll see an exciting advancement.

In the course of helping create the Johnson & Johnson Child Development Toys, Dan Simpson, our director of testing, has watched thousands of babies play with hundreds of playthings. And as he reports, nine months marks the beginning of a transition.

Up until now, your baby usually played with one object at a time. In fact, even if you gave him two toys at once, he likely explored each separately. At nine months, he still enjoys shaking and banging and poking his familiar one-piece toys. But he begins showing interest in multipart toys, too. He likes to grasp a separate object in each hand, hold them up simultaneously to compare them, and clap them together. He might also put a small object inside a larger one and take it out again. In short, he does more with two objects than he could do with either one alone.

This change truly is dramatic. It signifies your baby's physical ability to manipulate a different object with each hand. It marks his new cognitive ability to realize that separate objects can be related to one another—a sign of his burgeoning interest in how the world of experience is organized. And just as important, it opens up a new avenue for learning. For only by stacking and fitting and relating objects to one another does a baby come to learn important concepts like size differences (What's larger? What's smaller?) and spatial relationships (What's on top? What's underneath?).

MORE EVIDENCE

Our own research findings are corroborated by a study conducted by Jerome Kagan, Larry Fenson, and others. They looked at how children in four different age groups—seven months, nine months, thirteen months, and twenty months—played with a multipart tea set in individual lab tests. The youngest babies explored each object separately, as expected. So did the nine-month-olds. But 92 percent of the nine-month-old babies also engaged in simple relational behaviors like touching the spoon to the pot or the teapot lid to the side of a cup—and these were more popular than individual explorations.

LOOKING AHEAD

This interest in multipart toys grows steadily, and we'll have more to say about it in future chapters. For now, though, start adding toys with parts your baby can fit on or inside one another. When he puts two things together, delight in his prowess and encourage further experimentation. "Look, Justin, you put the ball inside the bowl! Can you take it out again?" Demonstrate different ways parts can be related, too. Don't be surprised if he doesn't follow your example right away. After all, he's just starting these explorations, and each step—small as it may seem to you—is a giant leap in his play and learning.

Growing through Play

UP HE GOES

Between nine and twelve months, your baby pulls himself up to standing by holding on to a support like a piece of furniture, your clothing, or the crib rails. He's well on his way to walking! But just like when he began to sit, he may have trouble getting down again—and might need your help for the first few weeks. For safety's sake, always supervise carefully when your baby is around flimsy or fragile furniture, or similar objects that might tumble over should he try pulling up on them.

THE BIG TOSS

Why do babies love to drop and throw things? No one can say with absolute authority, but we can make some assumptions. One, just as a baby practices holding objects many different ways, he needs to practice releasing them when and where he wants. Dropping and tossing are ways of letting things go that don't require much accuracy. And like any emerging skill, a baby enjoys practicing this new releasing ability again and again. Two, once a baby starts tossing things, he discovers that different objects move differently and make different sounds when they land. So dropping and tossing is a way to learn more about an object's properties. Contrary to popular belief, a nine-month-old does *not* toss things only to annoy or control his parents!

But tossing can become a fun game. Give your baby a few

different toys when he's in his high chair. He drops or tosses, you talk about the sounds each makes and retrieve them for another round. Careful, though. This game could go on forever if your baby had his way. Call a gradual halt when you've fetched enough and give him something else to play with, like a suction-cup toy stuck onto the high-chair tray.

HINT: What to do when your baby tosses all his toys out of the crib—then begs for something to play with? Make sure he has an activity center–type toy securely attached to the crib side.

SING WITH ME

Your nine-month-old likes to imitate you when you make sounds he knows, like *hi, oh-oh,* or *dada.* If you sing a musical tune along with these sounds, he likes it even better.

Imitation games like this seem really simple, but they aid language skills in lots of ways. When he imitates, your baby must listen very carefully to both you and himself, and then try to match the two sounds as closely as he can. So as he plays he practices concentration, listening carefully to speech sounds, making sounds—and he may even learn a few new words. So much from so little!

FUN IN THE WATER

Your baby has played with water almost from his first bath. He waved his arm . . . something moved and plopped against his skin. Later he kicked, and created more movement and new sensations. These early explorations mature into the scooping and pouring that mark true water play.

Most babies enjoy true water play once they can sit securely in the tub, usually between seven and nine months if you use a plastic baby bath. The family tub is probably too slippery unless you put a rubber mat on the bottom. And even then, your baby might like your supportive arm across his back to help keep him from sliding around. Once he gets his sea legs, though, water play blossoms. It's as beneficial as it is fun, too. In a nutshell, while playing with water your baby:

- · practices all kinds of arm-hand-finger skills and eye-hand coordination: splashing, scooping, pouring, filling, catching a bobbing toy or a pouring stream;

- learns scores of new words when you participate: _empty, full, wet, dry, float, sink, cold, warm;_
- discovers early scientific principles, such as flotation and water power ("What happens when I pour water over this paddle wheel?").

Water play is relaxing and absorbing. According to Joy Goldberger, a specialist in play with hospitalized and handicapped children, water play is particularly good for calming children who are tense or angry at being hospitalized, and for relaxing children with muscular tension caused by disease or disability. Of course, this absorption and relaxation are beneficial for every child from time to time.

Water play also leads to feelings of mastery. Water can be acted upon in so many dramatic ways, and every kind of play is successful. It requires no prescribed set of skills so there's no built-in failure potential. It lets your baby experiment at his own pace and succeed without pressure. So it's a nice counterpoint to the more structured toys and activities he also enjoys.

You can help by setting up play opportunities, by supervising to make sure everything's going safely, by providing a range of interesting water toys, by offering verbal encouragement and new words learning, and (of course) by joining in when you can.

For Outdoors
- A wading pool is a favorite. The molded plastic kind is more durable than the inflated ring type.
- For more confined spaces, or times when you don't want to use a wading pool, fill a large tub with water. Your baby sits outside to play—or even in this tub if it's large enough for him and some favorite toys.
- For more confined play (such as on a small porch), give your baby some toys and a plastic dishpan filled with water. He sits outside it to play.

For Indoors
- The bathtub is a natural. You can store favorite bath toys in a drawstring mesh bag and hang it over the shower head between playtimes so that the toys drip dry. Remember: This bag is not a toy; your baby could get entangled in the string.

- If your baby is none too secure in the regular tub even with a rubber mat on the bottom, let him play in the baby bath that you've put into the dry tub.

Good Toys for Water Play
- Plastic kitchen items like cups with handles, sieves and strainers, sifter, small bowls, and measuring cups. Make sure that your baby doesn't put any slender parts (i.e., strainer handles) into his mouth.
- Plastic cup you've punched holes in with a large nail.
- Nonwaterloggable balls (best for outdoor play).
- Commercial water toys. Those that let your baby manipulate water a variety of ways (i.e., scooping, pouring, squirting, "raining") and have removable parts that can be stacked and fitted together will get extra play throughout the next several months.

Poke holes in a plastic cup to create a dramatic rainmaker.

Water Safety Reminders

1. *Never* let your baby play in or around water without your vigilant supervision. There's always a chance of drowning.
2. *Always* drain a wading pool or other water-filled container after playtime. Any body of standing water is a drowning hazard—to neighborhood children as well as your own child.
3. *Never* let your baby play in the bathroom unless you're there. There are documented cases of children drowning in the toilet bowl.
4. Always supervise tub play closely, even if your baby is strapped into a bathtub seat. A recent issue of the *Accident Prevention Newsletter* put out by The American Academy of Pediatrics reports a case in which a baby in such a seat squirmed partway loose, and became lodged with his head underwater.

Research Update: Premies Catch Up

Holly Ruff and three colleagues at the Albert Einstein College of Medicine videotaped thirty nine-month-old prematurely born babies while each played with novel objects. They scored the babies for behaviors such as looking, handling, mouthing, turning the toy around, fingering it, transferring it from hand to hand, and banging it. When the researchers studied twenty full-term babies the same age, they found little difference between the two groups. So even if your baby was premature, you might still give him toys recommended for other babies his age.

12

YOUR
TEN-MONTH-OLD

Overview

T he first few months of parenthood are certainly filled with questions and problems, as you settle into life with a new (and very insistent!) family member. By three or four months, though, your baby likely entered a golden period, happy and cheerful, content to stay where she was placed. Things proba-

bly went smoothly for a while. But . . . night waking started again. And crawling, with its whole array of new problems. And this month your baby might make a fuss about going to bed. And soon she'll be walking. And she's ever so much more independent than she was as an infant. And so the visions of a new baby, that snuggly, dependent creature, start popping into mind.

Near the end of a baby's first year is the time many parents consider having a second child. (The next time is when the first child turns about eighteen months, and becomes quite contrary.) But many psychologists think this isn't the best time to add to your family, as we discuss in this chapter.

One puzzling—and annoying!—behavior that often arises this month or next is fighting the stroller. A younger baby usually sits quite complacently, enjoying the scenery and outing. But once a baby begins crawling well and standing with support (common around this age), and later walking alone, many struggle against confinement in this device; they'd much rather be out on their own. Your baby might try standing in her stroller, or fuss to be taken out every block or so when out for a walk. Naturally, standing in a stroller is dangerous, so you should always make sure she is securely strapped in. Just as naturally, you can't let her crawl around on sidewalks and pavements. Nor will you always have the time to take frequent breaks, particularly when your baby accompanies you on errands. This might be the time to leave her home with your spouse or a sitter if possible. If not, talk to her frequently to divert her attention from the stroller, make sure she has some toys to play with, and rush through errands as quickly as possible.

Uneasy bedtimes, stroller struggles, and other distractions aside, your ten-month-old continues to delight with her amazing skills. Now she makes a whole repertoire of sounds to communicate different needs or feelings. For example, she uses one group of sounds—usually short, simple words including *m* sounds, like *mi, imi, ama*—to ask for things she wants. Over time these may all merge into single words like *more* and *mine*. Another class of sounds may be used regularly to indicate dislike of foods or activities (like having her face washed); a third to indicate pleasure and surprise. It's fun to decipher her codes.

What your baby watches gives clues about her changing interests. At this age she probably enjoys looking at scenes as much as at individual people and objects, and shows particular fascination with other children at play. This is a further way she reveals her developing social skills, and is another preview of the expanded social life that toddlerhood brings. Since babies learn by watching and imitating, make sure your baby has plenty of social playtimes, even with children a bit older than she. Always supervise in case squabbles arise.

And now she does even more with her toys, and welcomes new ways of playing with you. On to ten months!

Uneasy Bedtimes

Whoever popularized the phrase "sleeps like a baby" either hinted at darker meanings or certainly wasn't a parent, because sleep problems are quite usual during babyhood. In Chapter 10 we discussed the night waking that commonly starts some time after six months. Now that your baby is in the final quarter of her first year, she may make a fuss about *going* to bed. There are several reasons why. Some are new, some are quite familiar and on-going. But what's different now is that, unlike the younger baby who almost always drops off when tired, at this age a baby can *purposefully keep herself awake*. In fact, according to British psychologist Penelope Leach, a baby sometimes fights sleep no matter how exhausted she is—and then gets so tense she needs you to help relax her into nodding off.

COMMON CAUSES OF BEDTIME SQUALLS

Major upsets: A dramatic event—a sudden illness, being separated from parents for several days while they travel—can understandably disturb normal sleeping habits for days or even weeks afterward. A formal study by Dr. Leon Yarrow at the National Institutes of Health found that sleep disturbances are quite common when a child returns home after a hospital stay, especially among nine- to twelve-month-olds.

Changes in routine: Less startling disruptions in the daily routine can likewise cause bedtime fussing. Babies are creatures of habit; they can be troubled by moving into a new room or sleeping in strange quarters when traveling (or even in the familiar nursery if the furniture has been rearranged). That's why a baby who has rare problems in her own home may raise a ruckus on overnight visits. Even non-sleep-related changes like starting in a new playgroup or day-care center or being cared for by a new sitter can lead to bedtime problems.

Separation anxiety: Add the phenomenon of separation anxiety (see Chapter 9, "Your Seven-Month-Old") to the ten-month-old's ability to stay awake at will, and you have a classic reason for bedtime blues. Since she rarely wants to leave you voluntarily during the day, she's certainly unwilling to separate uncomplainingly at night.

Then there are the occasional circumstances that prevent your baby from relaxing easily into sleep, like holiday overexcitement or an argument with parents as bedtime approaches. No wonder the trip to nodland may have some rocky starts.

PREVENTION SUGGESTIONS

As some of the aforementioned reasons imply, babies, like adults, can be too keyed up to sleep. One way you can help soothe bedtime struggles is to minimize the causes of baby "tension."

· Try to avoid introducing major changes in routine if you can. This might not be the best time for taking a trip (with or without your baby), or the mother's starting or returning to work outside the home.
· Keep prebedtime low-keyed, friendly, and enjoyable. No roughhouse. No fighting.

EASING SEPARATIONS

Since separation anxiety often creates fussiness, help prepare your baby for your nighttime departure. This is where a regular bedtime routine works wonders.

In our interviews with parents, we've found that many use the age-old soothing rituals: lullabies, nursery rhymes, a quiet time together in the rocking chair, a story, sucking on the breast or bottle. The warmth and familiarity of such activities relax your baby and make her feel loved. They also ease the transition from awake activity to sound sleep. And a regular routine helps your baby prepare herself for the idea of sleep, so the nightly leave-taking comes as no surprise.

Luckily, your baby is developing her own rituals for coping with your loss once you bid that final "good night." One is by sucking her fingers or a pacifier: Sucking is the basic comfort ritual in infancy. Another is by becoming attached to a special cuddly. Repetitive, rhythmic movements like fondling her hair or ears, or rocking on hands and knees, also help her comfort herself.

WHEN BABY CRIES

Preparations and care won't always guarantee an easy drift into sleep. No matter how drowsy and comfortable your baby is, she might give some complaining cries once you leave the room. As long as she doesn't seem too distressed, it's best to let them go unanswered. But if they build in intensity . . . Some professionals recommend you go to your baby, others suggest letting her cry it out. Our survey of parents found both these views supported. If you go to your baby, as we suggest you do, it's a good idea to be very calm and quiet, remind her that you're nearby, maybe stroke her back or bottom, and repeat your "good night." In general, make sure she knows that this is not get-up-and-play time. After a few of these reassurances, she (you hope) will drift into sleep. However, if your baby seems to be having strong and constant problems going to sleep, you should discuss them with her pediatrician.

HELPING YOURSELF

A baby's bedtime fusses very rarely signify a serious problem, but they can be annoying. You can keep your equanimity by reminding yourself that this is only a phase, and by not blaming yourself or your baby. Nightly difficulties have some real causes. And they're far from unusual. Despite other parents' rosy-hued reports of angelic bedtimes, our research guarantees that you are most emphatically *not* alone.

Be Careful of Bedtime Bottles

Although sucking is a traditional bedtime self-comforting ritual, avoid letting your baby fall asleep while sucking on a bottle (unless it's filled with water). As we reported in Chapter 8, nursing to sleep on juice, sweetened liquids, and even formula can cause severe tooth decay called *nursing bottle mouth*. A pacifier or your baby's thumb are preferred alternatives.

Harmless Habits—Or Problems?

Self-comforting rituals like sucking, rocking, and twisting her hair are usually positive signs that your child is becoming increasingly independent and able to cope with minor stresses. Most experts agree that using repetitive rituals to help get to sleep is quite normal. However, a few babies take things too far. It's less accepted when a baby frequently engages in such comforting techniques during waking hours. Banging her head against a wall or sitting in a corner rocking can mean that your baby is not getting enough stimulation from her environment or enough emotional attention and support from her parents. But how much daytime self-comforting is too much? No one can pinpoint the exact amount. You have to use your own judgment. If you think your baby engages in it excessively, talk to her pediatrician.

IS HEAD BANGING NORMAL?

Although you might think it odd, many a baby finds comfort in banging her head against the crib side. Again, this is accepted with little question. As British pediatrician Miriam Stoppard says, "This is rarely a sign of abnormality, and there's little risk of brain damage; what's more, the baby will grow out of it quite quickly." Many other experts agree.

Some books recommend using a crib bumper to protect baby from the hard crib surfaces. We disagree on safety grounds. Although the bumper will cushion her blows, a baby who can pull up to a standing position (as can most babies after nine months) might readily use it as a convenient step for climbing out of the crib. Then she could really get hurt! It's quite doubtful that your baby will hit her head hard enough to cause damage. However, if she's a vigorous enough head-banger to cause you concern, talk to her pediatrician.

Planning Your Next Baby?

Spacing of children is widely believed to have an impact on their development, especially on well-being and personality. But what spacing is ideal? Research in this area is turning up new—and changing—findings.

For years, the popular two-year interval between children was almost unquestioned. But research in the 1970s concluded that a three-year difference was best. By three years, it was felt, a child is independent enough of her parents that the newcomer poses fewer psychological problems than when the older child is just two years old. Now research reported at a recent annual meeting of the American Association for the Advancement of Science suggests different parameters. According to one study of over seventeen hundred teenage boys, conducted by psychologist Jeannie Kidwell of the University of Tennessee, Knoxville, the adolescents with siblings about two years away had the most negative feelings about themselves and their parents. Dr. Kidwell found the least negativism when the siblings were under one year or over four years apart—not the recommended three years.

Why such varied optimal intervals? It seems that the one-year-old is so young that she accepts a new baby as just a regular part of life, and can't remember a time when she was the sole star in her parents' eyes. On the other end, the four- or five-year-old is in school and has developed many interests outside the home. She has enough self-confidence that she is less likely to resent the newcomer as a wedge between herself and her parents.

KEEPING IT IN PERSPECTIVE

When you think about the best spacing for your children, we recommend that you weigh research as just one factor in the equation. Spacing studies may offer information, but they should never be the sole reason for making a decision. For one thing, no one knows *for sure* what the ideal spacing should be. Remember, too, that spacing studies might suggest what's optimal for a child—not necessarily for the entire family. You might have very good reasons for spacing at your own intervals: the mother's health or career, the family's financial condition, or your own judgment of child rearing. That's why even though Dr. Kidwell's study says that spacing of either under one or over four years is equally beneficial for the child, she concludes that "A spacing of five years is apparently optimal. It frees the parents from having to meet the demands and pressures of two children close in age and needs, and allows parents and children more time in one-to-one interaction for a far more supportive and relaxed relationship." Almost any parent of very closely spaced children will tell you that two babies in diapers can be quite a job! Close spacing can intensify early rivalry for parents' attention. Experts like Burton White and Haim Akmakjian generally feel that, as Dr. Akmakjian says, "The smaller the difference in age between siblings, the greater the rivalry."

ON THE OTHER HAND

Yet there's another side to this story. Several parents we spoke with extol the joys of close spacing. For instance, there are some less than perfect aspects of early childhood—night feedings, dirty diapers, and the like, things some parents like to put behind them. This consideration is likely to be especially important to a parent who wants to return to work as soon as possible, but to stay home until all the children have at least started nursery school. There's no denying that the closer together the children are in age, the sooner this parent will reach that point. Also, these early years pass, and siblings have a whole lifetime together. Often closely spaced children become best of friends as they get older, especially once sibling rivalry is no longer a key issue. When we talk to adults about their *own* sibling relationships, many report being closest to the sibling closest in age—and that is frequently two years or less. A close beginning can create a closeness for all time.

IN SUMMARY

Spacing your children is a personal matter. Since each family is individual, there can never be an absolute right or wrong interval. Don't take the latest guidelines as necessities. Anyway, you can't always follow such recommendations no matter how much you want to. It's a rare couple who can decide exactly when the wife will get pregnant again—and ensure that the conception will carry right through to delivery. More important than the worrying about spacing is giving each child plenty of attention and love, so that she feels valuable and secure. That truly leads to well-being!

More on Multipart Toys

According to psychologist Jean Piaget, your baby's intelligence develops in orderly, distinct stages, much the way her physical skills unfold. Piaget's theories say that a baby comes into the world unable to think in an abstract way. She likewise lacks understanding of space, of number, of cause and effect, of the ways that objects can be organized, and of other basic concepts. As a baby grows, she builds these concepts bit by bit. Piaget stressed that the way a child develops and refines these concepts is through play, especially play with objects.

PLAY = LEARNING

To summarize Piaget's theories, learning is an active, hands-on process. A baby needs hundreds—even thousands—of experiences handling objects: exploring their separate parts, arranging them from smallest to largest, stacking and nesting them, classifying them into groups, counting them and learning to label them. From such experiments a baby comes to master basic concepts. As Piaget put it, "To think . . . is to classify, to arrange, to place in correspondence, to collect, to dissociate, etc. But all these operations must be carried out materially, in actions, in order to be capable afterward of being constructed in thought."

Luckily, your baby's natural curiosity fuels such experiments. But to carry them out, she needs toys that have several parts.

FASCINATED BY ORGANIZATION

Another reason a baby favors multipart playthings near year's end is because she's becoming fascinated with *organization* and *connection*—what goes with what.

A ten-month-old has typically begun making more sense out of the world. She now realizes that there is a logic to many things. For example, she knows what familiar objects are used for—a bottle is for drinking from, a car for riding in, shoes are for wearing on the feet. (In contrast, a six-month-old would try using a shoe like a rattle.) She soon begins to realize that certain things belong in particular places: her socks go in the drawer, books and toys go on the nursery shelves. Unfortunately for parents, she won't put her things away for several months yet, but she is nonetheless understanding where they should go.

You'll notice this fascination even more clearly when your baby starts talking several months from now. The toddler loves to connect words with objects, and will constantly ask "What's dat?" She delights in connecting people with their possessions: "Daddy's coat," "Mommy's shoes," and most emphatically "*My* toy!"

Your baby's interest in organization extends to her play. That's why over the next several months she'll spend countless hours exploring the ways she can organize the parts of a toy: stack them, nest them, fit them together or on top of or inside one another. All these types of play can lead to concept learning, especially size differences and spatial relationships, while helping your baby develop precise eye-hand coordination.

JUST THE BEGINNING

Exploring relationships among toy parts is one hallmark of early toddlerhood. Your baby is just beginning. Naturally, some activities require greater physical and intellectual skills than others. So don't expect your ten-month-old to master the stacking skills of an eighteen-month-old. But don't be surprised if she tries!

We'll continue this important skills story in future chapters. For now, try the following game.

FILL & DUMP

A favorite early activity is putting objects into some type of container, taking or dumping them out, then repeating the process—sometimes over and over and *over*. Generally called "fill-and-dump," this game is so popular with the under-twelves because it's simple and mistake-proof: the opening in the container is much larger than the objects that go inside. Fill-and-dump is a forerunner of fitting things together, like a shape sorter, that require more precision. You can help your baby.

· Provide appropriate toys.
· Label your baby's actions and the materials she uses so that she learns many new words.
· Take turns—your baby puts in a toy, then you, then your baby. . . .

GOOD CONTAINERS: plastic mixing bowl, large plastic food-storage containers, small cardboard box without lid, basket, shoebox.

GOOD FILLERS: coasters, balls, plastic blocks, rattles, other smallish toys your baby can grasp easily. Make sure all are too large to fit entirely into her mouth.

Growing through Play

STAIRS—A SPECIAL FASCINATION

Once your baby is reasonably skilled at crawling and creeping, she tackles the staircase with a mountain climber's enthusiasm. Many ten-month-olds we know climb stairs over and over without becoming tired or bored. Great fun and great exercise!

Climbing up is much easier than descending. At first you'll have to transport your baby to the bottom again. Over time she'll learn (with your teaching and encouragement) to slide down feet-first on her stomach, slowing her descent with her hands and feet.

Whether you carry your baby down or she descends under her own power, you'll probably tire of stair climbing before she does. Don't let her pursue this fascination alone, though—the staircase can be very dangerous. Install safety gates at both top and bottom to keep it "off-limits" when you can't oversee expeditions.

THAT'S MY NAME!

Your ten-month-old responds to her name. Over the past few months she probably turned when you called, but researchers believe that the sound of your voice had more power than the words you used. She most likely responded to "Hey, you there," too. But now she is beginning to get the idea that she has a *name of her own.* Use it frequently in your conversations, especially in place of pronouns: "We're going out—it's time to put on Molly's coat" (rather than "your coat"). Aid name learning with simple games: You say, "Where's (Molly)?" When she points to herself, confirm her discovery with "There she is!"

HOLDING ON TO WHAT'S HERS

Here's a behavior that often perplexes parents. Your baby spontaneously holds out a favorite toy, you quite logically interpret this as an invitation to take it. Yet when you grasp the toy she looks surprised and pulls it back, getting quite annoyed if you don't release the proffered present.

She's not teasing you. There are good reasons for her seemingly split-second change of mind. For one thing, she probably had no intention of letting you take the toy from her. She extended it merely to get your attention or to show you a prize possession as if to say, "Look at what I have." Then again, she's just learning how to release objects at will, and isn't always sure of her ability to unfurl her hand voluntarily so you can take the toy. Either way, it's best not to snatch it over her protestations. Release it with a cheery "Thank you," or turn this into a gentle tug-of-war game, which most babies enjoy (especially when you let them win).

Research Update:
More on Stranger Anxiety

Recent chapters looked at aspects of your baby's social develop-ment like stranger anxiety and early friendships. Two studies add fuel to the notion that babies are more sociable than experts used to think. And once babies can crawl, they prove (at least in test settings) that fear takes a distant back seat to curiosity and budding friendliness.

In one study of ten-month-old crawlers, Carol Eckerman (Duke University) and Harriet Rheingold (University of North Carolina, Chapel Hill) sat mother-baby pairs one-by-one on the floor of a lab called the Starting Room. An adult female stranger sat on the floor of an adjoining Test Room. The baby was allowed to explore at will while a hidden observer monitored her actions.

The researchers first ran a trial using ten babies. While in the Starting Room, all the babies looked and smiled at the stranger. Five also crawled into the Test Room with the stranger, and one touched her. The researchers then duplicated the trial with ten more babies. This time, the stranger was told to smile at and even call to the baby when a baby looked at her. The result? Six of the ten babies entered the Test Room and four touched the stranger.

Eckerman and Rheingold found that *none* of the babies evinced any distress with the stranger. And just as significant, when the stranger responded to the baby's eye-contact, she evoked much more smiling and contact.

Barbara Lenssen at the University of New Mexico looked at another aspect of infant sociability. Does a ten-month-old show fear of strangers when the stranger is a baby?

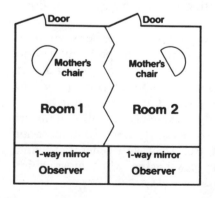

The testing room set up in Lenssen's experiments; adapted from Barbara G. Lenssen, "Infants' Reactions to Peer Strangers."

She tested forty-five crawlers in a two-phase experiment. In phase one, a baby was placed on the floor of a test room while her mother sat in a chair nearby. As in the Eckerman-Rheingold study, the baby could explore at will while a hidden observer monitored her actions. Then, in phase two, the mother placed her baby near her again, and a folding door was opened to reveal another mother and baby. Lenssen found that:

- No baby showed distress (such as clinging to her mother) in the strangers' company. On the contrary, every baby looked less at her mother, crawled farther away from her, and sought less maternal physical contact when the strangers were visible (phase two) than when baby and mother were alone (phase one).
- All the babies stared smilingly at the strangers; over 40 percent stared for about three-fourths of the test period. Nearly all the babies entered the strangers' room, and 75 percent touched the strangers.
- The babies also spent *considerably* more time looking at and touching the stranger-babies than the stranger-mothers.

What do we make of this? It could be that ten-month-olds are, in general, less fearful of strangers than eight- or nine-month-olds. Or it could be that in certain circumstances, when we look closely enough, babies are less fearful than other experiments might suggest they are in general. If we look on the positive side, these studies give evidence that, at this age, your baby is probably eager to explore people as well as toys. So give her lots of chances!

13

YOUR ELEVEN-MONTH-OLD

Overview

R emember your baby's earliest few months? It seemed that every day brought an advancement, like lifting his head from the mattress or offering that heart-filling first smile or batting his crib toys. Now this first year is drawing to a close, and, again, it's a time of monumental achievements. Climbing. First steps. First words.

Researchers have found a great variation in the age when important "firsts" appear. This month we talk about first words, because some babies start saying recognizable words well before year's end. But as you read about this extraordinary achievement, remember that there is a great variety in ages for first words spoken. The same is true for first steps taken, in our next chapter. We've seen walkers start as young as nine months, as old as sixteen months. Some children don't say recognizable words until eighteen months—even later. All fall within what developmental experts call the normal range. It's also important to remember that practically every child will learn to speak and walk no matter when he says his first word or takes his first step. And those who speak first won't necessarily end up the most fluent, just as early walkers don't automatically become the swiftest or most agile.

Other typical developments at this age include:

- Walking while holding a piece of furniture or other support.
- Making speeches of nonsense words and sounds. These lengthy babbles are filled with voice inflections, pauses and intonations—in fact, they sound very much like real speech. Such silly speech is often very sociable, and through it your baby is telling you how he feels about things and events. Pay attention when he babbles in your presence, and converse with him just as if he really were talking. It's one of the best ways he can hold a "conversation" before he develops a large speaking vocabulary.
- Understanding the meaning of "No." Most eleven-month-olds do, but they don't always obey you when you use it. Often a baby's urge to touch or explore is greater than his self-restraint. He may even handle a forbidden object while shaking his head and repeating "No, no, no," all the while. You should continue using "*No!*" to warn about important hazards, but you'll still have to accompany it with action, such as restraining him or removing him from the threatening situation.

Also, as your baby becomes more active, he exposes himself to added dangers, so we include more safety hints here as well.

First Word!

"Ball!" "Doggie!" "Mama!"

Your baby's first words are a major milestone, a sign that he's perched on the verge of language's boundless frontier. So his earliest "real" utterances are a cause for celebration.

IS HE REALLY TALKING?

As linguist Philip Dale of the University of Washington, Seattle, points out, parents are usually so excited by anything appearing to be a real word that they frequently read meaning into general babbling. But did Baby really say *Dada* to refer to his male parent, or is it merely language gymnastics? Dr. Dale proposes these criteria to distinguish between an accidental wordlike utterance and a true first word.

- A baby should somehow indicate that he understands the word's meaning (such as pointedly saying *Dada* in reference to his father).
- A baby should use the word consistently and spontaneously, not just in imitation of his parents.
- The word should be clear enough for adults to understand.

Using these guidelines, researchers generally agree that true first words usually appear between ten and thirteen months, with some babies starting younger and quite a few waiting until eighteen months or even later. Sara Wilford, director of the Sarah Lawrence College Early Childhood Center, reports that many children she sees, often boys, say their first few real words closer to twenty-four months. These children are normal, too.

Developmental psychologist Katherine Nelson at the City University of New York uses another language milestone to determine when a baby is what we might call "truly talking." Dr. Nelson proposes that a child truly talks when he has a speaking vocabulary of about ten words. In her research, children often reach this milestone between twelve and eighteen or more months of age, with an average around fifteen months.

WHERE DO WORDS COME FROM?

First words grow out of all the sounds your baby has used throughout this year, from newborn cries to six-month coos to nine-month babbles. Babbling is truly a universal language. Babies of every culture and race utter most of the same sounds—even if those sounds, like the click of some African dialects that American and European babies make, are never used again when real speaking begins. You have also helped set the stage for first words by talking to your baby throughout this year. He needs to hear language spoken in order to speak it himself.

No one can say with absolute certainty how recognizable words evolve from babbling. Different theorists stress different influences. Most agree, however, that three factors are involved.

1. The natural development of a baby's ability to make particular sounds. The easiest sounds tend to be consonant-vowel utterances like *ma*, *ba*, and *dada*.
2. A baby's inborn interest in imitating words and word sounds he hears frequently.
3. Parents' encouragement to repeat sounds and turn them into words.

As a case in point, let's look at *dada*, a common first word.

1. The *dadadada* babbling sounds are easy for a baby to make by year's end.
2. Babies often hear the word *Daddy:* "Daddy will be home soon." "Wave bye-bye to Daddy." "Hey kid, Daddy loves his big baby boy!"
3. Parents (fathers especially!) encourage a baby to say *Daddy*.

In fact, whenever a baby says *dada* even by accident, parents usually become ecstatic and encourage a repeat performance. The baby, delighted with this new power to amaze and amuse, complies, again parents react enthusiastically, so he tries again. . . . Over time, and with parents' encouragement and gentle repetition of the correct pronunciation, *dada* becomes *Daddy* and enters a baby's speaking vocabulary. Other common words probably evolve the same way.

Don't Overdo It

Although all babies love praise, an unusually sensitive baby may feel pressured rather than encouraged by overly enthusiastic response to early talking efforts. Boisterous plaudits might even inhibit further language attempts. So if your baby seems dazed by your excitement at his first words, you might tone down your reaction.

HOW YOU HELP

Once your baby is truly talking his language grows, as linguist Lois Bloom of Columbia University says, "one word at a time." You encourage this budding vocabulary and interest in communication (which is the essence of language) as you relate to him, especially when you play together. Talking to him, reading books together, and playing all kinds of language games, such as suggested in "Growing through Play," are all great. Also, praise his attempts at talking, and help him turn sounds into real words by modifying his pronunciation. You are your baby's guide as he enters the wonderful world of words. Help him enjoy and make the most of his blossoming skills.

Choosing a Ride-on

Soon your baby will be walking. Soon, too, he'll celebrate his first birthday. What's a good present? If you're like most parents we surveyed, you're probably thinking about buying him his first set of wheels. Twelve months seems to be a good age to introduce a ride-on toy, as long as you're aware just how the new toddler uses it.

From twelve to about fifteen months, toddlers rarely ride a toy in the conventional sense. Rather, they climb on. And off. And on and off. And on. They perch on it and survey their surroundings. They push *backward*—not forward. They signal for you to give them a ride. Don't push too fast; their balance is a little wobbly at this age. They get off and push it around the floor. They sit on it.

After fifteen months or so, riding toddlers begin pushing themselves forward. They also flip a ride-on upside down (if that's possible) and play with the wheels. These young toddlers are seldom able to steer accurately or use pedals, but they still enjoy being pushed. The ability to steer usually comes between eighteen and twenty-four months, pedaling a bit later.

FEATURES TO LOOK FOR

A first ride-on should be fairly simple, without pedals and non-steerable. Steering isn't an automatic drawback; it's just not a necessity. Pedals, however, get in the way, especially when the toddler pushes backward. There is such a staggering array of ride-on toys on the market that you might be dazzled—and frazzled—by all the choices. Parents and teachers we surveyed give high ratings to the following features. No one toy will have them all, so decide which you feel are most important for your child and you, and keep them in mind as you evaluate what's available.

Easy mount and dismount: Be sure your child can get off and on by himself, or else he'll cry for your help—and you won't always find it convenient to comply. Keep in mind that toddlers tend to walk onto a ride-on toy from the back; they can't swing their leg over the seat.

NOTE: Both parents and teachers rate this as the absolutely most important feature.

Covered storage compartment: Toddlers are collectors, and love to take special toys along with them. The compartment should be easy to clean, as all kinds of things—dirt, twigs, food—will find their way inside.

Contoured seat: One that cradles the child and prevents him from sliding off the back. Remember: at first he pushes himself backward on a ride-on toy. Be sure a backrest isn't so high that it hampers easy mount and dismount.

Concealed wheels: Or a wheelbase long enough that your toddler doesn't bump the front wheels with his toes.

Soundmaker: A horn, bell, or squeaker.

Stability: A ride-on shouldn't easily tip forward, backward, or sideways. To test a steering toy, turn the wheels all the way to one side and give a tug forward. If it tips readily, look for one with better balance. A ride-on should also be stable when turned upside down—a favorite way toddlers play with this toy.

Handles or steering wheel: These are better than reins. Toddlers need something solid to grasp.

Additional activities: Telephone, workbench, toys that fit into or onto the ride-on.

For you: A ride-on should be light enough to carry from room to room or indoors to out, small enough to store easily, and simple to wash.

TWO SHOPPING HINTS

1. Take your child with you when selecting a ride-on, to make sure he can mount and dismount easily and otherwise handle the toy. As with automobiles, test rides are definitely recommended.

2. Don't necessarily purchase the first ride-on your child falls for in the store. This immediate infatuation might be based solely on familiarity (his friend or day-care center has the same toy), or a cute face, or other fleeting affection. First love doesn't guarantee lasting play value. It's better to select a ride-on toy that's loaded with recommended features.

Can't find a dream vehicle with everything your child could possibly want—and that zips along as easily on carpet as on pavement? Don't despair. If you're also like the parents we surveyed, you'll probably own two ride-ons. Or more.

Watch Out for Falls

According to the National Safety Council's *Accident Facts*, about 250 children under the age of four died from falls in 1983; over 100 of them were infants under one year. Even though there are no exact numbers on nonfatal injuries, we know from our research with families that falls are dismayingly common. Safety researchers Jaan Valsiner and Claudia Mackie concur. In a professional paper on climbing skills, they state that the second year of life is particularly noteworthy for the rate of accidents caused by falls.

Your crawling, climbing, inquisitive almost-toddler is just entering this period and is too young to sense the danger that his explorations might bring. Help protect him against possible falls with these precautions.

- Supervise play whenever he's around items that he might climb onto. Bookcases can be especially hazardous, since a child can go from shelf to shelf as if on a ladder.
- Make sure furniture is not grouped so that the combination can act like steps. A young climber can scramble from safe

low table to higher couch to dangerous tall cabinet top. Be especially careful with stools and kitchen chairs—some are light enough for a baby to push to a countertop, then climb up. And over.

- Use the appropriate strap in the high chair, and even then, never leave your baby unattended.
- Never leave your baby alone on the changing table. (Remember: to help prevent accidental drowning, never leave him alone in the bathtub, either.)
- To make the crib safer, remove the bumper; your baby could use it as a step for climbing out. Keep the crib free of large stuffed animals that might likewise act as steps. (Also make sure the crib is free of cords that your baby might become entangled in.) Set the mattress at the lowest position and make sure you keep the sides locked in the upright position.
- Be sure all windows are kept closed, or that open windows have window guards, *very sturdy* screens, or other protective devices.

Growing through Play

CRUISING ON FURNITURE

Between eleven and twelve months, most babies walk while holding on to the sofa seat or coffee table, or other low, sturdy support. At first a baby usually shuffles along sideways while holding on with both hands, and frequently leans against the object so it helps support his weight. As skill and confidence grow, he holds on with one hand and stands further away from the object, using it only for balance. Some guidelines for helping make these early excursions safe and happy:

- Make sure the furniture is sturdy enough to support him!
- Clear low tables of ashtrays, bric-a-brac, and other things he shouldn't handle.
- Avoid using baby shoes. They make balance more difficult since they interfere with the sensations his feet gather from the floor. They can be slippery, too. You baby won't need shoes (to protect his feet) until he's fully walking.
- Avoid socks, too, unless the floor is carpeted. They're slippery on bare floors. However, there are socks with nonskid soles that overcome this problem.

- You can be a favorite support! Sit in the middle of the floor and let your baby cruise around you. Big hug for a circumnavigation!
- Praise and encourage his attempts. After all, moving from all fours to two legs is a real act of courage, and falls will be common. Your reassurance will tide him over discouraging moments. If you laugh off a fall with a friendly "Ooops," your baby will get up a lot faster than if you look frightened and say, "Oh no!"

NESTING PLAY

Nesting (at least in play terms) means fitting a series of open containers inside one another. It's a natural progression from simple fill-and-dump play—placing objects inside another object; however, it requires more dexterity and discrimination, because your baby must deal with the fact that the containers are closer in relative size. When you buy nesting toys, choose cups, bowls, or blocks. These are far easier to nest than shapes like stars or hexagons. Also look for sets of nesting pieces that stack securely on one another when turned upside down. Two play features: nesting and stacking!

All the pieces of a nesting toy set must be too large to fit into your baby's mouth. If any part can (and for some stacking/nesting cup sets the smallest cups are truly dangerous), throw it away!

The first few times your baby plays with a nesting toy set, he might find it easier to use just a few pieces—say, the largest, the middle size, and the smallest if the pieces are graduated in size. Add more as his skill increases. You might also demonstrate how the pieces fit and encourage your baby to try it himself. Mistakes like misalignments, attempts to insert large blocks into smaller ones, and the like, are normal. Remember that he learns by trial and error. It's best not to pressure him into following your demonstrations exactly or assembling the parts in the "correct" order.

PICTURE PLAYTIMES

Learning the names of objects is a central aspect of language development. And just like learning to *say* words, learning what words *mean* appears to involve three conditions:

1. A baby's growing intellectual abilities.
2. A baby's hearing a word used frequently in connection with an object.
3. Parents' praise and encouragement to identify objects by name.

Again like learning to say words, learning what they mean is most fun when done through play—such as these games with homemade picture cards.

Make a set of picture cards that show toys, eating utensils, clothing, familiar household objects, and the like. You can:

· Cut pictures from magazines or toy boxes and glue them onto file cards with nontoxic white glue.
· Take a clear, simple close-up snapshot of each individual item. Display it against a neutral background so that the image is clear and uncluttered.
· Draw the pictures yourself, with nontoxic felt-tipped markers.

You needn't write the name of the object on the picture at this age. This is a time to be playing with spoken words. Put the pictures into a container, like a small basket or a shoe box or small gift box or cigar-type box with lid. And use them in the following games.

· Your baby dumps out the pictures, then puts them back into the container one by one. Great fill-and-dump fun. You name and talk about the pictured object as he handles it.
· Hold up a picture, ask your baby what it is, repeat the name (pronouncing it correctly) if necessary, and then let him put it into the container.
· You can also use the pictures without the container. Talk about each one separately, as you might a picture in a book. Be sure to use the object's name in a variety of sentences.
· Put two or three pictures face up on the floor, and ask your baby to "Hand me the _____."

GOOD OBJECTS TO DRAW: These are taken from lists of first words babies typically understand, from psychologist Burton White, and first words babies typically say, from Katherine Nelson.

FOOD & DRINK	ANIMALS	TOYS
cookie	dog	ball
cracker	cat	blocks
apple	duck	doll
banana	horse	teddy bear
toast	bird	book

CLOTHES	VEHICLES	HOUSEHOLD ITEMS
shoes	car	clock
hat/cap	truck	chair
socks	boat	door
blanket	bus	telephone
coat	train	bed/crib

EATING UTENSILS	PERSONAL ITEMS	MISCEL- LANEOUS
bottle	keys	flower
cup	watch	pool
spoon		house
plate		moon

Objects young toddlers typically recognize and can say (or approximate) the names of, from research by Burton White and Katherine Nelson.

SAFETY NOTE: Always supervise your baby's play with these paper toys. He might chew—and choke—on a picture.

Research Update: Stick-to-it-iveness

A stimulating environment appears to aid a baby's perseverance. This was observed in a study by Dr. Leon Yarrow, from the National Institutes of Health, and his colleagues. These researchers observed twenty-five six-month-olds in their homes, and then, at thirteen months, tested these same children in a number of tasks, such as finding a hidden toy and relating two or more parts of a toy to one another. Dr. Yarrow found that those six-month-olds whose mothers

· touched and patted them frequently
· were involved in their play
· offered plenty of auditory stimulation
· gave their babies toys that responded with sound and movement to the ways babies typically explore objects

scored significantly higher on these task-directed behaviors at the later age. As the researchers sum it up, "These correlations suggest a link between a stimulating, responsive early environment and later persistence at tasks."

ON TO TODDLERHOOD!

Toddlerhood: An In-between Age

The ages from about twelve to thirty or so months are usually called *toddlerhood*. During this period, your child acquires an impressive array of new skills. You won't see them all right now—keep in mind that a twelve-month-old is quite different from a thirty-month-old.

Some abilities are essentially physical. A toddler begins to walk

between about twelve and sixteen months (some have even been taking steps as early as nine or ten months). Later she's able to run, to stand up and sit down, to jump, and to climb the stairs upright. At some point a toddler is able to throw a ball, to feed herself— even if she's pretty messy at first—and to help with dressing, at least with items of clothing that are easy to pull on (and off!).

Cognitive, or intellectual, skills also expand. Children begin really talking during toddlerhood, and in the latter part are able to carry on real conversations. Speech becomes a powerful tool for broadening their experience. A toddler advances her still-limited understanding of concepts like numbers, spatial relationships, and relative size.

SOCIAL AND EMOTIONAL ADVANCES

During the second year and beyond, toddlers further develop a sense of themselves as individuals truly separate from their parents and begin to have special feelings about their own possessions. That's why "Me do it!" and "Mine!" may become your toddler's watchwords at some point. Your child's love for you is growing, too. Once she can walk and say a few words, she's likely to toddle to the door when you return home, maybe calling your name and extending her arms to be picked up. She also takes great pride in sharing her accomplishments with you. On neighborhood strolls, she'll proudly bring you that just-plucked dandelion as if it were one of a kind, not one of many millions. And the first time (or even several times) she manages to complete that simple puzzle, she'll shout for you to come see what she has accomplished. Your toddler also shows how special she finds you by imitating things she sees you do. She may follow you from room to room while you clean, dragging some dingy cloth and earnestly "dusting" everything she can reach. Or she may parade around, beaming, while clutching your briefcase or purse. These simple imitations soon expand into the fantasy play that marks the latter part of toddlerhood and (especially) the preschool years.

Taken together, a toddler's advanced skills and enlarged awareness make her seem much more like a "real person." And she *is* considerably more capable and independent than when she was a baby. Despite such tremendous growth, though, a toddler is at an in-between age. She has left forever the almost total dependency of babyhood, yet it will take months or even years for her to "stand on her own feet" without the guidance of a caring adult.

THE FIRST ADOLESCENCE

In a way, toddlerhood has a lot in common with adolescence, the period between childhood and adulthood. And like a teenager, a toddler often shows the abrupt anger and frustration she feels with being in between periods of relative dependency and independence. Her reactions frequently swing from one extreme to the other. One night she'll quite capably feed herself; the next (and that's the night you really *need* her to be a "big girl") she acts as though she had never grasped a spoon. Sometimes she'll determinedly assert her independence in dressing, fighting against your help at every turn with "No!" or "Me do it!" OK, you do . . . and then, unable to pull on the recalcitrant shoe, she cries all the harder in frustration. But she still rejects help until she's too exhausted — physically and emotionally — to keep trying. There are times she'll march right out of your sight if you're not careful, or will gladly bid you adieu from the baby-sitter's side. Then other times she'll cry to be carried, or collapse into a panicky state of clinging dependence when you leave her for only a minute. There will be *plenty* of occasions when she'll whine for you to do things for her that, in her surer moods, she's been accomplishing all by herself for several months.

You may find these volatile shifts — from surges of independence to regressive babylike behaviors — confusing or annoying. *She* finds them scary — even painful. She so desperately wants autonomy . . . but you can imagine she is also terrified at the prospect of really standing on her own without the safety net of your security. Sometimes when you try to soothe her, she alternately pushes away from and clings to you, as if she's not sure what she wants at that very moment. Chances are, she isn't sure. At some point, the tantrums most parents dread will rear their thunderous heads — surely the most explosive expression of your toddler's emotional volatility. Losing control so violently, especially when one is struggling so hard to become autonomous, can be terrifying.

Toddlers clearly need guidelines and controls, even if they seem to fight against them. Yet they need opportunities to test just how far they can go, to see what they can learn by themselves, and to explore freely — but safely.

DEMANDING TIMES

Although you undoubtedly find it rewarding to enjoy and encourage the signs of your toddler's growing independence, you can't escape the fact that her skills, her experience, and—maybe most importantly—her understanding are still very limited. These limitations make her in some ways even more demanding than when she was a baby. Her memory is so short, her drive to explore so great, and her self-control so weak, that she'll probably touch the same untouchables day after day, maybe even hour after hour. Because of these, and the fact that she has a very cloudy understanding of time, your toddler is often extremely impatient. Some days she can't bear to wait even the thirty seconds it may take to pour her juice. "In a minute" or "Just a second" mean nothing to her. She wants it _now!_ She may fuss at you all the while you're preparing something to please her. And then, even after receiving your offering, she may show no thanks at all. There's no question that her behavior will occasionally drive you up the wall. Children can be very exasperating (as well as vivid, spontaneous, unselfconscious, and utterly charming) during toddlerhood.

FINDING YOUR OWN APPROACH

Obviously, it won't do to treat this spirited and ambitious creature the way we treat more helpless, docile babies. And just as obviously, parents can't expect a toddler to measure up to the standards appropriate for preschoolers, who have at least a basic understanding of concepts like right and wrong, and who can remember from one day to the next what's been forbidden. So in many ways, parenting a toddler calls for an in-between approach: flexible but firm.

Research scientists have been trying to discern why some parents deal with toddlerhood better than others. Of particular interest are the findings of a project conducted at Harvard some years ago by Dr. Burton White and his colleagues. These specialists studied the families of thirty-nine young children to see what parenting styles tend to be successful with toddlers. The mothers who seemed to be doing a particularly good job shared some important traits:

- They created a physical environment that was safe and stimulating for their children, rather than forcing their toddlers to live in a completely adult-oriented home.
- They understood and generally forgave the inconsistencies toddlers often show.
- They let their toddlers try most things the toddlers wanted, yet set limits calmly and firmly when necessary.

• They acted as play partners and learning consultants, answering questions, offering suggestions, and providing assistance "on the fly" when it was needed.

• And, interestingly enough, they did not spend long periods of time in formal efforts to teach their children.

In these ways, they encouraged their toddlers' independence while still providing protection, security, stimulation, and love. As a result, the children of these mothers appeared to be unusually competent and well-adjusted. Dr. White found that at three years, these children were in many ways more skillful than the average three-year-old. Their language was advanced. They had marked ability to anticipate consequences, to deal with abstractions, and to plan and carry out fairly complicated tasks. They were generally comfortable and confident in dealing with other people.

In the broadest terms, this is what we recommend parents aim for. There's no one perfect way to parent. Then again, there are few absolutely wrong ways. As parents know so well, raising a child is a complex process, with diverse factors—individual personalities, personal circumstances, and available time—intricately intertwined. As you and your toddler grow together, you'll develop your own parenting style that makes this challenging, wonderful, difficult, often perplexing, but always extraordinary time more rewarding for your whole family.

Toddlers and Parents

When your baby becomes a toddler it's a transition time for *you* as well—and one that may create inner conflicts: joy at seeing your child develop such sophisticated skills and blossoming independence, but a little sadness at losing the loving, more cuddly, dependent infant. Such conflicting emotions are natural and quite understandable. A toddler can also bring some new or increased fears. Safety usually leads the list. Your child's ability to toddle to things *she* wants and handle them in ways *she* wants also means that she's increasingly likely to get into potentially dangerous situations. Unfortunately, her new physical skills aren't matched by the ability to distinguish between breakable and unbreakable, safe and unsafe. A new one-year-old has almost no common sense—that will come with experience and patient teaching. So as parents of a newly mobile toddler, you have to balance your child's need to explore (which is a prime way she learns) with your need to protect her from harming herself or the family possessions. Childproofing helps enormously. Now would be a good time to reread the safety sections in chapters covering the baby months. We also offer ongoing suggestions throughout the next twelve months.

Other fears are a bit broader: How to provide the right atmosphere to encourage all kinds of development? The same guidelines apply as when she was a baby. Play with her. Make sure she has ample opportunities to explore new objects and places. Pay attention to her needs and desires. Praise her accomplishments, support her through momentary failures. Let her know she can count on you when she needs help or solace. All these help her understand how special and important she is both to you and as an individual. And they go a long way in building her trust in you and confidence in herself.

Even the best, most indulgent parents get angry on occasion. Children *do* try parents' patience. Toddlers especially can be challenging and frustrating as they test their blossoming independence. It may help to remember that your toddler often fluctuates between babyish and more mature behavior. She's also still very young, even though in many respects she seems infinitely older and more skillful than a baby. Maybe she falls short of your desires on occasion because you set your expectations a little high. A certain amount of "orneriness" is just typical toddler behavior (like dawdling, discussed later). As your irritation mounts, remind yourself that you might be requiring too much of her at the moment. You can also try to keep from losing your temper by considering how important it really is that she do what you ask. It may seem vital that she hurry to the store. But does it truly make that much difference today whether you get there in five minutes or in ten?

No parent will be calm all the time. So don't feel guilty. But do try as much as possible to keep from losing your temper. Sometimes a change of scene, a deep breath, and counting to twenty, or even a brief separation is the best way to keep a budding confrontation from turning into a conflict.

ANOTHER NOTE ON ORGANIZATION

Toddlerhood brings a change in how the remainder of this book is organized. Since the older children get, the more they seem to differ in developmental advancement, you'll see a little less to-the-month specificity. We'll continue gearing chapters to your child's age, but we'll tackle more toddler-universal topics, too, things like discipline and toilet learning, that won't be so tightly age-bound. On to Year Two!

15

YOUR TWELVE-MONTH-OLD

Overview

Walking is the big story. It is dramatic evidence that your baby has become a toddler, it makes him appear much more adult, and it offers even greater freedom to explore. Unfortunately, this wondrous mobility means that he's entering an especially dangerous epoch; accidents like poisonings are much more common now. You should take special steps to prevent poison-

ings. Also, his new-appearing maturity prompts many parents to think about toilet learning. We don't think twelve months is anywhere near the age to begin, as discussed later in this chapter.

Language development is the other major hallmark of toddlerhood, and soon you'll probably hear that first real word if you haven't already. There are several general ways to encourage and enhance this talent. Naturally, your twelve-month-old continues to explore the world, with ever increasing ability and understanding. Time for some new play suggestions!

Off and Walking

Of all the behavioral advances that may come near the end of your child's first year, walking certainly looks the most dramatic. Standing upright, alone and so independent, he suddenly *appears* older and more mature. This skill heralds his entering a phase so distinct it is given its own name—toddlerhood—thus marking the end of babyhood.

Even before your baby takes those all-important first steps, usually between ten and sixteen months, he has been pulling himself to standing with the support of the crib or playpen rail, or other anchor. For walking practice, he probably cruises from one end of the sofa to the other, moving hand-over-hand, or around the coffee table (be sure it has no sharp edges). These trial excursions strengthen his legs and help him learn to balance while standing. You can help, too, by walking with him, holding one or both of his hands.

Then . . . finally . . . when he himself is ready . . . come those first solitary steps. Bravo! Oops. He's down again. But he's well on his way to becoming a member of the upright race.

Babies show a great deal of individuality even in the earliest solo walking stages. Some take right to it, totally unintimidated by falls. Some are slightly put off by the inevitable mishaps and advance more slowly. Some prefer taking slow and deliberate steps, lifting their legs high into the air and bringing them down cautiously with long pauses in between. Others take a few running steps and then topple over.

TYPICAL PROGRESSION

New walkers assume strange postures—at least to our adult eyes—that improve their balance. They hold their feet far apart and point the toes in or out. This increases stability but it slows forward progress. They also hold up their arms, both for added balance and for protection in case of a fall. A baby's natural tendency to bend at the hip and knee brings his weight close to the ground. This also aids his stability while taking steps. A new walker may frequently look down at his feet for added control and reassurance.

As balance and coordination improve, and falls consequently are less frequent, a baby relaxes his arms and holds them closer to his sides. Finally they begin swinging right alongside his body in rhythm with the stepping movement of his legs. He adopts a more erect posture, too, bending less at knee and hip and bringing his feet closer together. Soon he stops hitting the ground flat-footed — with the entire sole touching the ground simultaneously — and begins walking heel and toe like an adult.

GOOD GAMES

Like crawling, walking is its own reward. There's nothing parents need to do to stimulate its advancement. Just be supportive, and let your baby know you share his excitement and enthusiasm. Here are some play ideas that help you all enjoy this liberating new skill.

• Both parents sit a few feet apart on the floor. Send your toddler back and forth, like a go-between. He might carry a "present" (a toy) from parent to parent. Reward his crossings with thanks and hugs.

• Take frequent strolls outside. The terrain of hard flat sidewalk and gently rolling lawn is quite different from floor and carpet.

• When your toddler begins walking with some skill, he'll delight in chasing you. Get down on all fours and hobble away, across the floor, behind the sofa, with your toddler in hot pursuit. Be sure to let him catch you!

Chances are, for the next several months your child will only be a chaser; he probably won't flee should you try to chase him because he doesn't yet understand why he should try to elude you. As play specialist Brian Sutton-Smith at the University of Pennsylvania puts it, "[This] seems to show that when we learn to behave socially, we first learn just one side of the relationship. Later we learn the other side. Then still later we put them both together. So here children learn the social relationship of chasing and escaping, first by chasing, next by escaping, then with both together.''

• Since the skilled walker often likes to carry something, invite him to be your special messenger. He might bring you something (unbreakable!) from the coffee table or bookshelf, or help you carry the laundry, or tote a single item (box of cereal) in from the car after a shopping trip.

• Most experienced walkers love a pull toy. Choose one that makes sounds when pulled so he can be sure it's following him without his having to turn around to look.

CHOOSING SHOES

Your baby's shoes are for function—not for fashion. So you should make sure they fit correctly. It's always best to take your baby with you to try on shoes, and to have them fitted by a professional. Be sure the soles have enough traction so that your newly walking baby doesn't slip. Smooth, firm soles should be roughed up with sandpaper or by drawing ridges across them with the point of a nail file. There's no clear consensus whether shoes should be firm-soled or flexible, like sneakers. Ask your pediatrician's advice.

Helping Language Grow

Learning to talk, much like most other skills, is a behavioral process that unfolds in a continuous pattern. Along the way are several important milestones (like first words) that appear according to every child's inner developmental timetable. You don't really teach your child to talk, just as you don't teach him to sit up or walk. But you certainly can enhance—and enjoy—this flowering ability. As you think about these suggestions, keep in mind that they apply to the entire toddler period—*not* just to the twelve-month-old. Remember, too, that first words can appear at sixteen months or later.

SOME GENERAL GUIDELINES

Talk to your toddler! This expresses your interest in him, and keeps the two of you in contact. Almost anything you and he do during the day can lead to language-helping conversations. During dinner preparations, tell him why you add certain spices to that pasta sauce, or why you knead the pastry dough. Talk about washing the car. As you undress him, a cheerful "Let's take off your shirt—lift up your arms," is much more educational and pleasant than undressing him in silence. Talk over the day's events at bedtime. *It's best if these are dialogues, not running monologues.* Encourage your toddler to enter in by asking questions and pausing for him to respond. Sometimes he won't—overtly. It doesn't matter. These conversations still help him feel close to you. At the early stages, he may just smile or gesture or make a sound. Later, he'll supply words; later still, enter into more equal conversation.

Researchers also agree that a toddler best understands words that are focused on what he can see, hear, and feel at the moment. Talk about concrete objects, describing them in as many ways as you can, repeating important words frequently, and using plenty of adjectives. Be sure to name objects for your toddler; he loves learning names of things well before he can say them himself. "A nice red cup, all filled with juice. Here's your cup, Benjamin." He might like to echo the word, too. At first he'll probably just say part of it, like *ca*, or might mispronounce it as *dup*. That's fine—it's a good start.

Keep In Mind . . .

- Talking should be light, easy, natural, and fun. Once you start sounding too much like a language teacher, it loses spontaneity and enjoyment dwindles for both of you.
- Gentle modeling and expansion are among the best ways to encourage talking and to bring your toddler's pronunciation closer to your own. If he calls out "goggie" when your neighbor's pooch races across the yard, you can chime in, "Yes, that's a *doggie*. He sure runs fast!" Or when the older toddler declares "Daddy go" after his father leaves the house, you might say, "Yes, Daddy has gone to the store. What do you think he'll buy?"
- It's probably best not to pressure your toddler as he's trying his new language skills. Admonishments to "Say *doggie* for Grandma, come on, say *doggie* for Grandma" when he's not in the mood, or not-so-patiently inviting him to repeat a word until he pronounces it correctly, may discourage his attempts to talk.

Language has been called the most powerful, the most versatile resource of civilization. By creating a rich verbal environment for your child, through the ways suggested here and countless others of your invention, you're helping him acquire one of his most valuable tools.

Time for Toilet Learning?

Your next-door neighbor insists her baby never needed a diaper after eighteen months. Your mother-in-law reports that your husband was completely trained by his first birthday. Your toddler *seems* so mature. You wonder: "Is twelve months the time to begin teaching a child to use the toilet?"

Well . . . It depends on the method you use, where you live . . . and when.

Attitudes about bowel and bladder training are different in different cultures and different times because concepts of toilet-training readiness depend on social and cultural factors as well as the child's physical maturation. For example, if you were a member

Time for toilet learning? Most likely not *at this age!*

of the Digo group living now in East Africa, you would have started soon after your baby's birth. So found Dr. Marten deVries from the University of Rochester and his wife Rachel, a pediatric nurse practitioner. The Digo mother's method involves holding the baby in a special position whenever she feels he's ready to eliminate, and prompting him with sounds. *This happens several times a day for several months.* How does she pick up these sensations? For the first two or so months, a Digo baby is in almost constant contact with his mother, in her arms or strapped to her back. (Because he doesn't wear diapers as we know them, he'd better learn when to go!) Also, toileting is easy. There are no Western-culture snaps or buttons or layers of clothing to pull down, no separate rooms to go to, no pots to sit on or lean over.

In the United States, our attitudes have changed drastically over the years. In the 1920s and 1930s, as reflected in the 1932 version of the government handbook *Infant Care*, mothers were also urged to start toilet training soon after birth. Experts recommended using methods such as a soap stick suppository. Absolute regularity was a must. Parents were exhorted to schedule bowel movements "twice daily, after the morning and evening baths, not varying the time as much as five minutes." This type of rigid reflex training partly grew out of the new movement in psychology called behaviorism. A baby could be trained by conditioning. It did work, but it was arduous for the parent, not terribly pleasant for the baby, and not too effective in bladder training. Early training was also stressed for a practical reason, to free a mother from diaper care, which was infinitely harder and more time-consuming than today.

Attitudes in American culture gradually changed from the 1930s parent-determined readiness to today's prevailing attitude of child-determined readiness. This change is partly based on what we're learning about children and partly based on practical issues. Now most experts suggest waiting until eighteen months or later to begin toilet learning. We agree. At that age, as Dr. T. Berry Brazelton points out, the child has the physical and emotional maturity to understand and accomplish the task fairly quickly, without a lot of frustration and failure and parent-child tension. Also, *he* is in control. The reigning method recommended today is more humane, too—naturally using a potty chair or the family toilet.

Another reason to wait is that starting early doesn't guarantee finishing early. Research has found that most children achieve reliable bowel and bladder control at about the same age (between twenty-four and thirty months) no matter when their parents began trying to train them. (Girls tend to learn toileting a few months earlier than boys.) Even diaper care, especially with today's disposables and diaper services, has become a minor consideration. So make it easy on yourself and your child and hold off for several months. We'll have more about this topic in future chapters.

Of course, you may need to think of a snappy comeback for your neighbor or mother-in-law.

Preventing Poisoning

Two facts make accidental poisoning a very real health hazard: (1) toddlers will eat or drink even the most foul-tasting or foul-smelling substances; (2) potential poisons are omnipresent. Based on their experience in poison centers, toxicant specialists George Armstrong, Mark Fow, and Joseph Veltri estimate that "The average consumer brings at least four hundred poisonous products into the home. Numerous plants, animals, and other toxic materials add to the poisoning potential." Take steps *now* to prevent accidental poisoning.

COMMON POISONS — AND PRECAUTIONS

Medicine. Statistics show that about 30 percent to 40 percent of the accidental poisonings of children involve medications. By far the most common culprits are vitamins and minerals, chiefly chewable vitamins; second are pain relievers, especially children's aspirin. These pleasant-tasting children's varieties are prime offenders because toddlers easily confuse them with candy. Other poisonous medications include rubbing alcohol, hydrogen peroxide, liquid cough and cold medicines (some contain as much as 25 percent ethanol, an alcohol), reducing pills, sleeping pills, laxatives, contraceptive pills, and almost all prescription drugs.

- Store *all* medicines in overhead cabinets — preferably locked ones — and in the bathroom. Keep the bathroom door locked from the outside when not in use. Never keep medicines in bureaus or bedside tables in your bedroom.
- Buy products that have child-proof caps whenever possible, and always replace these caps completely and correctly.
- Put medicines away immediately after taking them.

· Discard any medicine bottles that have missing or obscured labels.
· Never encourage your child to take vitamins, aspirins, or any medicine by calling it "candy."

Cleaning and Polishing Agents.   These are the second most common causes of accidental poisoning. Nearly all are toxic. Drain cleaners are especially lethal because they can burn as well.

· Never store these under the sink; instead, move all to an upper cabinet and lock this cabinet if you can.
· When using a cleaner, never leave it unattended even for a few seconds. Take it *with* you when you answer the phone or doorbell. Put it safely away if you need to go to the laundry room or other location.

Cosmetics.   About 10 percent of childhood poisonings handled by poison control centers involve ingestion of cosmetics. Perfumes, cologne, and after-shave lotion may produce serious poisoning because these products contain up to 90 percent ethanol. Even shampoos and deodorants are potentially toxic. It's best to store cosmetics as carefully as you do medicines.

Insecticides.   Always store roach powders and sprays and the like where your toddler cannot reach. Also, never use solid roach or rat poisons in low cabinets or other spaces accessible to your toddler. Find alternative ways to deal with pest problems.

Paints and Petroleum Products.   Turpentine, varnish, gasoline, and kerosene are all toxic. Always store them where your toddler cannot have access. A locked cabinet in the garage or utility room is best. Also:

· Keep the garage or utility room door locked from the outside when not in use.
· Leave these materials in their original containers or safety-approved cans. Never transfer them to soda bottles or other containers that normally hold beverages.

Plants. Many common plants have poisonous roots, stems, bark, leaves, flowers, or berries. Rid your home and yard of known toxic plants. The local poison control center can tell you which plants fall into this category. Also, store fertilizers, plant foods and sprays, and similar products where your toddler cannot get to them.

Alcohol. Wine, whiskey, and other spirits are fatal if consumed in large doses—and a toddler's tiny size makes a little dose large. Store liquor out of your toddler's reach. Also:

- Be careful where you set down cocktails.
- After a party, empty all glasses before going to bed. If you don't, your toddler might find them if he awakens and goes exploring early in the morning.

TWO MORE RULES

1. Post the number of the nearest poison control center and your toddler's pediatrician by *every* telephone in the house. Call *anytime* you suspect an accidental poisoning.

2. Keep a bottle of syrup of ipecac, used to induce vomiting, in your medicine cabinet. It can be purchased without a prescription at a drugstore. *Never,* however, give it to your child without the advice of a physician or poison control center. There are some types of poisoning where vomiting is not recommended. Always give the dosage recommended, and follow with a cup (or baby bottle) of cold water.

Growing through Play

UP IN SPACE

Most toddlers love to stack blocks, cups, cylinders, and similar toys into towers. And knock them down. And stack them up. It's fun, a great way to practice eye-hand coordination, and a mental achievement to boot. You can help by supplying appropriate toys and demonstrating this amazing feat. Join in, too. Take turns: You place a block, then your toddler, then you . . .

Stacking requires a meshing of physical and mental skills. On the physical side, your child must be able to place the second toy on top of the first *and* let go without knocking the toy off. That final step is the hard part, and one reason why early stacking attempts can be so clumsy. Here's where the type of toy makes a big difference. Stacking is much easier if the objects somehow fit loosely to-gether—say, a hollow end on one toy slips over a tapered protrusion on the other one—rather than merely rest on each other. Look for such toys when you shop.

On the mental side, the child must be able to conceive of vertical space, and realize that his towers indeed can go as high as his physical skills will allow. For a toddler whose play with toys has largely been horizontal, that's no small step. So don't worry if your twelve-month-old isn't interested in stacking. He'll begin when he's ready.

RIDES!

Your toddler is undeniably too young to enjoy (and endure) the roller coaster–log flume–space mountain–whirling teacups of the amusement park. But he's not too young to relish rides you can give him. So become an amusement park at home. Time-honored favor-ites include:

- Horseback rides, with you on all fours and your toddler grasping *securely* around your neck.
- Piggyback rides and shoulder rides; hold his legs *tightly*.
- Rides in safe, child-seat swings at the playground.
- Rides in a child-sized wagon. Make sure he always holds on to the sides. And don't push or pull too fast.
- Rides on wheeled toys.

Add variety with the following:

Beach Blanket Bingo: Your toddler sits or lies in the middle of a large blanket while you drag him across the floor or lawn. (Make sure there are no rocks or other hard things in the path!) If both parents are present, you can each hold two corners and *gently* swing the blanket back and forth like a hammock. Hold on tightly!

Boxcar Bonanzas: Sit your toddler inside a cardboard box with sides at least twelve inches high and push him around the room. You can go faster than if he were on a riding toy because the box protects him from accidental spills.

Daily Express: Or push your toddler around in a container (like a toy box) with wheels or casters on the bottom. Or tie a rope on one end and pull him. Don't have a rope? Use an old necktie. (Remove any rope or tie or strap when the ride is over; your toddler could get tangled in it.) Do you have two children? Tie together two wheeled containers to make a train. No standing in the aisles!

Bathtub Run: The outgrown plastic baby bathtub is a nice toddler-sized sled for snow or even grass. Punch a hole in the front, if needed, to attach a rope or strap. Again, remove the rope after play, and assure that there are no jagged edges around the hole.

SPECIAL NOTE: Pay attention to your child's reactions. If he seems to be becoming too excited, slow things down a bit.

LET'S LISTEN

A great game when you want to sit quietly for a few minutes, or to calm a toddler into nap time. Be very still and just listen. Listen carefully. Break the silence periodically to talk about things you hear. Start with the easy ones: "Shhhh. Be very quiet. Hear that? It's an airplane overhead." "Now what do we hear? I hear a truck rumbling by outside." "Can you hear that—it's a dog barking."

As your toddler becomes a more accomplished listener, add some less obvious sounds: the refrigerator's hum, the air conditioner going on and off, the television set blaring in the neighbor's apartment, the tinny, tiny voice sounds from the street. Just listen, and you'll probably discover many sounds you yourself haven't noticed before.

Research Updates

LANGUAGE SEXISM?

One way you encourage your child's talking is by imitating his speech sounds and inviting him to imitate yours (which he often does spontaneously). Many parents do this almost without thinking; however, a recent study implies that parents of boys maybe should pay more attention to what they actually do. Elise Masur of Northern Illinois University took in-home videotapes of eighteen mothers and babies ten to fourteen months. She found that mothers of boys imitated the child's miscellaneous nonlanguage noises (such as laughter, fake coughs, and tongue clicks) more often than his language-type sounds and words. Mothers of girls did the exact opposite. Does this make a difference? Well, this same study found that the children whose mothers highlighted speech-related sounds, rather than nonlanguage noises, were more likely to reproduce their mothers' conventional vocalizations and words.

HELPFUL GESTURES

Two Educational Testing Service studies of sixteen-month-olds by Marilyn Shatz and colleagues suggest that parental gestures have a significant role in holding a child's attention and maintaining the flow of interaction between parent and child. So use your hands when talking to your toddler.

16

YOUR THIRTEEN-
MONTH-OLD

Overview

Toddlers, like babies, love to explore and learn, and one object that's a favorite is her own body. There are many ways to build on this interest, as suggested at the end of this chapter in "Growing through Play." Young toddlers usually also explore body parts—like genitals—that parents might not accept quite so readily. There are different ways psychologists suggest you deal with this, as we discuss in this chapter.

Her skills and play interests in other areas blossom as well. Once she starts to talk, you'll see her vocabulary grow one word at a time. Language experts have found that these first words usually fall into some well-established categories which reflect what she finds interesting in her own world. Large muscle play, play with toys, play in the car—there are all kinds of expanded play opportunities you and she can enjoy.

Although skills growth spirals upward, physical growth slows dramatically after the end of the first year. Many young toddlers show a marked decrease in appetite, as we point out in the next section.

A Drop in Appetite

If your toddler's appetite is smaller than before, that's not only typical, it's also totally understandable. Even though a toddler weighs more than a baby, she doesn't need—or want—proportionally more food. The size of her appetite depends not on body size or age but on *rate of growth*. This slows dramatically around the first birthday. A baby generally doubles her birth weight by four or five months of age and triples it by the end of the first year. But from about twelve to thirty months, a toddler typically gains only six to eight pounds. It's logical that her appetite diminishes; she's growing far more slowly than before.

A toddler's growing independence can also affect eating habits. For one thing, the typical active toddler is too impatient to sit still for a whole meal; she'd much rather be out exploring as her newfound locomotion allows. For another, some toddlers deliberately refuse to eat as much as Mom or Dad would like, just to assert their autonomy. Here's the all-too-common scene. Many a parent, worried as a toddler's appetite drops, resorts to all kinds of wheedling, cajoling, and games to encourage "just another mouthful." The toddler refuses to eat as a means of controlling the situation. A vicious cycle can be set in motion: The parent strives even harder to encourage another bite, the toddler reacts with an adamant "No!" or a disdainful sweeping of food off the high chair tray. If you press the eating issue, you can create a nobody-wins situation.

You can prevent such confrontations by not making a big deal about eating. Many experts feel that it's the parents' rigidity, their insistence that a toddler eat everything *they* want her to, that can create real eating problems. At each meal (be it regular breakfast-lunch-dinner or a healthy snack), present your toddler with an array of nutritious tidbits, then let her decide what she wants and how much at a time. She may devour mostly protein at one sitting, then vegetables or fruits at the next. Don't worry. Even if every single meal may not be well-balanced, several meals over a period of days will probably add up to excellent nutrition. It's a *very* rare toddler who would deliberately undereat or starve herself when good food is available. Remember, though, that if you have serious questions about your child's eating habits—eating too little or too much—you should discuss them with her pediatrician.

How much food does a toddler need? Quite naturally, it depends on the individual. But chances are your toddler isn't underfed. If she has the energy to go from dawn to dark, to exhaust *you* every day, you can be sure she's getting enough to eat.

NOTE: Certain foods are inherently dangerous.

Exploring Genitals

Your toddler investigates almost anything she can get her hands on, and one "object" she finds especially fascinating is her own body. This body exploration began back in infancy and continues throughout early childhood. You can expect all kinds of poking and stroking, probing and tugging as your child seeks to discover what different body parts look and feel like, how heavy they are, how they move, and what makes them work.

WHAT ABOUT GENITALS?

Although this self-exploration is normal, you may feel a bit embarrassed when your toddler handles her genitals. That's not surprising. Most adults consider sexual organs in a quite different category from other body parts. Some parents may feel that genital play in toddlerhood is a sign of sexual development inappropriate for this tender age. Others are just plain puzzled by it. Whatever the cause of their discomfort, many parents question how they should react to genital exploration. We recommend you consider the following.

Most psychologists and child-behavior specialists believe that touching the genitals is a normal, healthy part of body exploration, and that parents should accept it as readily as they accept a child's exploring her hands and feet. Almost all toddlers do it. (As one of our researchers points out, one reason why genitals may be so fascinating is that they're nearly always covered up by a diaper or pants.) It's not a sign of precocious sexuality. No matter what your opinion of the specialness of the sexual organs, they are just another body part to your toddler (albeit, ones that might feel a little different when she touches them). Likewise, you needn't fear that a toddler who's allowed to explore her genitals at this age will never learn to share your personal feelings and beliefs about sexual privacy. She will when she's older and can understand you better. Right now your toddler can't appreciate your sensitivity.

DECIDE YOUR OWN APPROACH

Exploring the genitals is more than an issue of physical and cognitive development, however; it is intertwined with cultural, social, and religious views as well. The above information may answer some questions, but it isn't intended as a prescription for every family. You need to decide on your own approach, anywhere from openly approving genital play to ignoring it to discouraging it. If the latter, we suggest you do it calmly and matter-of-factly, with love rather than reproach. Your toddler is not being "bad." Merely curious.

Looking at Vocabulary

"Ball." "Bed." "Blanket." "Mommy." "Car." "Clock." "Cat." "Daddy."

Which word is a typical eighteen-month-old *least* likely to use? According to a now-classic study by Katherine Nelson at the City University of New York, the answer is *bed*. In this landmark research project involving eighteen toddlers, Dr. Nelson identified the first fifty *different* words each child spoke, then classified the words into five basic categories. She found that:

- 65 percent of the words these children used were nouns: 51 percent were general nouns (*ball, car, cookie, juice*), and 14 percent were specific nouns (*Mommy, Daddy, Baby,* pet names);
- 14 percent were words demanding or describing action: *look, bye-bye, give, up* (for "pick me up");
- 9 percent were modifiers: *red, all gone, dirty, mine, big;*
- 8 percent were what Dr. Nelson calls personal-social words: *please, no, want;*
- 4 percent are words that fulfill a grammatical function: *is, to, what, where.*

WHICH WORDS ARE POPULAR?

It's not surprising that nouns and verbs make up 79 percent of these spoken words. As Dr. Nelson, Eve Clark of Stanford University, and other language researchers discovered, a toddler talks about the here and now. Her early vocabulary naturally consists primarily of words that refer to objects pertinent to her immediate environment. Yet, every toddler hears and comprehends hundreds of nouns. Of all those, which are most likely to enter her speech?

In her analysis, Dr. Nelson found some fascinating patterns in the individual nouns that appeared in nearly every child's vocabulary, nouns that appeared in several vocabularies, and—particularly intriguing—nouns that very few or none of the toddlers used.

Many nouns are popular because a toddler can pronounce or approximate them easily. *Mommy, daddy, ball, dog, cat, bottle, cookie* (or *cracker*), and *car* appeared in almost all the vocabularies Dr. Nelson studied. But other nouns used by most of these toddlers— *juice, shoes,* and *socks,* for example—are not simple to pronounce. Still other easy-to-say nouns like *table, bed,* and *toy* (objects familiar to these toddlers) were almost never used. Likewise, when you categorize these first nouns, as Dr. Nelson did, you find some interesting omissions. Although *shoes* and *socks* appeared in most of the toddlers' vocabularies, other clothing items like *pants, sweater,* and *diaper*—just as familiar to a child—are missing. So familiarity and ease of pronunciation can't be the only deciding factors. One conclusion: toddlers generally use names of objects that they can act on, or that move in interesting ways.

With Dr. Nelson's subjects, toy words—*ball* and *doll,* for example—appear in a majority of vocabularies. Yet *ball* is far more popular because it is much more active and the toddler can do more with it. *Rattle,* theoretically a very familiar toy, did not appear in any toddler's vocabulary. The popular word *clock* makes interesting sounds and the hands move. A *crib* or *bed,* certainly more familiar in a toddler's everyday life, is static and therefore rarely a favorite early word. Almost no toddlers used furniture-type words like *stove, sofa, table,* or *window.* Yet smaller household items like *key* and *blanket,* things a toddler can move or act on, were reasonably common. Favorite words *car* and *cat* and *dog* are all active, but a *tree* (which did not appear in any vocabulary) is just "there." Even the favorite food words are *juice, milk,* and *cookie,* things that the toddler easily feeds to herself. A toddler knows what a shirt and a tree and a coat and hundreds of other nouns are. It's just that, spontaneously, she's less likely to include them in her early vocabulary of spoken words.

As language expert Philip Dale from the University of Washington, Seattle, sums it up, a young child's world is a small one. Change is important. Objects that move and change themselves — cars, clocks, animals — are likely to be the first words. And objects that a toddler herself uses or changes are the most important of all.

INDIVIDUAL DIFFERENCES

Although Dr. Nelson's study found common factors guiding early vocabulary growth, each child has her own reasons for acquiring the words she does. Each family (and toddler) has favorite foods that are likely also to become favorite words. What a toddler herself finds important or fascinating can help dictate her spoken vocabulary. Research studies indicate that a few children use only words they can easily pronounce, and avoid more difficult ones even if the objects are familiar and meaningful. Language expert Charles Ferguson of Stanford University has also found that, at the initial stages of vocabulary development, some children limit themselves to words that exemplify certain phonetic patterns. These might be words of only one syllable, or two-syllable words ending in an "ie" sound, like *doggie* and *mommy*. As with most aspects of development, these peculiarities are common — and help make every toddler the unique and special person she is.

YOUR OWN CHILD

For fun, keep a list of your own toddler's growing vocabulary. It can tell you a lot about what *she* finds important in her world. And it can be interesting to see how closely her first words match the types of words so popular in Dr. Nelson's study.

Helping Your Toddler Play

In chapter 14, "On to Toddlerhood!," we reported on a Harvard study that explored traits of "successful" parents. One noteworthy finding is that, even though such parents steered clear of formal teaching efforts, at three years their children were more intellectually advanced than the average child. Our Advisory Board members emphatically agree: Toddlers learn best through self-directed play, not formal instruction. So do Brenda Eheart and Robin Leavitt, the directors of Developmental Child Care Programs at the

University of Illinois at Champaign-Urbana. As they point out in a recent issue of the professional journal *Young Children:* "The adult's primary responsibility in facilitating toddler play is to be a supportive participant. A supportive adult responds to a toddler's initiations in play by expanding the scope of play while still allowing the toddler to take the lead."

Here are ways to best enhance learning, based on the guidelines Eheart and Leavitt use at their Infant-Toddler Center and on other expert recommendations. Some sound like common sense, but we've found that many well-intentioned parents—and teachers—unthinkingly take too formal a teaching role in toddler play.

Show your interest by talking: Talk about the toys your toddler is exploring and what she's doing with them, both when you play together and when you observe without participating. The younger toddler especially loves hearing her play reviewed aloud. For an older toddler, encourage her to talk about her play as well.

Expand play: Elaborate on what your toddler is already doing by suggesting new ideas or adding different props. Suppose she's playing with blocks. You might show how to build a tower, or hand her a container and start some fill-and-dump play. When she's rolling a small car on the floor, you might pick up another one and playfully show how to roll it through a large, tilted tube.

Introduce experiences at appropriate times: Adults can and should initiate some activities. It's best to wait until your toddler is finished what she's doing before embarking on a new play idea. It's also best to bring it up casually. If today's the first time you'll introduce ball-and-ramp games, start by talking about these toys, let her explore them as she pleases, maybe roll the ball back and forth between the two of you for a bit. Now try a little "down the ramp" demonstration.

Allow her to figure things out independently: As Eheart and Leavitt say, "You might be tempted to show a child which way a puzzle piece goes, but the value of the child's discovery is more important than a finished puzzle."

Give help when it's really needed: It's fine to step in with suggestions and encouragement when your child has a real problem. "I think this round piece fits here on the top. Why don't you try it? You almost have it. There! You did it!" Sometimes help should be more than verbal. If your toddler fusses in frustration after trying several minutes to negotiate the steps alone, lend a hand to solve the immediate problem.

Be a play partner when asked: Play with her as often as you're able. Likewise, when you're all fired up to play and she isn't, respect her desire (and need) to spend time alone.

Help her concentrate: Quite a few toddlers find it hard to concentrate on a challenging task, especially if it requires being still. If you sit with and encourage your child, she might be able to concentrate long enough to achieve the great satisfaction of completing a puzzle or constructing a really tall tower. Remember, though: don't pressure. Just encourage.

One final element in truly satisfying adult-toddler play is the thing parents offer even better than teachers: love. Let your toddler know how much you enjoy being with her, how proud you are of the wonderful things she does. This helps fuel her whole pleasure in play.

Growing through Play

GAMES FOR LEARNING BODY PARTS

One of the best ways to help your toddler learn about herself is the simple naming game that almost every parent instinctively plays. As you point to and name different parts of her face and body, add a few words about its function. "Here's your nose, Blair. What's a nose for? Well, we smell things with our nose." Naming games are ideal for bath time, changing time, almost any time the two of you play together. Over time, add all body parts—elbow, wrist, knee, genitals (if you like), nipples, and bellybutton (a favorite!).

Playthings add an interesting dimension to learning body parts because they help your toddler better understand the basic concept of a name. By using different things to illustrate *eyes*, for example, you help your toddler understand that an eye is an eye whether on a human, a doll, a teddy bear, a doggie, or a picture of any of these.

- Draw or paint a colorful face on a paper plate. Talk about the facial features, and encourage your toddler to point to them.
- Name and talk about face and body parts on a doll or stuffed animal.
- Whenever you and your toddler are reading a picture book together, talk about the different body parts of the characters. Remember that a favorite "book" is the family photo album. And should she snuggle up to you while you're

Stages of Comprehension

At what age does a toddler comprehend the names of different body parts? At what age does she use the name correctly in reference to a part? That depends on each toddler and on how often you and she play body-parts games. However, one study gives some guidelines. In this study, a toddler was judged as comprehending the name if she pointed correctly to that part on herself or her parent when asked "Where is (are) your_____?", or "Where is (are) Mommy's _____?" Parents of thirty-two thirteen-month-olds were asked if their children could comprehend the names of various body parts; parents of thirty twenty-month-olds were asked if their children could correctly name the same body parts. According to the parents, the following percentages of toddlers pointed to or named these parts correctly.

Body Part	%Toddlers Comprehending at 13 Months	%Toddlers Naming at 20 Months
Nose	22	67
Eye(s)	25	60
Hair	6	60
Ear(s)	3	57
Mouth	19	47
Penis	12 (of males)	47 (of males)
Feet (foot)	25	40
Tummy (belly)	12	37
Toes	9	37
Hand	0	37
Bellybutton	3	33
Finger	3	30
Knee(s)	0	30
Face	0	23
Leg	0	23
Cheek(s)	0	20
Arm	0	20
Tongue	0	13

reading a magazine, talk about the people in the advertisements.
· Let your toddler look into the mirror as you name parts of her face and body.

FITTING TOYS

Toddlers love—and benefit from—toys with several parts that they can fit together in numerous ways. In the toy store, you'll find lots of toddler items in which separate parts—a figure, blocks, cylinders—fit into a car, a boat, or other type of base. These usually work well. They're even better if similar round parts, like large hollow pegs, can fit together end to end. In fact, this end-to-end fitting is one of the most popular play behaviors we've witnessed in our toy testing labs.

End-to-end fitting is one of the most popular fitting behaviors we have seen in our labs.

As you and your toddler play with these toys, or even as she plays alone and you watch (and admire!), talk about what's happening. For example, "I'm putting the little boy into his red car," or "Good going! You put one peg on top of the other." Such comments help in some valuable ways. First, your compliments make her feel proud, which fuels her efforts to try new skills. Second, she learns new words such as colors and the names of objects. And third, she begins to understand important concepts like *on top of*, *inside*, and the like.

A set of plastic donut-type rings that fit on a spindle is a traditional toy that's well worth buying at this age. The rings will get plenty of play by themselves—as teethers, tossers, bath time diversions, and small toys for fill-and-dump and games of hiding and finding. Your toddler will also probably place a few over the spindle (perhaps if you demonstrate and encourage), although rarely in correct order for several months yet. The difference in size from one ring to the next is just too fine for most toddlers to discriminate. If she likes this fitting fun, give her just a few rings—largest, middle-sized, and smallest. Add more as her skills improve.

Research Update:
Learning through Touch

We often point out that toddlers learn by touching. Some recent experiments suggest just how important touch can be. In a test of twenty-five one-year-olds, Allen Gottfried (California State University, Fullerton) and Susan Rose (Albert Einstein College of Medicine) let each toddler play with five same-shaped objects— say, five stars. Then the objects were removed. A few seconds later, these stars were again put within the child's reach, this time scattered among five novel objects—for example, octagons. The stars and the octagons were about the same overall length, width, thickness, and weight. Then the lights were reduced until it was impossible to differentiate between shapes by seeing, and play was recorded using infrared light. Even in the dark, the toddlers handled, mouthed, and transferred the novel shapes from hand-to-hand much more than they did the familiar objects. A similar study by Peter Willatts, at the University of Dundee in Scotland, found that twelve-month-olds could tell the difference between shapes they could handle—but not see—in bags. In a study at Cornell University by Eleanor Gibson (Cornell) and Arlene Walker (currently at Rutgers University), the twelve-month-olds played in the dark for sixty seconds with either a hard or a spongy object. When shown two brief films, one of an object moving in a way characteristic of a rigid object, the other of an object moving like a spongy one, these toddlers looked longer at the film representing the type object each had handled in the dark. Now, these findings don't suggest that you should extinguish the lights at playtime! But they do show how much touch can lead to learning about the properties of objects.

17

YOUR FOURTEEN-MONTH-OLD

Overview

Even parents who blithely accept a baby's touching things that he has been told not to are often far less tolerant of the fourteen-month-old "defying" their admonitions. But as mature as he seems in some ways, he's still a baby in others, with a baby's limited understanding and (most importantly) lack of self-control. This is an age when discipline takes on new significance.

What method is best? That depends on each family; no book can give a blueprint for making every child accede to parental requests. One practice that is rarely effective, however, is slapping a child's hand when he reaches for a forbidden object. Yet too many parents resort to this—and just as many parents fail to take steps to reduce the types of temptations (for example, enticing objects on low tables) that can result in parent-child conflicts. We give some whys and wherefores, and our own discipline guidelines, in this chapter.

Another babylike behavior that many parents find inappropriate for the oh-so-independent toddler is sucking from a bottle. This may not be the best time to toss out those remnants of the infant year, as we point out on the following pages.

The toddler's social world continues to expand. Since he greatly enjoys getting together with his age-mates, this may be the time to start a playgroup if he's not yet a member of one. And even when he's with parents alone, he enjoys the play and learning suggestions found in "Growing through Play" at the end of this chapter.

Toddlers and Discipline

Discipline takes many forms, from your sharp "No!" as your toddler reaches toward the stereo buttons, to the big hug you give when he's done something that makes you especially proud. These and countless other actions are ways you guide your child's behavior. Most parents agree that the goals of discipline are to help a child learn to cooperate with them and with others; to follow their rules for acceptable and unacceptable behavior; and, over time, to become self-disciplined so control from others isn't as necessary. But there's less consensus—especially from experts—on the method that best achieves these goals.

A MATTER OF PHILOSOPHY

Parents should think of discipline in both the immediate and the long term. Long term refers to the overall approach you'll use throughout the preschool years. Should this be patient guidance that encourages cooperation, or a strict rule system that rewards right and punishes wrong—or some combination of the two? Should you only reason with a child, or should you also spank when you think it is necessary? How much, if at all, should you reward acceptable behavior? How much, if at all, should you punish unacceptable behavior—and what ways are not only effective in stopping unwanted behavior, but also least damaging to the child's developing self-concept? Different specialists will give different answers to these and the many other discipline-related questions because discipline is more a matter of philosophy than hard fact.

Parents must form their own discipline philosophy. This is usually based both on your own upbringing and beliefs and experience, and on information you gather from books and other sources. As you consider options, always keep in mind that discipline is *not* a simple matter. The opinions you read can vary widely. There's no guarantee that your toddler will cooperate the way that theories promise. Every child is unique. What works for your best friend's toddler may not work for yours; what works for one child in your family may not work for another. That's why it's best to be flexible in how you judge yourself and your toddler, and how you apply the particular philosophy you adopt.

LOOKING AT NEEDS RIGHT NOW

Whatever overall discipline philosophy you adopt for long-range results, you may well have some conflicts with your fourteen-month-old that demand immediate resolution. We recommend the following approach.

Be Clear.   In many ways, a fourteen-month-old is little more than a baby. He can't think ahead, and he's incapable of making any but the most basic discriminations and choices. So when you decide how you want him to behave, you should communicate your expectations as clearly as you can. Most of all, this means being brief. Tell him what you want him to know as simply and quickly as possible. Being clear also means setting limits *firmly* so that there's only one possible interpretation. As he reaches toward that hot oven door, grasp his hand and tell him, without equivocation, "No! Don't touch. That's hot, and it will burn. Burning hurts!" If you want him to stop throwing blocks, tell him so immediately, and be prepared to remove him—or the blocks—right away if he can't control himself. Again, a brief explanation of why that behavior is unacceptable helps him understand your prohibition. "Blocks are hard, they can hurt. We don't throw blocks."

Be Consistent.   The clearest rules will do no good if they're not applied consistently. Some inconsistency is inevitable, of course. From time to time, you'll be too distracted or tired to enforce a rule you're usually firm about. There may also be minor differences between the disciplinary rules of the two parents, or between your rules and those set by your toddler's other caregivers. This is inevitable. Try your best to keep these differences to a minimum. Serious inconsistencies can confuse your toddler and make it much harder for him to learn your rules. If you and your spouse are at odds, you should try your best to reach a compromise both can live with. Then, stick to your decisions. Discuss your views of discipline with your child's other caregivers and explore ways to bring their approach as close as possible to yours.

Reduce Temptations. In our interviews with parents, we've found that by far the most common reason for disciplining a young toddler was because he touched something he shouldn't: knick-knacks, glass objects, other breakables and valuables on tables and bookshelves, buttons on the stereo and TV, and plants. In most cases, these objects could easily have been put out of the child's reach. But the parents didn't, because (as they said) either they didn't think about it or they just didn't want to do it. Effective toddlerproofing can greatly reduce conflicts between parents and child.

It's understandable that you want to keep your own things displayed where you like, especially personal effects and family heirlooms that add to your home's unique personality. But if you do, you might be courting disaster. Most toddlers often have a difficult time keeping their hands off things—even those things they know you have forbidden them to touch. Toddlers do understand some "Don't touch" rules you set down. But that doesn't necessarily mean they will easily follow your bidding. Even if he knows your rule, his self-control is so tenuous and the object often so enticing that temptation gets the better of him. That's one reason why toddlerproofing is so vital. He *will* learn to obey you better over time. If you're firm and consistent, he'll touch less and less. And once he has completely understood and accepted these commands, he'll cooperate much more fully. So to make your life easier right now:

1. Put out of your toddler's reach things that he must not touch because they're dangerous or because he might harm them.
2. Make safe the things that you can't remove. Put safety caps in electrical outlets. Use trash cans with locking lids. Put mesh type safety gates on all stairways.

3. For things you can't toddlerproof—radiators, fireplaces, and the like—use the rules of clarity and consistency.

Try Some Substitutions. Your toddler is beginning to learn acceptable behaviors, even if he can barely restrain from touching certain things. Parents tell us that substituting an acceptable item for an untouchable can help. If your toddler won't leave the books on your bookshelves alone, give him his own selection of old magazines, dog-eared paperbacks, and the like in a special bin near your reading material. (Another hint: Wedge your own books in the shelves so tightly that your toddler can't pull them out.) Once you've cleared the coffee table of fragile objects, put on it a few safe objects that he *is* allowed to handle.

Criticize the Behavior, Not Your Child. When your child doesn't heed your rule, let him know that you are displeased with his behavior, not with him. It's better to say "I'm very angry that you broke the clock—I told you not to touch it," than "You're a bad boy!" The first gives him a clearer explanation of what he did wrong while still letting him save face. The second attacks his self-esteem, and does little to let him know why you're angry.

WHAT ABOUT SPANKING?

No matter how clear, consistent, and firm you may be, your toddler won't always follow your guidelines. One reason is that you may not be as clear or consistent as you think. Another is that, even though he understands your rules, he still lacks the self-control to avoid touching or doing what he vaguely realizes he shouldn't. Will a slap on the hand drive your message home?

It's hard to tell. Sometimes it might, if you have a basically cooperative child. Usually it won't. Parents we've interviewed frequently report, much to their amazement, that their child continues to touch a forbidden object even after having his hand smacked. A study of twenty-four mother-toddler pairs conducted by Michael Chapman (currently at the Max Planck Institute in West Germany) and Carolyn Zahn-Waxler at the National Institute of Mental Health found that spanking or slapping a child's hand was less effective in gaining his cooperation than was letting him know how much his behavior displeased his mother (sometimes called "love withdrawal"). This was especially true when this "love withdrawal" was combined with another technique, like physically restraining his urge or telling him "No."

We do not recommend slapping a child's hand. It is rarely effective, and if done hard enough can injure. Nor do we condone spanking. But we know most parents resort to it in times of frustration, particularly when nothing else works. That's natural. Spanking most likely has little long-term, negative effects if you use it sparingly.

As you think about these recommendations and your whole approach to discipline, remember that there is no absolute right or wrong way because each child, and each parent, is an individual. The most important thing is finding a style that your family is comfortable with.

For Further Reading

For more information, we recommend two classic books: *The Magic Years: Understanding and Handling the Problems of Early Childhood*, by Selma Fraiberg; and *New Ways in Discipline*, by Dorothy Baruch. You can find these in a good library or at the bookstore.

We've also found some excellent professional papers on this topic. If your public library doesn't carry these particular publications, you might try the library of a local college or university.

Chamberlain, Robert W. "Authoritarian and Accommodative Child-Rearing Styles: Their Relationships with the Behavior Patterns of Two-Year-Old Children and with Other Variables." In *Annual Progress in Child Psychiatry and Child Development 1975*, edited by Stella Chess and Alexander Thomas. New York: Brunner/Mazel, 1975.

Chapman, Michael, and Carolyn Zahn-Waxler. "Young Children's Compliance and Noncompliance to Parental Discipline in a Natural Setting." *International Journal of Behavioral Development* Vol. 5, (1982).

Pronunciation "Problems"?

You needn't be concerned if your fourteen-month-old doesn't say his words dictionary-perfect (that is, if he's saying any words at all).

Most speech sounds are difficult to make, particularly those that involve complex coordination of the tongue, lips, nose, teeth (if the child has any yet), and larynx. Sounds like *sh*, *spa*, *spra*, *ch*, and *th*, for instance, are frequently mispronounced even by three-year-olds. To compensate for this lack of control over all his language-related organs and muscles, a toddler frequently substitutes a simpler sound for one more difficult: *that* becomes *dat*, *pretty* is pronounced *pitty*, *chair* is changed to *care*, and the like. A toddler often has trouble with sounds at the middle and end of some words even when he can say the initial sound correctly. You may hear *basik* for *basket*, *baw* for *ball*, and *docket* for *doctor*. He might even mangle a word completely, using something like *benky* for her cuddly *blanket*, or *maw maw* for *lawn mower*.

One way to aid your toddler's pronunciation is by making sure you yourself pronounce words clearly—and completely. Even adults often let the final syllable of a word fade away when speaking.

Deciphering your toddler's almost–code words can be fun (and funny). But if you're in a hurry or a bad mood, his imperfect pronunciations might cause friction. How do *you* take it when your fourteen-month-old red-facedly screams *pinka* for the fourteenth time and you *still* don't realize that he wants you to turn off the terrifying lawn sprinkler? Or when he demands again and again, with amplifying volume, that you look at the *dya* and you have no idea he means flower? He becomes increasingly enraged by your apparent dullness, your own anger rises in direct proportion to his anger . . . At these times, your cool head can turn conflict back into normal conversation. Take a breath. Count to three, or seven or ten. Ask him calmly, again, what he means, and pay attention to every tiny signal he gives. These can help you decipher his meaning. Remember that he's trying his best. He may be just as frustrated as you are by his inability to pronounce correctly. And if you did get angry, a brief apology—nothing overboard—for your lack of comprehension might make you both feel better.

Bottles: Should You Stop Now?

Weaning your toddler from the bottle or breast started the day you gave your infant a spoonful of baby food. Another step was his beginning to eat table foods or finger foods, another was when you first introduced a cup. One step remains: Stopping the bottle or breast completely in favor of a cup (or similar container). If your toddler has yet to take that plunge, we recommend that you don't force the issue at this time.

Sucking the breast or bottle is more than just a way your child gets nutrition; it has come to mean love and warmth and security, too. Thus he may continue to suck for reasons of comfort even after he drinks fairly well from a cup and feeds himself solids. Remember that toddlerhood is a time of stresses and big adjustments. Your toddler often needs to comfort himself, and sucking may frequently be his chosen way. Nor will your fourteen-month-old be the only toddler on the block who isn't a one-hundred-percent cup-user. A study of 108 mothers of young toddlers conducted at The Johns Hopkins University found that only 30 percent of the children had completely given up the bottle and/or breast.

Your fourteen-month-old is still partly a baby. If he hasn't chosen the cup exclusively, we recommend you continue to wean gradually. The speed with which you do this should be determined as much by your child's readiness as by your own wishes. You might nudge him along unobtrusively if you think he's still nursing too much. Try substituting a cup for one breast- or bottle-feeding this week, another next week or a few weeks from now. He might accept this new cup better if it's offered by the parent who usually doesn't handle this feeding, too. Or maybe encourage a routine where your toddler uses a cup during the day, yet still nurses at bedtime and maybe early morning.

Bear in mind that weaning is a process—the process through which your toddler reduces his attachment to bottle or breast in favor of using a cup. There will be ups and downs throughout. A toddler often has increased needs to suck in response to temporary stress or change in routine. If he has just been sick or you've had a major change in your lives (like moving to a new house), he might want breast or bottle three times a day even though he had been down to only one. The age at which this process will (and should) be completed really depends on the child and his family. Many three-year-olds take a bottle at night. When your child is truly ready—maybe months, maybe years from now—he'll take that last step.

Growing through Play

HIDING AND FINDING

Most fourteen-month-olds (like older infants) love searching for a toy you hide. These games are like little mystery stories. There's the desired object that disappears, the dogged detective who tracks it down, and the thrill of final discovery. And like factual and fictional detectives, your toddler has to read clues and remember sequences of events to solve each case. Make sure your toddler watches you hide the toy when you play; otherwise, he won't understand that he's supposed to find it again.

Simple games: Hide a toy under something (diaper, small towel, inverted plastic bowl) or inside something (shoe box, cooking pot with matching lid, large boot) or behind something.

More advanced games:

- Hide a small toy in one of your hands and ask your child to choose.
- Take two hand towels. Hide a toy under one of them. Can your toddler find it easily? Try three towels.
- Take two large plastic cups or bowls of different colors. Hide a small toy under one. Can your toddler find it easily? Shuffle them around as in the old shell game.

Hiding and Finding

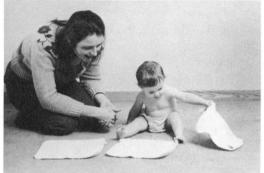

Hide a toy under something—say, a towel. Then, while your toddler watches you, remove it from this first hiding place and hide it someplace else. Ask him to find it. Don't be surprised if he looks in the first hiding place—then seems surprised when he doesn't find the toy there. This often happens. Some researchers theorize this is because a toddler this young can remember only one set of directions and the first sequence viewed is the most memorable.

However, other studies have found that he'll look immediately in the second place, much for the same reason; except that these researchers theorize that the most recent sequence is the one best remembered. Other studies have found a fifty-fifty chance where he'll search. Still other studies have found that a toddler is likely to search the first and then the second hiding place, suggesting that he can keep more than one set of instructions in mind and needs to act them out just as he remembers them.

HOMEMADE CONTAINER BANK

Since most toddlers love the challenge of fitting things through a slot, this toy's a favorite.

HINT: Rest the lid on top of the container; don't snap it on or close it tightly, or your toddler will undoubtedly have trouble opening the container.

You need:

- large, empty plastic container with lid (either hinged or separate)
- set of disks: coasters or jar lids (see SAFETY NOTE)
- sharp knife
- strong cloth tape

SAFETY NOTE: The disks must be at least two inches in diameter. According to current toy safety standards, disks this size are too large to fit entirely into a young toddler's mouth.

In the plastic lid, cut a slot long and wide enough for the disks to fit through easily. Line the slot with cloth tape if the edges are sharp.

LANGUAGE-BUILDING WALLS

Pictures and other things on your walls are more than mere decorations; they can double as a spread-out picture book that you and your toddler can "read." Make a routine (maybe right before you take your toddler to his room at bedtime) of carrying him around your home to look at all the things hanging on the wall. As his personal tour guide, you can name and talk about the pictured objects he's looking at.

Research Update:
You Can't Make a Silk Purse . . .

Researchers Megan Gunnar and Cheryl Stone at the University of Minnesota looked at how mothers influenced their toddlers' reactions to three unfamiliar toys. Previous tests with these same toys found that, when playing alone, the children had spontaneously enjoyed one (ferris wheel), had shown little or no enthusiasm for one (a talking robot), and had found one frightening (an animated cymbal-playing monkey). Gunnar and Stone discovered that no matter how much the mothers tried to interest their twelve- to thirteen-month-olds in the "scary" monkey the toddlers still avoided it. However, the toddlers took a far greater interest in the robot when mothers encouraged play with it than when mothers remained neutral. So even if you can't make a silk purse out of a sow's ear, your enthusiasm may help your toddler warm up to a toy in which he takes little interest on his own.

18

YOUR FIFTEEN-MONTH-OLD

Overview

Toddlers thrive on consistency. Major changes in their day-to-day routine can throw them for a loop. Parents and experts alike agree that a toddler adjusts with fewer problems if she is well prepared in advance, and if parents take special care to meet her needs in times of flux. This chapter looks at ways to help a toddler cope with major disruptions in her life.

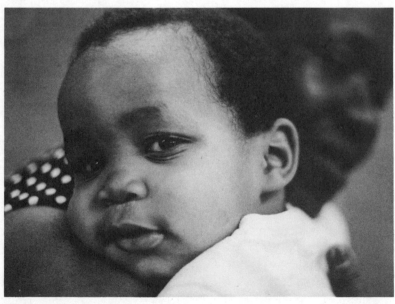

On a more positive note, a child this age is also getting better at handling stress herself, through self-comforting techniques like sucking a thumb or becoming attached to a toy. These may seem like babyish behaviors, but they're actually developmental advancements—signs that a child is becoming better able to regulate her own needs. You see other forms of this blossoming independence in her growing ability to feed herself. And, naturally, as her skills and understanding grow, so do play opportunities.

This month, your baby's doctor will probably continue with the series of immunizations that began at the two-month checkup. The fifteen-month-old typically receives an MMR vaccination that protects her against measles, mumps, and rubella (German measles). This is usually administered in the thigh. According to our pediatric consultant, Dr. Bill Waldman, about 25 percent of children have a mild reaction to this shot: low-grade fever and non-contagious rash may appear approximately ten days following the shot.

Coping with Major Changes

Here's how to help your child deal with two special situations that many toddlers face at one time or another.

STARTING DAY CARE

Today in the United States, close to half of mothers with children under the age of three are employed outside the home. The long-range influences of day care are under study; we report some findings in this chapter's "Research Update." But the short-term effect is clear: Most toddlers take a while to settle into the day-care experience, especially if they have had a parent (and it's almost always Mom) to themselves for much of the day.

You can help prepare your child for this experience in two primary ways:

- Talk up the wonderful times she will have with her friends and/or alternate caregiver, so that she goes into day care with an optimistic frame of mind.
- Introduce her gently and gradually to the new experience. If the care will be in your home, have the sitter come over for several days before you go start or return to work, so that she and your child can get to know one another with you in supportive attendance. If the care will be in another home or a day-care center, visit it several times, introducing your

toddler to the person (or people) who will be caring for her in your absence, and to the new setting.

Idea! If you can't afford individual care in your home, and can't find a day-care center or home you like, consider this option. Get together with another working couple or two who need day care and hire a caretaker to come to one of your homes and care for all the children (three is probably the maximum). For the particular location, you might choose the home most convenient to your workplaces, or the one with the nicest fenced-in yard. This is cheaper than individual home care, and offers you more control than a traditional day-care home. All the parents should interview prospective caregivers if possible. Share expenses: meals, equipment you might want to buy in common, and the like. The family in whose house the care takes place might pay a little less to compensate for wear and tear.

Remember that it will likely take your child several weeks— even months—to be completely comfortable with any new day-care arrangement. Expect some regressive behavior, and don't chide her for occasional babyishness. With your loving support, she'll wean herself into this alternate care arrangement.

MOVING TO A NEW HOME

When Packing. Talk in an upbeat way about the imminent move: the cartons and what you're putting in them, the new house and your toddler's new room, the adventure, the excitement. Keep these explanations simple and geared to your toddler's level of understanding. Also reassure her—frequently—that she'll be taking her toys, that Grandma will continue to visit, that Mom and Dad and Barkey and Cat-Cat will all be together in this new place. When you have the time and patience, ask your toddler to help you pack things she can't ruin, notably her own books, shoes, toys, and the like. Being involved in this way makes her feel more like a willing participant in the project. It's a good idea to pack your toddler's things, including bedding and room decorations, in their own cartons; mark these cartons clearly and keep them together as best you can. On moving day, have the movers load these cartons and your toddler's furniture last, so that they can be unloaded first at your new residence. Then while one parent (or other adult) oversees the remainder of the unloading, the other can set up your toddler's bed and start unpacking toys and other personal things so that she has a safe place to nap or play. Try to have the bulk of her room set up by nightfall. She'll appreciate sleeping in a comfortable place surrounded by familiar objects the first night in her new home.

Pack a special suitcase to keep on hand both for the ride to the new house and for unpacking as soon as you get there. It should hold things like a change of clothing, clean diapers, caretaking items for diaper changes, sleepwear (in case she should want a nap on arrival), and a few beloved books and toys. On the morning of the move, add a bag of nonspoilable finger foods for snacks, and a bottle or thermos of juice or other liquid refreshment.

On Moving Day. Have one parent look after the movers, the other after your toddler (and other children if you have them). She'll probably be anxious about all the bustle, and will need reassurances that everything will be fine. This adult will also need to make sure your toddler doesn't get underfoot of those sofa-toting moving men. Single parents: Ask a friend or relative to give you a hand.

In the New Home. After the hectic moving day is over, invite your toddler to help you unpack her possessions. It might delay the process, but it will make her feel more involved in the new house, and help her learn where her things are now kept. Also take her on frequent trips throughout the new house, showing her where plates and sheets and other things are now stored. Above all, try your best to maintain her regular daily schedule and family routines. In the midst of all the new experiences moving can bring, these bridges to the past are welcome indeed.

Thumbs, Pacifiers, and Security Blankets

Parents are a young child's strongest source of security and comfort; indeed, they're practically a baby's sole source. But this just won't do for the increasingly independent toddler. Although she still depends on parents when times are roughest, she provides her own solace through "comforting habits"—like sucking thumb or pacifier, or hugging a security blanket. These are just part of a lifelong ability to regulate and care for the self. We adults, too, have our own ways of comforting and relaxing ourselves.

Comforting habits serve important functions, says Janice Gibson, Chairman of the Department of Psychology and Education at the University of Pittsburgh:

"First, they allow toddlers to reduce the tensions of growing up. One-year-olds have far more pressures and conflicts to deal with than they had when they were younger. Second, comforting habits allow toddlers to regress briefly when they need to. Third, comforting habits contribute to toddlers' sense of self by giving them new ways to increase their independence when independence is a major goal."

COMFORT THROUGH SUCKING

Sucking remains a powerful way most younger toddlers comfort themselves. If yours sucked a pacifier as a baby, she'll probably continue as a toddler, at least for a while. In a study at the University of Wisconsin, Milwaukee, Richard Passman and Jane Halonen (currently at Alverno College, Milwaukee) found that 20 percent of twelve-month-olds and 14 percent of eighteen-month-olds they studied were still attached to a pacifier (see the table on page 238). This soon passes. Numerous studies indicate that children naturally give up pacifiers—almost always by twenty-four months—as they develop other ways to comfort themselves. Self-comforting is a skill that grows increasingly sophisticated as your toddler matures.

Are you embarrassed by your toddler's attachment to her pacifier? Have friends been casting disdainful glances, or relatives been wondering aloud when this nonsense will stop? Ideally, you should recognize the importance your toddler places on this object and just live with your own discomfort. But your feelings deserve respect, too. You might compromise by gradually weaning your child away from the pacifier. First you might restrict its use to home, car, and other private rather than public places. Later, try keeping it for when your toddler is in a particular area of the house—like the upstairs or her bedroom or playroom. Later she may be ready to use it only at nap and bed times. This process may take months, so don't force the issue. Remember, too, that even without your help in weaning, your toddler won't take her pacifier with her to college—much less grade school.

In fact, thumbs and fingers tend to far outstrip pacifiers as sucking favorites after infancy. And these you can't take away even if you want to. Nor do we recommend trying to stop this behavior in toddlerhood by putting bad-tasting preparations on the offending digit. These don't work as intended. But your habit-breaking attempts can build up your toddler's tension, since they show that you don't approve of this habit, and that can cause her to suck even more. As with pacifiers, thumb or finger sucking subsides on its own, even if more slowly than you might wish.

ATTACHMENTS TO SECURITY BLANKETS

A security blanket (also called a lovey or cuddly) helps many toddlers get through tense times. This is well-named; as Passman and Halonen found, 60 percent of the eighteen-month-olds were attached to a real blanket, and half of these children were judged by their parents as being strongly attached (see the table on page 238). Other favorite security objects are stuffed dolls and animals, cloth diapers, and other cuddly-type things. Some toddlers become attached to hard toys and objects, too, or to more than one object. Like an old friend in a new place, this security object is reassuring because it offers familiarity with no surprises. And best of all, the toddler herself is in complete control of it. If your child adopts one, be sure it goes with you to unfamiliar settings, to the playgroup or day-care center (at least the first few days), on trips and vacations—anyplace where she might be initially uncomfortable. Make sure the baby-sitter knows where to find this special security toy.

Soft cuddlies have a few built-in problems. They get filthy, and some toddlers are so attached to a particular cuddly that they hate having it washed—presumably cleaning ruins its familiar, precious smell. To minimize problems, wash it with unscented soap or detergent as infrequently as your own personal standards of hygiene allow, and don't use a fabric softener sheet. Another problem: Cuddlies can wear out, so try to get a duplicate at the start. If it's a soft toy, buy a twin. If it's a special blanket or other piece of cloth, you may be able to cut it in half as insurance against the day when the first becomes too disgusting and threadbare to save. This replacement will never feel or smell or look exactly like the original, of course, but it's a lot better than nothing. You might even tie or sew the old and new versions together until this replacement is broken in. Then—and with some toddlers, only then—can the first be cast away.

MORE METHODS

There are plenty of other ways toddlers comfort themselves: rocking rhythmically on hands and knees (or on top of a prized teddy bear), banging the head against the crib side, fondling hair, and stroking a piece of cloth against the face. These repetitious motions help a child relax herself, just as rocking often soothed your baby. Many a toddler devises ways peculiar only to herself. We suggest you accept them. Since they help *her* cope with tension in the way she knows and likes best, discouraging them can cause additional stress. When you accept her tattered blanket, raggedy doll, or dripping thumb, you're supporting her increasing resourcefulness to help herself.

A final word. The very occasional toddler adopts a self-comforting habit that you might find too unorthodox for your own taste. Also, a very few toddlers rely on self-comforting habits so excessively that they cut themselves off from both the comfort and the stimulation other people can provide. If you have serious questions about your child's habits, discuss them with her doctor.

Percent of Children with Some Degree of Attachment to Inanimate Objects*

Object	Age (in months)				
	12	18	24	30	36
Pacifier	20%	14%	0%	2.5%	3.8%
Blanket	22%	60%	56.2%	52.5%	57.5%
Hard object (toy or bottle)	14%	28%	11.2%	11.2%	10%
Pacifier and blanket	10%	12%	0%	1.2%	3.8%
Pacifier and hard object	4%	8%	0	0	0
Blanket and hard object	2%	26%	7.5%	11.2%	8.8%
Other objects	58%	36%	40%	46.2%	41.2%

*These data were gathered from interviews with 690 parents of children ranging from infants to five-year-olds. Adapted from: Richard Passman and Jane Halonen, "A Developmental Survey of Young Children's Attachments to Inanimate Objects," *The Journal of Genetic Psychology* 134, (1979): 165–178.

Steps in Self-Feeding

Independence in eating! Most parents look longingly toward this day of nonspilling self-sufficiency with cup and spoon. When will it be? It depends on your own child, of course, and how often she gets to practice. The following highlight typical behavior development.

CUP

Most fifteen-month-olds have trouble lifting a cup steadily from the feeding tray and replacing it after they've drunk. When drinking, the average fifteen-month-old tips the cup by rotating her wrists; she's apt to tip the cup too far and too quickly, spilling some contents. A lidded cup with a spout prevents liquid disasters. The eighteen-month-old lifts the cup to her mouth more steadily and drinks well. By twenty-one months, the average toddler handles a conventional cup quite well, and can lift, drink from, and replace it on the tray with almost no spillage. She also tends to tip the cup by rotating her fingers rather than her entire wrist.

UTENSILS

The average fifteen-month-old lacks the wrist control needed to use a spoon correctly. She has trouble scooping up food effectively and as she brings the food to her mouth, she turns the spoon over in midair and spills most of what she managed to scoop. An eighteen-month-old is more skilled; she fills the spoon more easily and guides it to her mouth more steadily. She also lifts her elbow when raising the spoon, which affords greater control. But she still tends to rotate the spoon somewhat as it approaches her mouth. It's not until twenty-four months that most toddlers insert a spoon into the mouth without spilling.

The under twenty-four-month-old obviously isn't ready to use a knife; a conventional fork isn't really appropriate, either. Spearing a bite on a fork might be easier than scooping with a spoon (and the tidbit doesn't fall off as easily), but the sharp fork prongs are dangerous. Also be careful about letting your toddler use disposable plastic utensils. Many are brittle and break far too easily.

HELPING HER ALONG

The transition from total parent feeding to total self-feeding involves lots of mess and experimentation. Although you'll often be tempted just to do it all yourself, remember that your toddler needs lots of practice to perfect her self-feeding skills. A plastic tablecloth beneath the high chair protects the floor. It's also perfectly natural for toddlers to play with food at this age. You'll still need to take over when you're in a hurry or when you serve really messy or soupy foods. If she insists on trying to feed herself, compromise by giving her another spoon to hold.

A few parents report success with special self-feeding spoons. Some are specially angled. Some have a free-spinning bowl, so that as your toddler rotates her wrist, the bowl rights itself automatically. You might investigate other special toddler utensils now on the market, too.

NUTRITION GUIDELINES

By this age, your toddler is well into eating a modified adult diet, as long as the foods are cut into bite-sized pieces and that certain very chewy foods—such as chunks of steak and other similarly textured meats—are avoided. According to the American Academy of Pediatrics, it's best if she has three regular meals and two snacks a day. Remember that her intake might vary—one day she'll seem to eat next to nothing, the following day she might seem to stuff herself. Actually, this isn't too different from adult eating habits; we rarely consume the same number of calories or amount of food each day.

To ensure proper nutrition, make sure you offer your child variety from the four basic food groups. These are:

- Meat, poultry, fish, eggs, peanut butter, cooked dried beans, usually about two servings each day. A toddler-sized serving is usually about only one-half ounce.
- Dairy products: milk, cheese, and milk products. This will usually be in the form of milk (unless your child is allergic to cow milk and uses a milk substitute). The average amount is two to three cups daily.
- Fruits and vegetables, about four servings a day. These servings are much smaller than adult portions—about one tablespoon per year of the child's age. Thus a one-year-old needs only about four tablespoons a day. An exception is fruit juice high in vitamin C, such as orange juice. This should be about one-third cup a day. Apple juice—a real toddler favorite—also supplies essential nutrients.
- Cereal, grains, pasta, and bread, about four servings a day. A toddler-sized serving is usually one-fourth to one-third an adult-sized portion. Portion sizes are hard to gauge, since bread, crackers, pasta, and cereals each contain different amounts of nutrients. However, most toddlers eat large amounts of grain, so chances are your child is receiving adequate helpings.

As you see, the total amount of food is quite small compared to adult nutrition. But as we've said, toddlers are not gaining weight nearly as rapidly as babies and thus require proportionally less food. Also, the above are only average amounts. Each toddler—like each baby—has her own nutritional needs, and only your baby's doctor can help determine whether *your* toddler's diet is adequate.

In terms of snacks, think of these as mini-meals. Ideally, they should be as healthful and nutritious as your toddler's general meals. Avoid foods and snacks high in sugar; these fill your child with empty calories and can also lead to tooth decay. Also remember that not every meal will represent all four major food groups (neither does every adult meal). The above are daily averages, and over each day or successive days your toddler's total intake should balance out—provided you offer her nutritious foods. Remember: You cannot force her to eat—and should not try to. No-win fights will likely be the result if you do. However, if you are worried that your child's diet is lacking in important nutrients because of her idiosyncratic eating habits, discuss these with her doctor.

Growing through Play

RAMPS AND ROLLER GAMES

If your toddler loves balls and toys that roll (and most toddlers do), add novelty to her play with some ramp games. They're fun ways to practice eye-hand coordination and locomotion skills.

Short Ramp

Short Ramp.   This is good for play on low tables as well as on the floor. The ramp can be a large book, a large cutting board or "counter saver" from the kitchen, or any similar large, flat plane. Prop up one end on a few books, a small box, or a comparable object.
   • Roll a toy down the ramp for your toddler to catch. Try reversing roles, too.

Long Ramp.   This is for floor play. It can inspire more exercise — and excitement. You'll need a plank and a support.

   • *Plank*: Spare shelf from the bookcase, long piece of cardboard, firm couch cushion, etc.
   • *Support*: Cardboard box (about nine to twelve inches high), plastic milk crate, upside-down plastic dishpan, toddler-sized chair (rest the plank on the seat)

HINT: An indoor toddler slide is a great ramp for these games!
   • Simplest: You roll a toy down a ramp. It races across the floor . . . and your toddler chases after it (crawling, creeping, toddling, whatever) and brings it back to you. Or she sits or squats at the ramp's bottom, catches the descending toy, then carries it back to you for another round.
   • Change roles. This time your toddler rolls the toy down the ramp and you chase it. Or you catch it at the bottom. A variation for older toddlers: For fun, after snaring the toy, roll it back up the ramp for your toddler to catch.
   • You and your toddler each hold a rolling toy on the top of the ramp. Ready . . . set . . . *go!* Release the toys . . . down they zip . . . across the floor they fly. Whose went fastest? Farthest? This is a good game for siblings to play. For variety, see who can retrieve her toy first and bring it back to the top of the ramp.

HINT: Make a rattling roller by putting some blocks into an empty oatmeal box.
SAFETY NOTE: Always supervise ramp games. Left alone, your toddler might try to walk up or slide down the ramp. Most of these homemade versions aren't stable enough to be safe.

FUN WITH TUBES

Cardboard tubes create play possibilities. You and your toddler can peek at each other through a short tube (perhaps one from an empty roll of paper towels) or whisper to one another through it. Or use it as a telescope for exploring the room. Longer, stronger mailing-type tubes are fine toddler bats for hitting big objects, like a beach ball lying on the ground. And they're not too hard should she chance to swat a playmate with them.

SAFETY NOTE: Make sure your toddler doesn't stand or walk around while peering through a tube. She might fall or bump into something. And always supervise if the tube—like that from a paper towel roll—is narrow enough to fit into her mouth.

A large mailing tube and rolling toys small enough to fit inside it make a dramatic duo. You can buy mailing tubes at the stationery or office-supply store. Open both ends. Tennis balls are great for these games. So are transparent plastic balls with spinners inside.

· Tilt the tube and drop a ball into one end; your toddler chases it when it emerges. Or you hold the tube and let your toddler drop the ball.
· When your toddler plays alone: Tape (use masking tape!) the tube to the outside of the stair banister, slanting down and low enough for your toddler to reach easily. She can place the ball in one end, then chase it after it pops out the other. For a change of play, set a box or basket on the floor under the tube to catch the balls.

SAFETY NOTE: Ping-Pong balls are *too small!* Your toddler might put them into her mouth.

Fun with Tubes

Research Update:
How Day Care Affects Behavior

How does day care affect a young child and her family? The surprising answer is: Apparently not as much as you might think, individual differences aside. Researchers who look at this question cannot hope to isolate and measure the precise impact on any one child's social, emotional, and intellectual development. Yet when certain criteria are examined, it appears that maternal employment is not the negative influence it was once feared to be.

EFFECT ON PARENT-CHILD ATTACHMENT

Ann Easterbrooks (Tufts University) and Wendy Goldberg (University of California at Irvine) studied seventy-three single-child families, all with twenty-month-olds. About a third of the mothers had not been employed since the child was born, a third were employed part-time (an average of eighteen hours a week), and a third were employed full-time. All the fathers in this study had full-time employment.

To help determine how the mother's employment affected family relationships, Easterbrooks and Goldberg looked at two measurements. The first was parental perception. Each mother and father was asked individually how she or he thought the mother's working influenced the child's relationship with her mother and her father. As the following data show, the families with employed mothers overwhelmingly thought that the mother's employment had a positive or neutral impact on their parent-child relationships.

Impact on the Mother-Child Relationship
- 67 percent of the mothers and 74 percent of the fathers said the impact of the mother's employment was entirely positive
- 6 percent of the mothers and 22 percent of the fathers said it had no impact
- 26 percent of the mothers and 4 percent of the fathers said it had a mixture of positive and negative effects or entirely negative effects

Impact on the Father-Child Relationship
- 58 percent of the mothers and 64 percent of the fathers said that the impact of the mother's employment was entirely positive

- 18 percent of the mothers and 34 percent of the fathers said it had no impact
- 23 percent of the mothers and 2 percent of the fathers said it had a mixture of positive and negative effects or entirely negative effects

The second measurement was parent-child attachment. Easterbrooks and Goldberg assessed this by observing how the child related to her parents when confronted with a stranger or an unfamiliar situation. (This is a widely used experimental technique for studying attachment.) The researchers found that:

- In families where the mother was not employed or employed part-time, almost 90 percent of the toddlers showed secure attachment with their mothers, about 70 percent had secure attachment with their fathers.
- When mothers were employed full-time, 83 percent of the toddlers had secure attachment with their mothers and 59 percent with their fathers.

So there appeared to be almost no difference regarding attachment to mothers, a small reduction in attachment to fathers when the mother was employed. Why is there a difference between attachment to the two parents? It's hard to pinpoint. One guess is that most toddlers in our society are closer to their mothers, since mothers traditionally have the larger role in child rearing.

The Easterbrooks and Goldberg study is especially significant because it looked at toddlers only (as compared to most studies, which look at a range of age groups), and because the vast majority of these children were cared for by sitters rather than in day-care centers. This is the most common situation for children under two years. Other evidence confirms these findings. Joanne O'Connell, director/research coordinator of the Institute for Human Development at Northern Arizona University, reviewed studies covering a cross-section of children from six months to five years of age. She found no significant difference in the mother-child bond between home-reared children and those cared for in groups or day-care centers. In fact, the similarities in behavior between the groups far outweighed any observable differences.

You should keep in mind that any study that tries to assess complex interpersonal relations has built-in limitations. Nevertheless, these findings do suggest that toddlers whose mothers are employed can be just as close to their parents as toddlers of non-employed mothers.

Another common concern shared by mothers is whether the child will form a stronger relationship with the substitute caregiver than with her. Studies have explored this as well, using among other standards a variation on the attachment experiment described earlier. It has been found that when children are confronted with a stressful situation in the presence of both their mother and their caregiver, they overwhelmingly turn to their parent. So it seems that if your child is cared for by another, chances are you won't be replaced in her affections.

EFFECT ON INTELLECTUAL DEVELOPMENT

Many studies on intellectual development have been conducted with children from low-income homes. On the whole, children in day care showed definite and long-lasting gains over similar children who were not cared for outside the home. (Some studies, however, suggest that such gains disappear by about eight or nine years.) Several other studies of middle and upper-middle income children find no appreciable differences in intellectual development between care-reared and similar home-reared children. One research study of two- to four-year-olds by Alison Clarke-Stewart at the University of California at Irvine found that children in day care tend to be more advanced in language skills and knowledge of the world than those who stay at home. Again, we caution you not to read too much into these findings. Most of these studies have been done with children in group care or day-care centers, and with children older than toddlers. All in all, though, it appears that day care for older children doesn't hinder learning.

EFFECT ON SOCIAL SKILLS

Many parents logically assume that group care improves a child's ability to get along with other children. This can be hard to evaluate. To determine a child's social skills, most research studies historically have looked at isolated test situations in which two or more young children interact. The evidence is mixed. Some find that day-care-reared children tend to have better social skills, others that home-reared children do, depending on the specific variables examined. And since few toddlers are cared for in groups, the effect on their social skills has rarely been studied. But numerous studies do show that toddlers enjoy playing with their peers, and that positive interactions greatly outnumber negative ones.

IN SUMMARY

So what does all this mean? We agree with the conclusion Dr. O'Connell reached: "No consistent adverse effect of out-of-home child day care has been found by over a dozen child development investigators." Even though most studies are done with children in day-care centers, the few that explore other care situations, like Easterbrooks and Goldberg's, generally concur. Obviously the quality of the care is important—an indifferent caregiver or poorly run center will definitely be inferior to your own care. But just as obviously, a child isn't automatically disadvantaged just because her mother works outside the home.

19

YOUR SIXTEEN-MONTH-OLD

Overview

When you think about how important the abilities to make friends and get along with others are to us adults, it's not surprising that the foundations for these skills develop very early. In the second year of life, a toddler's relationships with his parents are definitely the most important to him, but he's actively developing relationships with members of his own genera-

tion, too. This chapter looks at these unfolding social skills, and ways you can help friendships form even at this early age.

A toddler's social relationships both within and beyond the family certainly influence his overall development. So does the nature of the relationship between his parents. Research confirms that your child is quite sensitive to feelings flowing around him, and that incidents of anger, love, and other emotions definitely affect him.

On the language front, the typical sixteen-month-old has a speaking vocabulary of over fifty different words. (Remember that this is an average; many toddlers this age have yet to start truly talking.) Even so, you'll likely see your child call every man "Daddy," or every four-legged animal "doggie." There are several reasons why he might make this "mistake," as we discuss in this chapter.

When Toddlers Play Together

Picture the scene. Two typical mothers and their sixteen-month-olds get together in one of the family's homes. Greetings are exchanged, toys are brought out, all four gather in a room for a nice social visit. Now . . . what probably happens?

Chances are, the toddlers will be more interested in each other than in their mothers—or even in the toys. Studies conducted both in laboratory playrooms and homes have found that in the above situation, the toddlers direct much of their attention to their peers—even if the children haven't spent much time together previously. Contrary to what was once thought, most sixteen-month-olds really like spending time and interacting with their age-mates.

GETTING STARTED

When two toddlers are introduced, some dive right into playing with each other, others are a little shy, and need to stay close to Mom or Dad initially. They prefer to size up the new situation from a secure base. Soon, though, curiosity usually takes over and they become more sociable. If shyness persists, you might try to help ease your child into interacting with his potential playmate. Maybe sit on the floor and talk to the other toddler, or play together with a toy. Gradually involve your toddler at a pace he accepts, without placing undue pressure on him. This is much better than admonishing him for being shy, or telling him to be a "big boy" and go play. He might view this emphatic push into socializing as a sign that you're rejecting him, and cling all the more. You also help by exuding your own comfort with the situation. If you and the other parent are friendly and relaxed, your children will pick up on the positive atmosphere.

WHAT TO EXPECT

First encounters with potential friends usually involve less personal interaction than playtimes where the toddlers are well acquainted. But whether the children are new friends or old, you'll probably notice the following behaviors.

Watching.   All toddlers spend a lot of time looking at things. This is far from time-wasting; toddlers and adults alike learn a lot just by looking. Sometimes your child will stare openly at the other toddler, sometimes he'll keep watch out of the corner of his eye while he appears to be concentrating on another task. Perhaps surprisingly, researchers Jaipaul Roopnarine (Syracuse University) and Tiffany Field (University of Miami School of Medicine) found that the amount of time toddlers spend watching each other usually *increases* as they become more familiar.

Solitary Play.   When your child has a friend over to visit, the two toddlers will often play separately near one another, maybe each with his own toy. They're probably enjoying this "togetherness" the way you and your partner might enjoy sitting and reading in the same room, each aware of the other although no interaction takes place between you.

Parallel Play.   If you observe solitary play closely, sometimes you'll notice that it entails a certain amount of interaction. Often two children who appear to be ignoring each other are in fact playing with similar objects in similar ways—which means that they're not only noticing each other, but also silently modeling one another's behavior. This is called parallel play.

Imitation.   Toddlers also like to imitate one another more overtly. Claudia Davis and Carol Eckerman at Duke University found that the sixteen-month-old toddler pairs they studied spent 14 percent of the time together imitating each other, and that one-fifth of all their interactions contained some type of imitation. In a study at the University of Guelph, Ontario, Canada, Leon Kuczynski found that the most common imitations included copying one another's sounds: laughing, cheering, shouting, sighing, squealing, and the like.

Play with Objects. When they're together, toddlers spend a lot of time playing with toys. Sometimes each plays with a toy alone, quite unrelated to what the other toddler is doing. Sometimes this play involves subtle or direct imitation. Toddlers also share toys and play together. Usually, the bigger the toy and the more it invites shared play—such as a toddler-sized slide or a curtain to hide behind—the less the children fight over it.

Toddlers often show or offer toys, too, as a way of engaging in social interaction. (After all, they don't have the verbal skills to break the ice with words.) Often a toddler won't wait for his friend to make the invitation, but will snatch a toy away. This may look like burgeoning selfishness, but it's a common part of development. Grabbing toys is thought to be a way your toddler discovers how much power he has in relation to another person, and thus is a way he helps to define himself. Many psychologists consider it a positive step in developing his self-concept. At sixteen months, you don't need to step in when toys are snatched. Let the two children work out this possession struggle themselves. However, if one child is always having his toys taken away, you might encourage him to stand up for his rights and not surrender the prize every time. Or even suggest he take it back. Of course, if toy-grabbing escalates into a fight, you should intervene in the ways we suggest later.

WHAT IS THE PARENTS' ROLE?

Peer play helps your toddler develop simple social skills that continue to mature as he grows. It also helps him learn many other things, among them new games. It's undoubtedly fun. Peers enjoy silly toddler-type things like jumping off the bottom step twenty times in a row and wearing pots for hats—activities parents often enter into with far less enthusiasm. You don't really need to do anything special to encourage your toddler's social skills, aside from making sure he has contact with his age-mates, and that the toddlers have plenty of toys to play with. But neither should you leave them to their own devices.

One reason toddlers need supervision is they often treat one another like objects, and explore each other with hands and mouth the way they might a toy. Usually these pokes and probes and tugs are gentle enough so that you needn't pay much mind. But if they're rough, you should intervene for both toddlers' sake. Stop the child as you explain to him that he *must not* pull hair, *must not* poke a child in the face, *must not* bite. Biting *hurts*. Pulling hair *hurts*. He should be *gentle*. Be clear and emphatic, not angry. Let your child know that his behavior is unacceptable without giving him the feeling that you're rejecting him. It's also important to be calm in dealing with this type of normal toddler behavior. Your overreaction might make the toddlers overreact as well.

Remember, too, that two toddlers can get into just as much trouble as one. So when your child has a friend over, keep both children in sight or check on them very frequently. Don't let a long silence lull you into thinking you shouldn't disturb them when they're so contented. They might be absorbedly stuffing toys into the toilet.

WHAT ABOUT FIGHTS?

Naturally, toddler age-mates don't get along perfectly all the time. Yet the amount of aggression, toy-snatching aside, is much less than you might think. In fact, in a study of nineteen-month-old pairs by Judith Rubenstein (Boston University Medical School) and Carollee Howes (University of California at Los Angeles), the toddlers acted aggressively toward one another only about 3 percent of the time. Keep in mind that these aggressive acts tend to increase with age.

Sometimes the aggression will be mild pushing or name-calling ("Bad boy!"). Toddlers usually work these out for themselves — often by pushing or name-calling right back. However, if one toddler begins pushing hard, biting or kicking, or clobbering the other child with a toy, it's time for you to step in — and swiftly. This doesn't mean that you should rush in shouting; your cool head is needed to help both children calm down. Nor do we recommend spanking the offending child. It's a little illogical to strike a toddler while asserting, "Don't hit people!" As is the case when toddlers explore one another too roughly, your intervention should be prompt, firm, and above all, calm. Be sure to soothe the hurt child, too, if his parent isn't there.

Usually these toddler squabbles are brief and quickly forgotten. If they become too frequent (maybe because one of the toddlers is getting tired and a bit cranky), a change of scene might help. You can march everyone off to the kitchen for a glass of juice, or initiate a trip to the backyard sandbox.

EACH CHILD IS AN INDIVIDUAL

As you observe your toddler with his age-mates, keep in mind that every child is an individual, and that every toddler-pair or small group won't interact exactly the ways research studies suggest. Some children play together more cooperatively than others — that's a fact of personalities. Some like to be near one another, yet spend little time in actual interaction. That's natural, too. But even if your toddler seems to ignore his pal when they're together, chances are he's enjoying the companionship. He's learning a lot from it, too.

Toddlers and Family Emotions

Almost every parent intuitively knows that young children pick up on feelings and emotions flowing around them. One recent, complex study of twenty-four families gives insights into how sensitive a toddler might well be.

This particular project was conducted at the National Institute of Mental Health by Mark Cummings, Carolyn Zahn-Waxler, and Marian Radke-Yarrow. Each mother reported how her child responded to incidents of anger that the child observed *as a bystander* over a nine-month period. For the most part, these anger episodes were parents arguing between themselves, or a parent shouting at or spanking the toddler's older sibling. Some findings:

· These toddlers reacted with visible distress to over 70 percent of the anger incidents they witnessed. They evidenced their anguish through cries, worried facial expressions, or words expressing concern (46 percent of the episodes); or by becoming angry themselves, and scolding or hitting the offending parties (24 percent of the episodes).
· The more a toddler witnessed his parents arguing, the more likely he was to become angry himself. The researchers hypothesize that frequently viewing such incidents threatened a child's sense of security regarding his social environment.
· The toddlers studied were significantly more likely to respond with distress when someone was hit (such as when the

*Toddlers are quite
sensitive to angry words
between parents; family
spats can frighten them.*

parent spanked a sibling) than when people merely argued
or otherwise expressed anger.

Such findings suggest that if you and your spouse are having
problems, it would be best to shield your toddler from the anger and
outbursts as much as you can. You needn't present false faces that
everything's rosy, but you should try to confine serious disagreements to private quarters. Also, whenever feasible, discipline your
older child away from your toddler. Your toddler usually can't
understand why you're angry or why such reaction might be called
for; all he sees is your anger—and that can frighten him.

Realistically, you can't—and shouldn't—shield your toddler
from every expression of anger. There's no evidence that viewing
occasional outbursts has lasting ill effects. You can help calm your
child by telling him "Everything is OK," and reminding him that

"I'm mad at your sister, not at you." Nor is a falsely sweetened world desirable. Toddlers learn from observing a range of emotional behaviors. However, this study does reinforce just how sensitive your toddler can be both to your emotions and to the relationship between his parents.

What about when toddlers observed episodes of affection between parents, or a parent and the toddler's sibling? This same study found that 30 percent of the time, the toddlers reacted with smiles, laughs, or other expressions of pleasure. But, surprisingly, they became angry in 23 percent of the instances. This generally happened when the incident interfered with the toddler's attempt to draw an affectionate response from his parents, or interrupted an affectionate episode in which the toddler was engaged. It seems that a toddler becomes a bit jealous when the affectionate attention he wants at that moment is given to someone else. Try to let him be first in line for hugs.

Is Every Man "Daddy"?

"Daddy!" your toddler squeals excitedly as his father steps into the kitchen. You beam. "Daddy!" he cries with equal enthusiasm to the sixteen-year-old boy behind you at the supermarket checkout. Red-faced, you hasten to reassure your toddler (and, not incidentally, the other shoppers!) that "He's not daddy, dearest." Then maybe you wonder: Does he really think every man is his father?

It's highly unlikely. A toddler often uses a single word to refer to several different objects if they share some common, obvious feature. For instance, he might call every round object *ball*. Or everything with four legs is a *doggie*, be it a pony, lamb, puppy, or cow. He may use *fly* as the name of all small things from insects to raisins to polka dots. *Car* can refer indiscriminately to any wheeled or moving vehicle. Of course, every man may be *daddy*. Or maybe he's more restrictive. If his own father has glasses and a mustache, he may greet as *daddy* only men who share these features.

Language specialists generally call this *overextension*. There are several possible reasons why your toddler uses the same word for two or more objects.

THEY ARE THE SAME—TO HIM

Your toddler is still grasping the concept of a particular object's name. Learning names is a complicated task. When you point to and name a ball, for instance, he must figure out which of the features defines this as a "ball." Is it the shape? The size? The colors? The material from which it is made? The fact that it bounces or rolls? Or some combination of these? As your child learns the names of objects, he builds mental concepts and groups things into categories. Eventually he learns that balls can be big or small, hard or rubbery, red or blue or striped; however, they all are round and bounce or roll. But before he gets this concept down pat, he's bound to say "ball" to other objects that fit some or all of these criteria. This can be quite reasonable. Suppose your toddler sees his first orange. He might logically think that an orange really *is* a ball.

LIMITED VOCABULARY AND OVEREXTENSION

As the case above illustrates, your toddler sometimes overextends a word like "ball" because he probably isn't entirely sure what is and what isn't a ball. That's only one reason, though. Scores of researchers have found that toddlers overextend even when they *can* differentiate between two similar objects.

One explanation is that a toddler recognizes that the objects are similar, but he doesn't know the name of one of them. In the case of *daddy*, your toddler almost certainly knows that every man is not his father. Yet, he might not have learned the more general word *man*. Because he loves to talk and name things, he naturally substitutes the closest word in his vocabulary. In test situations, toddlers shown pictures of a dog and another four-legged animal (like a horse or cow) often call both of them "doggie." Nevertheless, when asked by the experimenter to "Show me the dog," the toddlers almost always point to the correct illustration. In these cases of overextension, your toddler's ability to say words lags behind his comprehension and categorization skills. He realizes that horses aren't dogs and all men aren't his daddy. But the words *horse* or *man* haven't yet entered his speaking vocabulary, so he does the best with what he knows.

Will correcting these overextensions help speed up the process? Research findings are mixed. One thing *is* certain: You don't need to. Overextension isn't a problem; it's a part of natural language development nearly every toddler exhibits. And it can tell you a lot about your own child's thought processes, which is one reason so many experts study this phenomenon. The general ways you support your toddler's language learning—looking at books together, naming things casually in the course of a day, talking to him—help develop his comprehension and speaking vocabulary.

OTHER POSSIBLE REASONS

Surprisingly, though, toddlers sometimes call two different objects by the same name even when both words *are* in their speaking vocabulary. There are several possible reasons why. Some experts theorize that the toddler has occasional problems with retrieving words from memory, so he mentally substitutes a more familiar word. We adults often do this as well. When you can't think of that exact word you want— "It's right on the tip of my tongue"—you use one that more readily comes to mind. Other theories say that a toddler often shifts his basis of perception. (A simple example of this: A hat is a hat, and a book is a book. But a book is a hat when balanced on the head.) In a study at the City University of New York, Katherine Nelson and Judith Hudson (currently at the State University of New York, Albany) theorize that, especially in fantasy play, older toddlers sometimes rename familiar objects because they draw metaphorical relationships between different things.

One other reason for overextension is that, at this age, most toddlers are still speaking only in one-word utterances. Thus, the word *daddy* might mean in one case "my daddy," and in another case "a daddy." When your toddler talks, you need to rely on his gestures and the context of these utterances to decipher their meaning. The process will become easier when he starts speaking in phrases—which is most likely just a few months away.

Growing through Play

BEGINNER BALL GAMES

A ball is probably the single most indispensable item for active toddler play. It can be rolled, bounced, thrown, caught, kicked, whacked with a stick, dropped through a hoop, chased after—and more. Collect a variety of balls for your toddler; different ones lend themselves to different types of play, depending on their size and material. And different children play with balls in different ways, depending on the *child's* size and skills and interests. Here are some games and ideas appropriate for younger toddlers.

· Simplest: Roll a ball for your toddler to chase and retrieve.
· You and your toddler sit a few feet apart on the floor and roll a ball back and forth. His aim might be off a bit, but he'll have fun trying. If he has real trouble keeping the ball on course, sit with your legs spread widely—they'll define a nice large funnel to trap the rolling ball.
· For the child who has lots of power but poor aim, play rolling games in a narrow hall. You can sit farther apart, and the walls prevent the ball from straying.
· Safe throwing: Use a pair of rolled-up socks as a ball. Invite your toddler to toss it to you. He'll probably throw it any-where—even behind him—but the soft socks won't damage anything. He'll also improve his aim with practice.
· Inflated beach balls are a special treat because they're so large (and therefore look "heavy" to a toddler), but are light enough for him to carry easily. Roll a beach ball back and forth between you two (or three or more). Hold your toddler under his arms so that he's standing, and swing him gently back and forth so that he "kicks" the ball.

Remember that balls plus ramps and balls plus tubes are terrific play combinations.

FUN WITH AROMAS

Give your toddler's nose an education! If he likes to join you for your morning wash-up, introduce him to the smells of soaps and colognes and after-shaves. When you cook, let him sniff spices like vanilla and bay leaves, or ingredients like mayonnaise. For added adventure, you might counterbalance these pleasant aromas with some that are less attractive: garlic, smelly cheeses, and the like.

CAUTION: You should avoid having your toddler sniff jars of crushed spices or other powdery substances, like pepper. He might acci-dentally inhale some fine particles. And remember that neither he nor you should inhale the fumes from ammonia, bleach, gasoline, and similar products.

Sniff-it game: Here's a way to introduce your toddler to many different smells at one sitting. Take a number of cotton balls, sprinkle each with a different aromatic liquid, and hold them under his nose one at a time while you talk about them. Ideas: cooking extracts like vanilla, lemon, and almond; colognes and perfumes; fruit juices; vinegar and juices in which things have been pickled. Just make sure your toddler doesn't *eat* these yummy-smelling puffs. If he insists on trying, you might dab the aromatic liquids on a sheet of blotting paper and let him sniff that.

PEEKING HOUSE

Just like older infants, toddlers love playing all kinds of versions of peekaboo. For a twist on this favorite game, make a Peeking House. Take a large cardboard carton, cut off one long side, and in the remaining three sides cut one or more peep holes. These can be different sizes and shapes if you like. Just make sure each peep hole is large enough for your child to see through with both eyes, but too small for him to fit his head through. To play: Stand the box up with the open side to the back; your toddler sneaks behind and peeks out at you. Peek right back!

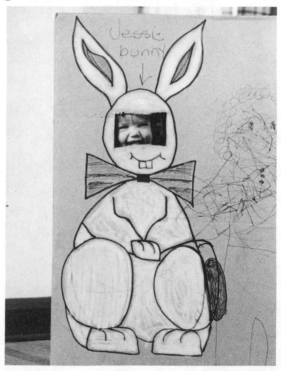

Peeking House

HINT: Your older child—or even your toddler if he likes crayons—can decorate this house.

Research Update:
"Tools" and Problem Solving

As part of a University of California, Los Angeles, study of sensorimotor development, researchers Claire Kopp, Marian Sigman, and Arthur Parmelee looked at a young child's ability to use a "tool" in solving problems. The problem: How to retrieve an out-of-reach toy. In one test, the toy sat on the far end of a piece of cloth. All the subjects successfully pulled the cloth to get the toy from ten months on, with their skill—measured by how easily and quickly they solved this problem—generally increasing with age. In another, the child was given a separate rakelike tool. Only 20 percent of the fourteen-month-olds and 47 percent of the sixteen-month-olds figured out how to use the rake to bring the toy within reach. It seems that when the "tool" isn't directly touching the toy, the children have more difficulty seeing the relationship between the two objects.

20

YOUR SEVENTEEN-MONTH-OLD

Overview

Defiant behavior! As your toddler nears the middle of her second year, she may well step up her drive to prove her independence and maturity. She purposefully handles things that she knows she shouldn't. She takes forever doing something, realizing all the while that you want her to speed it up. Soon she'll express contrariness myriad ways that we discuss in the next

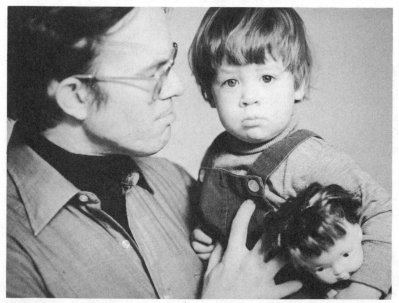

chapter. All these mini-rebellions are partly means to let you know that she wants to be the boss—at least some of the time.

On the other hand, though, many acts of defiance have a benign rather than vengeful foundation. A seventeen-month-old handles some untouchables because she lacks self-control. She dawdles on a walk because she's too small to take large steps, and because she lacks an understanding of time that's necessary for her to truly understand the importance of hurrying up. You need to take her developmental limitations in mind when judging her behavior. But you have needs, too. We offer hints to encourage cooperation whatever the reason for her seemingly uncooperative behavior.

Other problems parents often confront during the toddler year revolve around bedtime and sleep. Many toddlers continue waking during the night—and calling for parents—as we first discussed in an earlier chapter. Or they do whatever they can to stretch the bedtime routine, postponing that final "good night" as long as you're willing. Or they wake up early, and that chirpy 6:00 A.M. voice is *not* music to your ears. We look at some ways of handling these in this chapter as well.

More on Discipline

As we said in an earlier chapter, most disciplinary "problems" involve your toddler's touching something that she shouldn't. By this age, she's beginning to understand that the stove and some other items truly are "hands-off." Nonetheless, she still doesn't always obey your sharp "*No!*" as she reaches for the kitty or a plant or other thing she'll almost certainly *not* handle with care, because she still has little self-control. Brian Vaughn (University of Illinois, Chicago), Claire Kopp (University of California, Los Angeles), and Joanne Krakow (Mount St. Mary's College, Los Angeles) found that eighteen-month-olds show very limited restraint when specifically asked not to touch enticing objects within their reach. This self-control increases dramatically as a child's intellectual, social, and—perhaps most surprisingly—*language* skills mature.

LANGUAGE AND SELF-CONTROL

Language gives power. A vocal toddler generally influences other people more effectively through statements and admonishments and requests for help than a baby does through cries and gestures. By the same token, language gives a child more control over her _own_ behavior. You'll notice this more clearly over the coming months. For instance, your child will use language to defuse momentary angry feelings. Yelling at you or calling you "Bad! Bad!" releases emotions that, with a less-verbal child, are usually let out only through hitting and kicking and other physical acts. (However, these physical acts may well still occur even after a child can talk.) You'll also notice that your child will use language to restrain herself from touching forbidden objects. Suppose there's a delicate figurine just begging for tiny hands. The barely vocal toddler will likely grab it even though you've told her "No, no, don't touch," countless times. She likely knows that she shouldn't, but she has real trouble controlling her urges. The toddler with more sophisticated language skills often tries to restrain herself by talking through the desire out loud. "No, no. Don't touch. Nice dolly. Don't touch. No, no." This self-spoken warning frequently relieves her urge to touch it. It's not always effective at the early stages, though. Many a child will repeat "No, no, don't touch," while picking up the figurine. Her level of restraint also depends on her mood, personality—and, obviously, the desirability of the forbidden object or activity. Nonetheless, it's true that toddlers mishandle less when they can partly control themselves through talking.

This power of words is difficult to explain, because the theories of language's relationship to behavior are quite complex. Different theorists express different viewpoints. However, most specialists agree that language and thought are inextricably entwined, and that these verbal-intellectual skills influence behavior. Once a child can think and can represent actions through words (either spoken aloud or internally), she doesn't always need to carry them out physically. The ability to talk can relieve the need to act.

It may also be that the words themselves have some magical quality. Hearing these words, even when she herself is saying them, may have the same effect on a child as hearing them spoken by her parents.

ENCOURAGING COOPERATION

Sometimes, though, the often-uncooperative toddler touches forbidden objects purely to defy you. She doesn't really care so much about the item—but she knows full well that touching it bothers you. This is her way of expressing power over the situation, and over you. One way to reduce this defiance is occasionally to let her handle things that she normally isn't allowed to. This helps her see that you are basically on her side, and that you are willing to share your prized objects with her—as long as she's gentle. Such experiences also hasten the day when she will be somewhat careful with breakable objects even when you're not around.

The trick is to set up a situation that's safe both for her and for the touched object. Supervise carefully so that she doesn't throw or otherwise harm it, and patiently teach her how to handle things with care.

- Sit your toddler on the sofa or a soft carpet and let her handle an attractive figurine (not a really valuable one!). Show her how to hold it "carefully."
- Let her pat or stroke the kitty while you hold it. Show how to pet "gently."
- Hold her in your arms and let her touch the clock on the mantle.

These are exciting experiences for your toddler. She senses that you trust her, and that you're sharing with her things that you care about. You shouldn't expect too much, though. Remove the object from her grasp at the first sign that she might exceed your handling standards. Don't snatch it away or scold her; these kinds of actions give her the message that she can't deal with the situation on her own. You already knew that. Remind her that she may touch this object *only when you say so,* and that she'll be able to handle it again soon *only with your help*. Let her know, too, that you're proud of what she's been able to do.

SPOTS ON PUNISHMENT

The traditional way parents punish a child for "bad" behavior— sitting her on a step or in the corner, confining her to her room, even spanking—usually don't work for a toddler under about twenty-four months of age. For one thing she rarely does something intentionally to bother you, or because she knows it is forbidden; rather, she does it because she lacks self-control or the knowledge of "right" and "wrong" behavior. Sometimes she'll even repeat the behavior that she knows bothers you (like pouring milk on her feeding tray) just to try to understand *why* it makes you so angry. She doesn't understand that her behavior is wrong. She doesn't understand why she is being punished. Therefore, the punishment will do little to discourage her repeating the anger-provoking behavior in the future.

Even so, there will be times when she defies you again and again, and you'll both get increasingly angry. These are the times to separate. She might go to her room or other safe place—not as traditional punishment, which she won't understand, but as a chance to let you both cool off.

Sleep Roundup

Hints and help with common dilemmas.

BEDTIME ROUTINE

By seventeen months, chances are you and your toddler have established your own successful routines for easing her into sleep at day's end. Terrific! This routine is not only relaxing, it also gives your child some uninterrupted time with one or both parents. But . . . have you begun to notice that the routine is somehow becoming longer and longer? It's possible. Most toddlers like this bedtime togetherness so much that they encourage you (subtly or overtly) to add another song or story or good-night bidding to still another stuffed animal—until half your evening is gone. So beware the sweetly devious routine-stretcher! You need to set a limit on just how long you want this to last. Remember, once a routine is established, most toddlers insist that the exact same procedures be followed every night. They won't like it if you skip a single step (but they'll be more than happy if you add some!). Should the routine become too long for your liking, it can be hard to shorten it again.

SETTING A BEDTIME

We definitely suggest establishing a regular bedtime for a toddler, even if only to ensure that parents themselves have time alone for each other, or for doing things that they need to get done without having to care for their child. As Dr. Susan Doering, a social psychologist, told us,

> A toddler needs a regular bedtime so that she'll get enough rest, but her bedtime may be even more important to her parents than it is to her. Parents need privacy and time to

themselves, and above and beyond this, the parent who has been keeping up with the toddler all day wants simple relief. To recover your sense of humor and enjoyment of yourself as an independent adult—not to mention your ability to relate to your spouse as an equal, a partner, and a lover—you _need_ to be free of your toddler at night. Don't feel guilty about wanting your child out of the way by a certain hour, or about feeling annoyed when she has trouble settling down; these are natural reactions. But when your child is having trouble going to sleep, try not to communicate your impatience to her. She'll settle into sleep sooner if you respond helpfully, but matter-of-factly, to her needs.

Don't be surprised if your toddler doesn't drift off quickly once you've settled her in her crib at bedtime. Data gathered as part of the New York Longitudinal Study of Temperament and Development, as reported by Antonio Beltramini and Margaret Hertzig, found that 26 percent of the one-year-olds required more than thirty minutes to fall asleep. A dim room light and some favorite crib toys help keep these toddlers quiet and sleep-bound.

THE EARLY RISER

A toddler who rises with the sun and crowing roosters may not be a joy to the parent who wants to sleep longer. Naturally, you can't _make_ her sleep more. But if you put some soft toys and vinyl—not paper—books in her bed the night before (maybe after she falls asleep), she might play alone happily for a while. A night-light might be necessary on winter mornings; after all, you can't expect your toddler to amuse herself in the dark. Another tactic is to bring your toddler into your bed if your room is _completely_ toddlerproofed: And that includes _no_ medications in the bedside table, _no_ cosmetics out on surfaces, and the bathroom door securely shut. If you're not quite ready to get up, you and she may share a book or a song in your bed. Or maybe let her play on the floor with some favorite toys. Toddlerproofing is necessary in case you should fall back to sleep again.

Some books and magazine articles we've read suggest putting food into your toddler's crib so that she can snack upon waking. We strongly oppose this idea because there's always a possibility that she'll choke on what she's eating. For the same reason, it's important to assure that there's never anything in the crib small enough to fit into your toddler's mouth. Never string anything across the crib or playpen at this age, either. Your toddler could get entangled in it.

Dealing with Dawdling

It takes a toddler a *long* time to do just about anything. Her self-fed mealtimes seem to last hours. Baths may go on until she's all "pruney." When you walk from the house to the car, she stops to explore just about every pebble, twig, and leaf in her path. If you try to hurry her along, she may insist on standing rooted to the sidewalk—or being carried. She may even throw herself on the ground.

There are lots of reasons for this dawdling. The most basic is that it's hard for some toddlers to move quickly. They may lack the muscle coordination to move along as fast as you like. Some toddlers are very persistent, too; they have a hard time switching activities (especially when they're enjoying the one they're doing at the moment). Toddlers don't have a very clear concept of time, either. They're basically unable to think in terms of getting somewhere sooner or later. They live in the absolute present, the attraction of the moment is all there is. With so much to explore, no wonder she dawdles.

Of course, dawdling can also be a form of self-assertion, a way for a toddler to express herself by setting a pace that suits her, and even a clever way to manipulate a situation without being downright uncooperative. So dawdling that happens at home—taking forever to finish a bath, for instance—is best dealt with the same way you deal with other assertive behaviors. Avoid confrontations, arguments, and anger. Let your toddler know in a firm but calm way that it's time to finish what she's doing. Also try to gain cooperation by turning the situation into a game: "Let's see if you can finish taking off your sock before I put your shoes in the closet." If all else fails, take the matter into your own hands *before you get angry*.

Dawdling in public can be a little different. You may feel embarrassed by your inability to control your toddler, and disinclined to insist she hurry for fear it could lead to a fight—even a tantrum. If you need to get somewhere quickly when you walk, take along the stroller or backpack so you can pop her inside when need be. But suppose you and she are out for a walk with no specific destination, so you haven't brought the stroller, and time is drawing very short. The best policy is to keep walking at a slow, steady pace. Turn around frequently to make sure your toddler isn't doing anything she shouldn't (like eating a leaf). As long as you keep progressing, she'll more or less match your pace because she's probably afraid of your getting too far away.

It's best not to threaten abandonment by resorting to that standby of exasperated parents: "Bye, bye, I'm leaving you." You'll likely terrify her. Also, you know, of course, that you never really *will* leave her. So if you threaten, and she doesn't respond, and you don't (and you shouldn't!) follow through, she'll realize that you're bluffing. She may start doubting your other commands, too. Rather, encourage her to keep walking, occasionally offering a supportive remark like "I know there are lots of interesting things to explore. But it's time to go home. We must go have lunch." If you have a free hand for her to hold, this will help guide her at a quicker pace. You might also play a game: She holds one end of a belt, you hold the other, and you pretend to be her puppy. "Woof, woof, I'm hurrying home to get my dinner." You might even find that this kind of walk with your toddler is fun.

Growing through Play

TOUCH TOURS

As you well know, your toddler loves to touch things. In fact, at times it's almost impossible to stop her! You can help her become more aware of her sense of touch by drawing her attention to the things she handles. You needn't do this in a formal way; rather, sometimes when your toddler is busily exploring your body, talk about the softness of your lips, the scratchiness of Daddy's beard, the fuzziness of Mommy's hair, the hardness of your fingernails. When she's playing in the kitchen while you cook or wash or whatever, talk about the objects she's handling, or hand her new ones that have interesting textures: a pot scrubber, a vegetable brush, a peach or kiwi fruit. Try your best to describe the object and its textures so that you help focus her attention. Plus, you'll introduce some new words.

You might also take your toddler on touch tours. Carry her around the house, stopping frequently to let her handle items normally out of reach: wall hangings, carvings on the banister post, knickknacks on the shelves and dresser top, and so forth. Because of your close supervision, you can let her touch even delicate objects she rarely gets to feel otherwise. Outside, lift her up to reach things like tree leaves and the brickwork on buildings. Or walk with her, and invite her to touch tree trunks, step railings, and other textured materials. Pause to touch and talk about the same things.

SIMPLE SCRIBBLES

Many seventeen- or eighteen-month-olds like to scribble with crayons. At this age, they're interested in exploring and making marks, not in creating a picture; they enjoy dabbling for a few minutes, not working industriously. In other words, it's not the time to ask your child to draw you a landscape. And since toddlers aren't the most careful of creatures, you should always stay by to confine your child's creative urges to the page rather than the wall, and to make sure she doesn't nibble on her art materials.

Choose jumbo crayons about a half inch in diameter. These are easier for a toddler to hold (she usually grasps them like a drumstick), and less likely to break. The nonrolling type stay close at hand. Make sure crayons are nontoxic—your toddler will probably put them into her mouth. When she does, remove the crayon while reminding her that crayons are for drawing, not eating. She'll learn this rule after a while. (If she continues to insist on tasting her art supplies, maybe she's not yet ready for crayons. Try them again in a few weeks or months.)

Give your toddler large sheets of paper to draw on. Best is a giant pad, available at an art supplies store—it holds the page steady and gives her plenty of room. You can keep single sheets stationary by taping them to the drawing surface: high-chair tray, table top, or the (uncarpeted) floor.

COMING DOWN THE STAIRS

At this age, you can help your toddler learn some safe ways to come down the stairs. One way is on her bottom, in a sitting position, maybe holding the banister rail uprights for added support. Demonstrate how to advance one step at a time, "pulling" yourself down with your legs and feet. Another way is to come down backward, facedown on all fours, again step by step. Most toddlers love to learn this skill by watching an (admired!) older child. Remember, though, that stairs are still dangerous at this age. *Always* supervise these descents, and be sure the staircase is blocked by safety gates when you're not around.

Research Update:
Sorting Skills

Give your toddler a jumble of red blocks and blue coasters, and chances are that before long she'll spontaneously sort them into their two distinct groups. Why? No one can say for sure. Maybe she's interested in order and organization, and enjoys creating some with her playthings. Perhaps she revels in the rewarding feeling that comes with meeting this self-imposed challenge. Possibly it's merely because she *can*, and she enjoys grouping things. Whatever the reason, it's clear that toddlers like to sort, and that this play is a reflection of their growing skills to comprehend the differences and similarities between objects, and to form mental categories.

Toddlers tend to sort along two main criteria:

1. Physical properties like shape, color, size, and texture
2. Functional qualities, which include the potential actions and uses of objects

Sorting by physical properties tends to start even in late infancy. In a study at Brandeis University David Starkey gave each baby in his study a set of eight objects; each set consisted of two groups of four objects each (four blue clay balls and four yellow plastic pillboxes). He found that the babies tended to touch first all four of the same objects, say the balls, before touching any of the boxes. Also, 13 percent of the nine-month-olds and 44 percent of the twelve-month-olds demonstrated some observable object grouping. More of this sorting occurred when the babies were given objects that differed in at least two qualities—size and color, for example—than in only one quality, such as shape. As evidence, the babies sorted the set of blue clay balls and yellow pillboxes much more successfully than they did a set of four flat yellow ovals and four flat yellow rectangles. Other studies with toddlers confirm that young children are most successful sorting objects when the two sets differ in size, color, and form than when the sets differ in only one physical property.

Yet if things become too complicated, this can hinder sorting skills. In a study at the Children's Hospital of Philadelphia, Linda Spungen and Joan Goodman tried a sorting experiment with eighteen- to twenty-four-month-olds. In the first level of the task, each child was asked to sort two types of small objects (clay balls and plastic animals) into two different containers. About 77 percent of the children were successful. In level two, the task was to sort four groups of small objects (plastic cars, plastic people, wooden pegs, blocks) into four containers. Only 30 percent could do it. It appears that there were just too many variables for the children to deal with at once.

Because sorting is so much fun, give your toddler opportunities for sorting games. Choose multipart toys that allow for sorting. Mix a set of small toys in a box and let her sort them again—maybe into two separate containers. Make sure it doesn't get too complicated until she has lots of experience. A simple set might contain two groups of identical objects—say, blocks all one size and color and plastic coasters all one size and color (a different color from the blocks), or maybe plastic disks one color and plastic squares another color. Maybe later try a set consisting of three groups of identical objects. You'll also see her spontaneously sort objects—maybe by color, maybe by shape, maybe by size, or maybe by one dimension and then another. She might sort her set of painted wooden blocks along one property (say, color), then mix them up and sort them by size or shape. Sometimes the criteria won't be cut-and-dried. Should the cookie go with the coaster because they're both round, or with the roll, because they're both food? Hmmmm . . . .

Don't be dismayed if your toddler isn't interested in sorting right now. First of all, this is a developmental skill, and some children come to it later than others. Second, your child may be more interested right now in large motor acts like running and climbing, or be fascinated with toys that have nothing to do with sorting properties. This shouldn't discourage you from offering sorting-type toys; just don't feel that it's a setback if you have to put them away for a later day. Eventually, with practice, your toddler will be able to move into helping you sort things around the house—like pairing up socks and dividing the silverware into those neat little compartments. Now, that's a practical skill!

21

YOUR EIGHTEEN-MONTH-OLD

Overview

Specialists at the Gesell Institute of Child Development at Yale University have a theory that stages of emotional equilibrium tend to alternate with stages of disequilibrium. These stages come generally (and we stress *generally*) in half-year cycles. A typical steady twelve-month-old enjoys several months of relative calmness and satisfaction. But starting around sixteen or

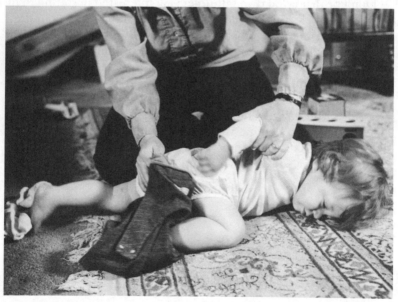

seventeen months, he begins a difficult era. His wishes are strong, his needs are demanding, so parents can expect plenty of stormy times. This period of disharmony usually starts subsiding around twenty-one or so months, so that by the second birthday, the toddler is again at relative ease with himself and the world. Around twenty-eight months, the cycle begins repeating itself.

The Gesell Institute researchers believe that these states of disequilibrium result chiefly from changes that go on within the child himself, and most particularly because of a discrepancy between ability and desire. For example, right now your toddler likely has a strong wish to do things for himself and be independent, but he lacks the ability to satisfy these wishes and needs. He's not able to undress himself as he might like; nor is he mature enough to bathe unaided, or walk beside a busy street without holding your hand. So he frequently becomes frustrated and angry—and that can result in a tantrum. A few months from now, his skills will be in better synchrony with his desires. He'll have made mental and emotional strides that help him handle frustration better. So he tends to be at peace with himself—and, by extension, with the world.

We generally agree with this observation, although we disagree somewhat with the timing put forth by the Gesell Institute of Child Development members. Children are such individualists that each has his own cycle and rhythm. However, don't be surprised if your toddler is especially contrary now, and periodically out of sorts for months on end. It seems to be a common aspect of development.

Most pediatricians like to schedule an eighteen-month checkup. At this visit, your toddler will most likely receive another series of immunizations:

- A dose of oral polio vaccine (OPV). This causes no reaction.
- A DTP (diphtheria-tetanus-pertussis) booster. Typical reactions include fussiness and a low-grade fever within four hours, and maybe a sore leg within twelve hours (if the shot was given in the buttock or thigh). Most reactions are lessened if the child is given acetaminophen, such as Children's Tylenol, two hours after the vaccination is administered. Call the doctor of your child has more severe reactions.

Quite Contrary!

Your eighteen-month-old enters a new phase on his journey from babyhood to childhood. Now halfway between the almost total helplessness of the newborn and the relative independence of the preschooler, he may intensify his struggle to grow up. He appears almost driven to assert himself, as if to convince everyone—himself included—that he is definitely no longer a baby.

Self-assertion often takes the form of contrariness. The typical eighteen-month-old tries to prove he's maturing by refusing to let you control him. He doesn't resist at every turn, of course, but it can certainly *feel* as if almost any issue becomes a battle. You ask him to come for lunch. "No!" he shouts. You invite him to walk with you to the library. He pouts, stamps his tiny foot, and yells "No!" His need to assert his independence is so strong that he even says *no* to things he wants to do. You offer him a favorite cracker. His eyes light up. He reaches while declaring "No!" and takes it all the same. You might conclude that he doesn't even know what *no* means. He does, most definitely. It's just that he wants to defy you on principle, and wants to have the cracker, too. His solution is simple. He does both.

DECLARATION OF INDEPENDENCE

A toddler's contrariness is his declaration of independence, his way of telling you he wants to make decisions for himself. In general, he's not contrary in a conscious effort merely to aggravate you. It's just that you're so big and powerful, he's so small and relatively powerless. It may help to think of his rebellion as a fear—fear of losing his unfolding sense of himself as a separate, independent person unless he digs in his heels and forces you to recognize that he's growing up.

MANY WAYS OF DEFYING YOU

This defiance may pop up in almost any situation—and encompass any tactic. Saying "No!" is one expression of resistance. He also squirms so that you need four hands to dress him. He runs away from you. He pulls out of your grasp, kicks and screams at you, sometimes even goes all stiff—or all limp—when you try to insist he do something. Likewise, different toddlers have different ways of reacting to parental control. A feisty child may defy almost every request, and throw tantrums over practically every demand you make of him. Another child might demonstrate contrariness in less vigorous ways, such as refusing to eat or nap. Some children who conform on the outside are actually angry on the inside at the parental pressure they feel. Though they usually cooperate with your requests, they're likely to express their defiance in sneaky ways: breaking things, pinching a baby brother, or kicking the dog when they think no one is looking.

FRICTION IS INEVITABLE

As your patience stretches to the snapping point, remember that this defiance is not only typical, *it's also a sign of growth*. Your toddler's awareness that he can choose *not* to do something is a step toward learning that he can choose *to* do something. The ability to make decisions for oneself is a vital part of self-reliance and maturity. Just about every one-year-old passes through a phase of contrariness that tends to subside—temporarily at least—around his second birthday. At that point, he's more secure in his identity, more sure of himself in lots of ways, and his drive to imitate and cooperate grows stronger than the desire to oppose.

Even if you accept that contrariness reflects a striving for independence that's essential to your toddler's development, this defiance will occasionally infuriate you, making it tough to keep your temper. But it's important to try. When you react too harshly, you risk prolonging the struggle or upping the emotional stakes, whatever the particular incident. You also add to the strain that is an inevitable by-product of this stage. As often happens, parental overreaction can trigger more violent toddler reaction—and when both of you are out of control, no one is in charge. This can terrify your child. Although he strives for independence, he would likely be scared to sense that he couldn't fall back on your strength and control when he himself is so stressed.

Still, all parents have been driven to the edge—or even over—by their toddler's contrariness. If you've reacted with furious yelling, or even a spanking, you need to get back in control. Calm yourself, then your child. Explain why you got so angry. Maybe even apologize for losing your temper. Reach out and offer some physical comfort, like a hug. This can certainly make you both feel better, offset your initial anger, and reassure him of your love. The next section offers hints for avoiding reaching the boiling point.

TIME CURES

After all is said and done, *time* is the real cure for this contrary phase. Your toddler is growing with each balk and fume toward the day when he'll react to life more calmly and confidently. The more composure you can muster, the better off your whole family will be.

Getting Your Nay-Sayer to Obey

You want to nurture your toddler's growing independence without denying your need to maintain authority. How do you accomplish both? *Make your goal ultimate cooperation rather than instant obedience.* If you don't expect your toddler to comply with your requests at once—and you shouldn't, because often he won't no matter how much you insist—you can avoid major confrontations. You can also help get your nay-sayer to obey with these guidelines from professionals and parents.

LET HIM DEFY—TO AN EXTENT

Expect your toddler to be contrary whenever you ask him to do something. Then you'll be pleasantly surprised should he comply at once. When he doesn't—well, then, you figured he wouldn't so you'll be less annoyed.

Whenever possible, make your requests in advance so that he has a chance to defy you. For instance, five minutes before you two must run errands, drop the bombshell casually. "Ian, time to put your coat on. We're going to the store soon." Don't get angry if he shouts "No!" or stomps away. The reason for the advance warning is to *let* him defy you. A few minutes later, repeat your statement. If he balks again, you might reflect his feelings: "I know you're angry. You don't want to leave your crayons. But we have to go shopping. It's time to get dressed for outside." These brief statements convey your compassion and support, which might soften his resentment at having to do your bidding. At the same time, you help him learn that feelings can be expressed in words rather than acted out.

NOTE: These reflections can help soothe things when you don't have time for an advanced warning, too.

If your child still refuses to cooperate after you've given warnings and reflected his feelings, now's the time to act. Pick him up firmly, but coolly, and make him put on the coat. You might repeat that you understand he's angry or disappointed. Try not to argue, though.

Heated words probably won't make him any more compliant—in fact, they might have the opposite effect.

At times, action alone works even better than words. Instead of asking your toddler to do something—like come up and take a bath—communicate your request with gestures and action. Walk over to him, give a friendly smile, pick him up in a loving way, and carry him off. Or go over and hold out your finger. It's surprising how often a toddler will simply grasp an outstretched hand or finger and go along, no questions asked.

Remember . . . As we said in "More on Discipline" in the last chapter (page 262), spanking or otherwise punishing your toddler for this defiance will do little to discourage it in the future—but it will make both of you feel bad. You're much better off separating from one another until you both cool down.

MAKE COOPERATION FUN

You can also try to gain cooperation by turning obedience into a game. For example, instead of asking him to put his blocks away, try "Let's see who can pick up the most blocks and put them into the box. I have one!" A friendly "I'll race you to the stairs!" might entice him into going up for a bath. If you get him as far as the tub before he balks, try putting in a new water toy for added inducement. Does he now act contrary by refusing to get out of the tub? Do some magic with a towel. Make it into a turban for your head, a fuzzy overcoat for a fanciful animal (your hand, peeking out of the folds), a bedroll for a water doll. Then invite him back on dry land so he can wear a turban, too, or wrap up just like dolly.

Sometimes you can chant him out of a *no* mood. You say, "Let's put on your shoe." He says "No!" You chant, "No, no, no, no, no, yes, yes, yes . . ." Or make it silly. You say, "Let's put on your shoe." He says "No!" You say, "OK, let's put on your fire truck!" "No!" "Let's put on your teddy bear!" "No?" "Let's put on dolly's shoe!" "Yes!" "Oops—doesn't fit. Let's see if *your* shoe fits."

NOURISH AUTONOMY

You can often avoid battles *and* nourish your toddler's drive to make his own decisions by giving him a simple choice. Let him choose between the red shirt and the blue-striped one, and he might forget about refusing to put on his shirt at all. Avoid the confrontation about a prelunch washup by letting him decide whether he wants to wash hands in the kitchen *or* the bathroom. At clean-up time, the choice of picking up his blocks *or* his cars may get him working willingly—while you pick up whatever he didn't choose. Keep it simple. Asking "Which shirt would you like to wear today?" will probably confuse him and prompt a "No!" Instead, offer only two choices, making sure that *you* find both acceptable so you'll go along with his decision.

One of the best ways to encourage cooperation is to let your toddler do things himself. He's already taking over a lot of his own feeding. Let him wash himself as much as he's able and try helping you with dressing. We'll have more to say about these self-help skills in upcoming chapters.

Beginning Toilet Learning

Toilet learning—or, as many people call it, toilet training—is a step toward personal independence. Many parents dread this period as one of tears, fights, frustration, and guilt. It's true that these used to be standard—mostly because parents tried to teach toileting at too young an age, and because they expected success too early. As we suggested in a previous chapter, eighteen months is probably the earliest age to begin teaching toileting. The key word here is begin. Toilet learning is far more complicated than you may have thought, and control over bladder and bowel movements requires a maturity that the typical eighteen-month-old does not have. Few toddlers are able to master it until after two years of age.

One significant reason is that the younger toddler generally lacks the necessary physical skills. Eliminating in the toilet rather than diapers involves a complicated series of physically related steps. Consider urination. First step: Your toddler has to sense that his bladder is full. (A child has no control over this developmental step; it's a function of his maturing autonomic nervous system.) Next step: After he realizes his bladder is full and feels the need to urinate, he must consciously hold back for a brief period (by using one of the large voluntary muscle groups). Babies cannot do this; they automatically urinate whenever the bladder is filled. Toddlers are physically able to after some point; however, they have to learn to hold back. Next step: While holding back, he must get to the nearest bathroom, remove his clothing, and sit on the potty or toilet. Then, after struggling to hold in the urine, he must let it flow out. This involves contracting the diaphragm and some other abdominal muscles while simultaneously relaxing. And you thought it was easy! It is to adults, because we have all the necessary physical skills and because we go through these steps almost automatically. It's much tougher for a toddler.

Physical maturation aside, few young toddlers are motivated to master toileting. There is little inherent reward for eliminating in the toilet. In fact, there is plenty of reason not to bother. After all, it's a lot easier to pause, go in your diapers, and then continue with what you were doing than it is to hold it in, tell Mom or Dad you need to use the toilet, go to a special room, and fumble with buttons or snaps or elastic waists. Luckily, there *are* some incentives. One is to please parents. If your toddler is going through a contrary period, as many eighteen-month-olds are, this is not a strong motivation right now. Another is the desire to be "grown-up." This is usually more important to a toddler as he approaches his second birthday. A third is the desire to be dry and clean for his own comfort—not just to please you. This, too, generally comes at a later age.

One more thing: Starting toilet learning early certainly doesn't guarantee ending early. Dr. T. Berry Brazelton conducted a ten-year research project in which he studied the toilet learning of 1,170 children. Whatever the age parents started teaching toileting, Dr. Brazelton found that:

- 90 percent of all the children achieved initial daytime success between twenty-four and thirty months of age; the average age was 27.7 months;
- Reliable day training was demonstrated at the average age of 28.5 months;
- 80 percent of these children achieved nighttime success between thirty and forty-two months, with the average age 33.3 months;
- Surprisingly, 50 percent of the children who started toilet learning at eighteen months or before still had not achieved reliable day- and nighttime control by thirty-six months.

Other studies generally agree with these findings. All this is to say that we think eighteen months is a good time to start taking preliminary steps, but *not* to teach toileting in earnest.

GETTING READY

Probably the first and most important thing is to help your toddler understand what toileting is about. He has worn diapers all his life, and has eliminated in them whenever he wanted. Now he needs to understand what urine and feces are, where they come from, and where you want them to go—eventually.

A young toddler urinates or moves his bowels automatically. He doesn't realize when he is going to or even that he has done so. Between fifteen and eighteen or so months, he starts connecting the feeling of needing to eliminate with the product of these actions. For instance, he might clutch himself before he urinates, or, if naked, look at the puddle he produced. Help him understand the connection and learn the appropriate words. You can usually tell, for example, when your toddler is having a bowel movement in his diaper: He stops all activity and gets a very concentrated look on his face. Use such opportunities to label matter-of-factly what he's doing: "BM? Billy making a BM?" This helps make him aware of the feeling of defecation and the word that goes with it. When you change his diaper as usual, you might show him the bowel movement and name it again before flushing it away.

NOTE: Some toddlers get upset at seeing their bowel movements disappear down the toilet. If yours does, flush the toilet after he leaves the bathroom.

Another preparatory step is to help your toddler understand how people use the toilet. He probably joins you in the bathroom occasionally; many toddlers go through a phase when they get so upset at losing sight of Mom that bathroom togetherness is the rule. Chances are he sometimes trails Dad into the bathroom, too. Use these occasions to tell him what you're doing, and why. Second and third children usually learn toileting earlier than first-borns (in Brazelton's study, about one to two months earlier), and part of the reason is that they observe big brothers or sisters using the bathroom and want to imitate them. If you feel uncomfortable with bathroom togetherness, you might arrange things so your toddler occasionally sees older playmates using the toilet.

We suggest you keep toilet talks casual and positive. As you chat about what you do in the bathroom and what he's doing in his diapers, avoid acting as if his body products were dirty or "yucky." If you do, he might become ashamed of urinating and defecating, and start hiding from you when he soils his diapers. Later, when you *want* him to tell you before he needs to toilet—so you can help him—he may be afraid to let you know.

THE POTTY CHAIR

The final preliminary step is introducing your toddler to the potty chair or toilet seat he'll use later. The point now is to get him accustomed to it, not to force it on him. Talk about how he'll be using this seat when he's older, "So you can go to the bathroom like grown-ups do." Let him sit on it fully dressed if he wishes. He might perch his doll or teddy on it, or use the pot as a hat for a month or so. That's fine, too.

There are two main types of chairs now on the market: one sits independently on the floor; the other affixes over the regular toilet seat. We recommend the floor model for beginners. On his own potty chair, your toddler has his feet planted firmly on the ground, which can make him feel far more secure. Also, he doesn't need your help to mount or dismount, or need to climb up steps to the larger toilet seat just when he's struggling to keep urine or feces inside.

NEXT STEPS

The next step? Be patient. Your toddler will let you know when he's ready to start using the potty chair. He'll display physical readiness by staying dry for longer and longer periods of time; maybe through his nap. He'll show intellectual readiness by beginning to use the words you've taught for urination and bowel movements, and by actually telling you he's urinating and defecating as he does so. These usually come a few months from now—so we'll pick up the subject again in a later chapter.

Growing through Play

[This section was prepared with the help of Donna Brink Fox, PhD, professor at the Eastman School of Music, University of Rochester.]

YOUR TODDLER AND MUSIC

During the early years, music is both a means and an end, a fun way to help learn things and a purely expressive behavior important for its own sake. Here are some ways you can help nurture and enhance this almost surely innate affinity.

SETTING THE MUSICAL STAGE

Musically speaking, toddlerhood is a time for experimenting, for exploring, for sampling all the wonders that music can add to life. It's assuredly *not* the time to begin formal education, even if you would like ultimately to steer your child toward a musical career. Rather, the best way to encourage a "serious" love of music in your toddler is to be interested in it yourself.

Researchers Jeanette Jenkins, William Kirkpatrick, and others have found a consistent relationship between musical development and the home environment. Put simply, a child whose parents value music, who listen to music frequently and play musical parent-child games, generally has an increased enjoyment in and aptitude for music. Parents are role models. When you spend time involved in music, and particularly when you share music with your child, you tell him that such activities are valued.

LISTENING TO MUSIC

Because today's parents have access to so many kinds and sources of music, there's no limit to what we can bring to a young child's listening experiences. Try all kinds of records, Broadway to Beethoven, calypso to classical, and jazz and blues and religious chants, too. Be sure your toddler has opportunities to listen to and watch people playing instruments like the piano and guitar. This helps him see that music doesn't only come from inside a machine. That's also a reason why you should sing to your child. Some hints:

· Make a few songs part of the bedtime routine.
· When he's getting fidgety in his car seat, launch into some favorite familiar tune, especially one that has lots of repetition ("Old MacDonald," "Yankee Doodle," "She'll Be Comin' Round the Mountain When She Comes"). If you encourage him, he might join in and croon, babble, or sing a few words, depending on his skill level.

Teachers often bring chants and invented songs into many other activities. For example, they chant "This is the way we wash our hands" to the tune of "Here We Go 'Round the Mulberry Bush" when cleaning toddlers' hands after arts play. Or they sing stories, or parts of stories, instead of speaking them. These can be very simple words and tunes—or even familiar tunes with new words inserted. Teachers find that singing helps hold a child's attention and enhances his developing vocabulary. Simple tunes can make it easier to learn and remember words. It's no secret that adults, too, often recall advertising lyrics more easily and powerfully than merely spoken statements. Also, how many of us still relate the letters of the alphabet to the tune of "Twinkle, Twinkle, Little Star"?

MOVEMENT AND INSTRUMENTS

If listening is one of the major building block skills of a musician, movement is frequently the way children indicate they're listening. Movement is a visualized response to sound.

Turn on the stereo and dance with your child. Sweep him into your arms and dance in front of the mirror. Hold his hands and pretend to be Fred Astaire and Ginger Rogers, or the Tango Twins. Or dance separately. Try a happy dance. A mad dance. When you're too busy to join in, your toddler will also like dancing by himself, devising his individual choreography.

Toddlers are also ready for simple rhythm band instruments: maracas, cymbals, rhythm sticks, a xylophone, and the like. Here are some you can make.

Clappers: Screw D-shaped cabinet handles onto two blocks of wood, each about six inches long, three inches wide, and one inch thick.

Shakers: Fill a metal screw-top spice shaker with some jar lids too large for your toddler to put into his mouth (in case he should open the shaker). Another favorite: *loud* baby rattle.

Clappers

Shakers

Cymbals: Two cooking pot lids that don't have rims on the underside.

Drums: Give your toddler a small cooking pot and a wooden spoon.

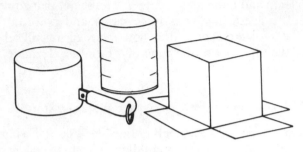

Drums

HINT: Cooking pots and lids and baking pans are wonderful instruments, but constant music play will dent and batter them. It makes sense to buy your toddler his own set at the thrift shop or flea market. If you like, store these and other instruments in a large cardboard box with appropriate decorations—musical notes, a drum—on the outside. Draw them with markers, or cut pictures from magazines and glue on.

Have a parade! You, your toddler, and any other children and adults available can march around clanging and shaking and tooting and ringing. . . . It may not sound like a symphony to you, but this cacophony is nourishing an early love of music.

STARTING TO SING!

Toddlers explore the possibilities of vocal production. Often they experiment with long-short, high-low, and fast-slow combinations of sounds. Or they sing as they play, making up strings of syllables. Sometimes they add real words to these strings. Later they include fragments of songs they've heard before. Sometimes children borrow the rhythm, sometimes the words, less often the melody. As they approach preschoolage, children draw their own song-making closer and closer to singing structured songs. The more you sing and play records, the more songs your child has a chance to learn. Songs with lots of repetition tend to be favorites.

CHILDREN'S RECORDS

Besides all the recorded music *you* like, your toddler enjoys some special children's records with simple songs and musical activities geared for his age group. These are also fun for you and he to listen to together, and they'll give you ideas of other musical games appropriate for toddlers. The Wee Sing series is excellent. Each record or cassette is accompanied by a song book so you can easily learn the lyrics. Members of our Advisory Board also recommend the records of children's songs made by Woody Guthrie for their fine examples of words and tunes. Another favorite: *Wake Up and Sing: Folk Songs from America's Grassroots*, selected and adapted by Beatrice Landeck and Elizabeth Crook. Other favorite performers for this age group include Bob McGrath, Tom Glazer, Ella Jenkins, Kevin Roth, and Raffi.

IN SUMMARY

Music has charms that soothe the savage breast or infectiousness that inspires inventive movement. It's personal and it's social, a part of each culture's heritage. And through such early music play as described here, you're helping pass it along.

Research Update:
More on Separation Protests

Several studies have found that separation protests generally begin to decline at about eighteen months. At this age, the child has the understanding that the absent parent really will return, and has developed routines that help him cope better with the separation. But keep in mind that this intellectual progress is just one factor that governs separation anxiety.

In studying ninety-three children aged sixteen to twenty months, Joseph Jacobson (Wayne State University) and Diane Wille (Indiana University) found that familiarity with the routine of separation and eventual reunion doesn't necessarily make separations easier. The toddlers who had a moderate amount of child care outside the family (four to nineteen hours a week) seemed to protest separations the least. Those who had little extrafamilial care (under four hours a week) protested more, and those who had a lot (twenty to fifty-four hours a week) seemed the most anxious. It seems that understanding object permanence—that parents who leave can be counted on to return—does not *in itself* make separations easier.

As you might imagine, there are plenty of emotional issues involved in separation and reunion, and these can be hard to isolate for examination. For example, not every study finds this "security" difference among children who spend little, moderate, or lots of time away from their parents. Jacobson and Wille themselves point this out. Each study deals with a different group of subjects, and each group (indeed, each individual toddler) has varied quality of care both inside and outside the home. Many experts, including members of our Advisory Board, maintain that the quality of alternative care certainly affects how easily a toddler separates from his parents. Then again, as always, individual differences come into play. So don't be surprised if your eighteen-month-old still needs lots of reassurance when you must leave him, even though he does understand, at least intellectually, that you'll be coming back. Many factors affect how he feels about your leave-taking. This may be an issue for some time to come.

YOUR NINETEEN-
MONTH-OLD

Overview

As your toddler plunges headlong in her desire to grow up, she'll undoubtedly meet many frustrations that temporarily overwhelm her. When her defenses are at their weakest, she'll likely dissolve in that dreaded aspect of toddlerhood: temper tantrums. Nearly all children have them, despite parents' best efforts to keep things on an even keel. Still, there are ways you can

reduce the frustrations that might lead to a tantrum, and handle the outbursts that do occur, as we discuss here.

On a happier note, this is the age when you might see a huge surge in your child's language development. Her vocabulary increases dramatically, and soon she starts putting those single words into simple sentences. Now she's far easier to understand than before—and you'll feel even more like she has joined the talking majority. She shows other intellectual advance by becoming interested in shape sorters and puzzles. Her greater dexterity also enables her to remove some items of clothing, particularly shoes and socks and elastic-waist pants. She might also pull off a tape-held disposable diaper. Later she'll unbutton shirts and sweaters well before she can button them herself. If you want to guard against her undressing in public, make sure she wears hard-to-remove clothing like overalls instead of stretch-waist pants, crew-neck sweaters instead of v-neck, laced shoes tied with double knots and the like.

Sometime during this part of the second year, many toddlers become a bit possessive—even overpossessive. Ironically, this is an advancement in learning, not a sign of burgeoning selfishness. So much going on!

Surviving Temper Tantrums

I am a parcel of vain strivings tied
By a chance bond together
—Henry David Thoreau

It's doubtful that Thoreau was thinking about toddlers, but his eloquent words capture the essence of many nineteen-month-olds. The struggle to grow up *will* be terribly frustrating at times. Your toddler drives herself to try things beyond her abilities—turn a doorknob, ride a big kid's bike—so she fails a great deal. She wants to make her own decisions, so your sensible regulations and limits antagonize her. You're not going to let her remove her shoes in a park where there's broken glass; but sure enough, she'll want to, and she'll feel unfairly hindered when you interfere. Frustration is a fact of life, and toddlers have not developed the coping strategies to handle it. That's why temper tantrums can be so common.

A temper tantrum is like a blown fuse. It's both a sign that the frustration load has become too much for your toddler to bear, and a means—albeit an explosive one—through which she blows off steam. For many toddlers, the tolerance for frustration is periodically so low that almost any issue sets them off. The cracker you give her snaps in two. She stares in horror for a few seconds, then flings the pieces across the room and throws herself on the floor, screaming so loudly you're sure she'll set off the smoke alarm.

Some toddlers are definitely more tantrum-prone than others, but even the happiest, most easygoing children have occasional storms. Likewise, some children have relatively mild tantrums, others rattle windows and send cats scurrying. Tantrums often start midway through this second year, then ordinarily subside and swell in periodic patterns throughout early childhood. They rarely disappear completely. Adults have them occasionally; we feel like having them more often than we give in to the impulse. We have other ways to express our anger and frustration: slamming doors, swearing, yelling, or. . . . We also have better checks on our emotions and several ways to control our feelings or calm ourselves before we reach the exploding point. But a toddler doesn't have these or alternative methods of coping with frustration. When her feelings get out of control, a tantrum might be the only release.

A POUND OF PREVENTION

You can't always prevent tantrums, no matter how diligent and caring you may be. Nonetheless, you can likely reduce their frequency. The key is helping your toddler control her frustration.

· Try to keep her out of situations where she's likely to feel overwhelmed. You know that she's going to try grabbing candy bars at the supermarket checkout. So try giving her something healthful to snack on as you approach the cash register. And try to avoid taking her shopping if it coincides with her mealtime or naptime—times when she's at her most vulnerable. You know that certain toys are frustrating her at the moment: The "dressing skills" doll she was content to hug last month now begs her to try buttoning and zippering, but she can't! Put them away temporarily. Maybe bring out some tried and true favorites to see whether she finds new play value in them. Toys that are too complex for her current skills will probably frustrate her. So will toys that she can't use without your help, like a rocking horse she is unable to mount and dismount all by herself. These are better hidden away for a while, too, if your toddler doesn't raise too big a ruckus at their sudden disappearance. Her older brother's toys and other possessions that are inappropriate for the toddler should now be kept in his room, not the mutual playroom, if at all possible.

· Offer support and assistance—without interfering—when your toddler seems really to need it. This can be a fine line. Jumping in at every tiny sign of a setback *creates* frustration for the I-want-to-be-independent toddler. At the same time, don't assume that she really does want to do *everything* herself. When you see or hear your toddler becoming frustrated with something she's trying to do, try to determine what it is that's disturbing her. Then help in a way that lets her feel successful about the task. This will take some trial and error. Be aware that sometimes when you offer aid, she may give up trying and insist *you* do it. Careful! If you take over totally and don't do the job to her exacting standards, she'll go over the top again. Gently encourage her to work *with* you to finish whatever caused so much frustration, maybe mentioning that it *is* hard to do. Or offer alternative activities that are equally pleasing.

· Pay attention to the signals that tell you she's exhausted, hungry, overstimulated, or otherwise reaching her limit. See that she has a nap, or at least a quiet time, when she's becoming too tired. A snack (healthful, please!) can appease a tantrum-provoking appetite between regular meals. Guide her to a quieter activity when she's becoming too wound up. You might read to her as you snuggle together on the sofa, or give her a refreshing bath. As teachers and other experts have told us repeatedly, water play can have a very calming effect on toddlers. Be sure you *always* supervise!

· Take care not to thwart her unnecessarily yourself. It's amazing how often parents say "No!" without really thinking, or forbid something—like letting a toddler eat vegetable soup with her fingers—without any really powerful reason. (In fact, a mother we know told us that her husband secretly recorded her on a portable videotape camera for a few days, then played it for her to see. She was appalled by how often she gave negative responses—quite innocently—even when they weren't called for.)

ONCE A TANTRUM IS UNDERWAY

There are two basic approaches to controlling a tantrum that's underway. You can ignore it. Or you can try to hold and comfort your child during the tantrum. This second approach may work on very mild tantrums, but it's impossible—and inadvisable—for major ones. After all, the out-of-control toddler can hit and kick pretty hard. Then again, at the height of a storm, she may refuse any kind of comfort at all. Probably the best method for a forceful tantrum is to ignore it until it begins to subside, then to comfort your toddler.

There are a few ways to ignore the tantrum. Stand silently by, watching with interest as you might a television program. Or go about your business quietly, as if there weren't a banshee wailing on the floor. Sometimes your toddler—as out of control as she seems to be—draws comfort from your presence. If things get too bad and you feel your own anger rising, leave the room. You might calmly announce your departure with something like "I understand how angry you are. I'm going to leave you until you cool off. Let me know when you're ready." Simple, *short*, soothing statements of this type tell your toddler that you aren't angry, that you're still in control, that you understand how upset she is, and that once she calms down (which you are telling her she has the ultimate power to do), you'll be ready to pick up where you left off. She'll probably absorb your feeling despite her rage, and that may help her calm down. Don't overdo your explanations, and don't try to argue her out of a tantrum. That won't work.

Leaving the room has other purposes. You'll probably feel better not watching this heart-wrenching display. Your absence might calm your toddler, especially if the tantrum is partly a play for sympathy—as tantrums can be. Walking away also prevents you from throwing a tantrum of your own. Your toddler's screaming and screeching will undoubtedly make you pretty angry at times. If you lose your temper, though, suddenly both of you will be out of control. She'll learn that she can't count on you when the going gets rough, and you'll develop some pretty bad feelings about yourself, especially if you end up shaking her or yelling at her, or even spanking her.

Probably the most common reason your toddler throws a tantrum is because you refuse to let her have something or do something she wants. Leaving the room means that you won't succumb to her demands. Giving in can be a big mistake. Suppose you've said "No" to another cookie, and she has a fit. When you try to quiet her with "OK, OK, here's a cookie," she'll soon figure out that tantrums are effective for getting what she wants. Now, trying to control you is *not* the only reason a toddler throws tantrums; frustration is the major culprit, as we said. But the two are interrelated, and sometimes tantrums are partly an attempt to control you. Stand by your original decision as often as possible.

That's the ideal, but realistically, every parent gives in on occasion, especially with public tantrums. (More about this in the next section.) Don't feel unduly guilty. But if this happens too frequently, you'll be giving your toddler a confusing message. Make sure giving in is the rare exception.

COMFORT TIME

Sooner or later it's comfort time. Tantrums can be frightening; after all, it's pretty scary to lose control. Your toddler will appreciate help in returning to normal. Depending on her individual temperament, she might want to be held, talked to soothingly, or simply left alone until she's ready to make the overture. Each child has her own way of reestablishing contact. If you've remained calm, the storm clouds will usually disperse as quickly as they gathered.

Tantrums and Special Situations

Even parents who easily handle the day-to-day home tantrums have a tough time with the following situations.

PUBLIC TANTRUMS

Parents tell us that, by far, public tantrums are the worst, and the supermarket is usually the most common place for them to occur. These are the situations when parents are most tempted to give in to whatever the toddler demands, or to bribe her into being quiet: "Here, Jenny, a nice yummy chocolate bar!" You'll consider anything to regain peace, especially since you feel other people are judging your parenting ability. You're sure each is thinking: *Can't they even control their own child?* It's hard to ignore your toddler as you might at home, both because she's such a public display and because you fear that other adults will brand you as uncaring, unfeeling, unfit. A dilemma, indeed. Will giving in teach her that tantrums are effective? Most likely, if you do it often enough. How often is that? No one knows. Ideally, you should do everything to avoid resorting to bribes and concessions. Try to stay as cool and calm as you endeavor to do in private. Talk to her quietly. Focus on her behavior, not on your own feelings. If she's really in a state, it's best to scoop her up—if you can without harm to yourself—and take her to a quieter place. Maybe go to your car if it's nearby; or to a corner of the store, so at least you're not the center of attention. Keep telling yourself *not* to get angry, *not* to be embarrassed. It might help. But if you should give in on occasion—well, that's just the way life goes. Don't agonize over it later. Parents aren't perfect. Remember, too, that if you *do* lose your temper, things will get a lot worse and you'll really draw looks—and comments. Do your best to remain in control.

TANTRUMS AND EMPLOYED MOTHERS

"Why me?" moaned one mother. "Why is my toddler fine all day with the sitter, but at home she throws a few tantrums every evening? Does she store them up?"

Sort of. Tantrums are funny things because, in a way, they reveal how close your toddler is to you. That is, your toddler feels safe throwing a tantrum in your presence because she trusts that you will remain in control while she's out of it, and that you still love her. She may not be so trusting of the sitter. She does everything in her power all day long to avoid losing control, since a sitter can't care for her the way a beloved parent does. When night comes and she's back in your safe company, everything boils over. Actually, this isn't very different from adult behavior. You're probably a lot freer to make mistakes in front of and share your failures with your spouse than with an employer or casual friend.

Of course, there might be another reason. Your toddler may realize that you're a pushover, and that tantrums get her what she wants. Are you?

End-of-day tantrums can be especially trying. You're tired, and you're looking forward to some pleasant family togetherness time. They are bound to make you feel extra guilty. It's easy to feel that tantrums are a condemnation of both parents' working outside the home. Try to keep these situations in perspective and handle these tantrums with the same approach as you do at other times. Also try to enjoy a quiet, stress-free time when you and your toddler reunite at day's end by establishing a shared activity, like looking at books together. Put off dinner a little longer. Have a snack if you're both too hungry to wait. Certainly, emotional sustenance is as important as physical.

Tantrums are among the hardest problems of toddlerhood. Almost no parent ever feels that he or she constantly meets these challenges well. Yet, most do. When you make an effort to recognize your toddler's needs, to respect her complicated feelings, and to provide a calm, loving framework within which she can express her volatile emotions, you go far to help her weather these stormy stages.

Putting Words Together

As we've said before, the following ages are based on the hypothetical "average" toddler, and *no* toddler is average. Some nineteen-month-olds are already using short sentences, others haven't said first words yet. This broad variation in skills is well within the range of normal behavior.

Your child's first real words were a cause for celebration, undeniable proof that she was on her way to joining the speaking society. Her vocabulary most likely grew slowly for the next few months. She struggled to master one word at a time. These early words almost always referred to specific, immediate objects and actions. Now a change is in the offing. At some time soon, you'll notice some exciting language developments.

First will be a dramatic growth in vocabulary. During the second half of this second year, your toddler's understanding broadens. She gradually appreciates that words are symbolic representations of objects, actions, and thoughts; she uses words to refer to things that *aren't* immediately present. She grasps more clearly the social and communicative value of words. She's beginning to crack the code of what language is and can do. After this happens, and the age varies from child to child, her vocabulary grows by leaps and bounds.

Then a month or two later comes another advance: She starts putting two words together to form a simple sentence. This is an impressive milestone, indeed! For one thing, it reflects your toddler's growing awareness of relationships between separate objects or events, which gives you some insight into her intellectual development. Even more importantly, she can *express* these relationships. Now she's much easier to understand. For instance, when she was only speaking in single words, she might say "car." You had to decipher: She wants me to look at the car? She wants to go in the car? She doesn't like the car? Now that she can talk about the relationship between two concepts, she's much clearer. When she says "Daddy car," you can narrow the list of possibilities. She's probably referring to her father's car, or is noting that her father is in the car. "Big car" and "Car go" and "Me car" tell you many more things than the single utterance "car."

BEGINNING SYNTAX

The way your toddler orders these words shows that she has some grasp of *syntax*, the rules by which words are put together to express meaning. Studies by Susan Starr (Yale University), Martin Braine (New York University), and several other linguists show that toddlers almost always order their words as adults do. For example, consider the standard subject-verb-object form of simple English sentences. It tells us who (the subject) is doing what (the verb) to whom or what (the object). Your toddler largely follows this rule. When she wants you to look at a flower, she's far more likely to say "Look flower" than "Flower look." You can usually rely on her chosen word order to give you clues to her intended meaning. "Daddy car" gives you one type of message. Daddy is the subject, car is the object, and the verb is implied. You can mentally fill in the missing words and assume she means something like "Daddy is in the car" or "Daddy owns the car." When she strays from this format and says "Car daddy," this doesn't make sense if you take car as the subject and daddy as the object. More likely she's expressing something else, such as "Look at the car, Daddy."

WHY SO SHORT?

Almost all first sentences contain only two words. Even though a child can typically produce subject-verb, verb-object, and subject-object sentences, she rarely utters subject-verb-object all in one sentence. She obviously understands how to order these three forms correctly; why does she stop at two words? Language specialist Moshe Anisfeld of Yeshiva University believes that three different words is just too difficult at this stage. After all, a sentence is the product of coordination and planning. The words have to be chosen mentally, organized, given the desired intonation, and then produced. As Anisfeld says, "Naturally, the larger the number of components, the more difficult the internal processing. There is thus a cognitive constraint on length."

AMAZING EXPRESSIVENESS

Obviously your toddler doesn't stick only to simple subject-verb or verb-object utterances. As researchers have found, children express many different categories of thoughts with two-word sentences. Many expressions are *demonstrative;* that is, they're intended to draw attention to objects. Examples include "See juice." "Here flower." "That dog." In Susan Starr's study of twelve toddlers, almost 40 percent of their utterances fell into this category. Demonstrative sentences reflect a child's interest in classifying and naming objects, an interest that is actively encouraged by parents. Toddlers also talk about the quality of an object: the *red car, big bottle, wet dog, broken toy.* They dwell on people's possessions: *Gramma scarf, my ball, Mommy sock.* They love talking about action: *throw ball, Billy hit, me jump.* They make requests, or comment on the recurrence of a particular object or event: *more cookie, more clown, do again, another one.* And, yes, they make value judgments and express feelings: *Bad boy, no bed, me good.*

REALISTIC LIMITS

These language gains *are* dramatic. Remember, though, that your toddler is just beginning to express herself more clearly. You'll still need to pay attention to her gestures and voice tones to decipher her meaning. You also can't be sure that you and she are always on the same wavelength. As linguist Christine Howe (University of Strathclyde, Great Britain) points out, adults shouldn't always assume that children are expressing meanings that an adult expresses or are necessarily using language as an adult would. Children's thought is organized in a fashion unlike adults'. We don't *really* know what meanings a child is capable of conceptualizing, or for what purposes a child may use language. This can make our job of interpreting a bit harder, since we need to rely on all the available clues. But it also makes a child's language so delightful. She'll put together words that sound wonderful, and even if we can't comprehend their meaning, she undoubtedly can. Exactly what *does* she mean by "juice nose"???

Me! Mine!

"Me!" and "Mine!" will likely become your toddler's motto at some point, as she loudly proclaims ownership of her possessions — and very often of those belonging to other people in her immediate domain. Although it looks to all the world (especially to in-laws!) like she's becoming selfish and spoiled, most probably she's not. Temporary overpossessiveness is one way that your toddler reveals her developing sense of self.

During her second year, your child starts recognizing that certain objects belong to her, others to Daddy or Mommy or Brother. She talks about her possessions as "Mine!" and emphatically distinguishes between "mine!" and "yours." Sometimes this sense of possession prompts shouts of "Mine!" or "No!" when someone else, especially a sibling or another toddler, tries to play with her toys. Rather than piggishness, such outbursts reflect her immature sense of personal identity. Since one way she defines herself is through possessions—*my* shoes, *my* coat, *my* cookie, *my* toys—she naturally feels a bit threatened when a part of herself is snatched away. Over time, though, she'll become more secure in her self-identity as she develops a fuller, more mature understanding of herself. Then she'll be more relaxed about sharing her worldly goods.

Because this possession need can be so powerful, you shouldn't force her to share toys at this age if she would rather not. Sharing will come in time. You might, though, gently encourage her to give another child a chance with the truck or the doll she's hoarding when she's finished playing with it. This helps sow the seeds of sharing, especially when you point out how pleased the other child is to receive this temporary present. It also gives the other toddler a chance to play with something that she, too, wants.

Another thing: *You* needn't surrender objects—like that cookie you're nibbling—just because your toddler commands that it's "Mine!" After all, things don't become her possessions just because she demands them. She needs to learn what is *not* hers as well as what *is* hers. A gentle "No, this is my cookie; you have your own cracker" helps get this message across.

But why is she so overpoweringly possessive at first? you might well ask. Well, think about the other skills she's been developing—skills like walking or saying the first word. At every new milestone, she tended to overdo it a bit. The same is true about the steps in discovering who she is.

Growing through Play

EARLY PUZZLES

Teachers we've interviewed swear by puzzles because, as these professionals point out, puzzle play has so many benefits, like building eye-hand coordination and helping a child develop important concepts like size differences; shapes; spatial orientation (which side is up?); positional relationships between separate parts of an object or entire objects in a scene; and matching (the solid shape to its hole). The forced correctness of a puzzle offers nice contrast to the free-range toys, like blocks and cars and dozens of others, that have no single "correct" way to play with them.

Toddler puzzles should have trays into which the pieces fit. They come in two main types.

Island puzzles: Each removable piece is a complete object (an animal, a vehicle, etc.) that fits into its own well (or hole) in the tray. A nineteen-month-old may be ready for three- to five-piece island puzzles. She might need a little help completing each one the first few times. And if she's really proficient at solving island puzzles, she'll probably enjoy those that have more pieces.

Jigsaw puzzles: Each piece is a component of a whole, and all the pieces fit into the same large, shallow well in the tray. Simple jigsaw puzzles are usually introduced between about twenty-four and thirty-six months. It's best to hold off until your toddler is old enough to try one without frustration. Remember, she's not "behind" if she's on the late side.

Teachers suggest you keep the following in mind when you shop for puzzles.

1. The pieces should be easy to remove. Knobs and handles help. (EDITOR'S NOTE: Make sure these handles on first puzzles are sturdily attached. Some puzzles have been criticized by the Consumer Products Safety Commission because the handles fell off too easily, and were swallowed by some toddlers.)
2. Colors should be bright and clear.
3. Pieces should fit into the wells easily.

You might also keep in mind the following:

· We've found that some toddlers are real "puzzle-people," others have little or no interest. That's natural. The nonpuzzlers acquire the puzzle-play benefits through other kinds of fitting/matching/sorting toys.

· Puzzles that display familiar scenes, objects, people, and the like have extra usefulness because they give you opportunities for naming games and simple story-telling.

· If your toddler is having a hard time with a puzzle, resist the temptation to complete it for her while she watches. If you step in so quickly and completely, the play value will be lost; she also might come to depend too heavily on your helpful intervention whenever she faces a minor difficulty. Instead, give some hints and words of encouragement: "How about if you try the boat over here. Let me turn the tray. You almost have it. There! It fits! You did it!"

SHAPE SORTERS

Shape sorters are a very popular form of early puzzle. Instead of flat pieces, they have three-dimensional shapes that are fitted onto some kind of base or inserted through holes. Like some puzzles, simple shape sorters can be quickly mastered and forgotten. It's better if the shape sorting feature is incorporated into a toy that has other built-in activities, such as a bucket for fill-and-dump, a water or sand toy, an activity truck, or the like.

Some shape sorters add complexity by offering many more than the basic circle, square, and triangle shapes. This may look like a good idea, but such shape sorters are almost always too advanced for the nineteen-month-old. It's better to find a shape sorter that offers other types of play as well.

Shape Mastery. At what age can you expect your child to insert shapes correctly? That largely depends on her individual rate of development, how much practice she has, and the particular shape sorting toy she uses. We do have some insights, though. Researchers have studied shape mastery using a *form board,* a simple island puzzle with three pieces: circle, square, and triangle. The circle is the easiest shape for a toddler to fit because it presents no orientation problems. By contrast, a square or triangle has to be turned a certain way to fit into its well. According to form board studies reported by the pioneering developmental specialist Arnold Gesell:

- At eighteen months, 75 percent of the toddlers tested correctly inserted the circle; 45 percent inserted the square; and 48 percent the triangle.
- At twenty-four months, 100 percent of the toddlers inserted the circle; 90 percent inserted the square; 97 percent inserted the triangle.

Research Update:
Coordinating Skills

Your nineteen-month-old might be on the verge of a learning breakthrough, according to a study by Eugene Goldfield from Connecticut College. He tested eleven toddlers at sixteen, eighteen, and twenty months of age to see whether each could retrieve a cookie from a transparent cylinder by using a hand-held rakelike tool. None of the children could do this at sixteen months; less than 20 percent could at eighteen months. But more than 60 percent of the twenty-month-olds fished out the cookie. It seems that twenty-month-olds could control two independent activities simultaneously—maneuver the cylinder and the rake in separate hands; and could coordinate the two systems—orient the rake correctly to retrieve the cookie. Goldfield had similar findings with a related test. This newfound ability to fuse two systems into a single skill is, as he puts it, "A considerable advance over earlier trial-and-error groping and sets the stage for more efficient learning."

YOUR TWENTY-
MONTH-OLD

Overview

As toddlers learn more about their world, they also come to
realize that it can be threatening as well as supportive.
Many develop fears ranging from dogs to doctors, loud
noises, baths, dark passages, heights, and strangers. Parents may
be inclined to dismiss certain fears as silly or babyish, or see them
as a sign of overall timidness or sissiness (especially in a boy). Yet

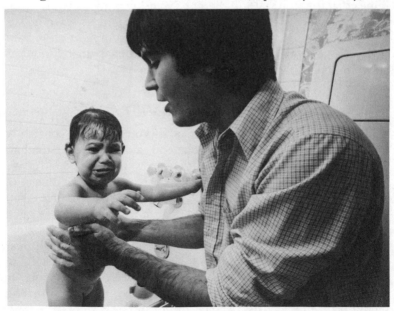

when looked at closely, a toddler's fears aren't too different from an adult's.

Another puzzling behavior common during the latter part of this year is a toddler's insistence on eating one food only. Despite your probable gut reaction that this must be stopped, experts recommend going along with your child's desires, as this chapter discusses.

The twenty-month-old is also moving right along in his language development, yet he continues to mispronounce some words that seem well within his articulation ability. We give insights into this behavior on the following pages. Play grows too. At this age, your toddler has the fine motor skills that let him insert a playing card through a slot; the large motor skill and coordination to toss a ball with fairly good aim. (He has probably been throwing balls since early toddlerhood.) He also shows a shift away from imitation and toward true fantasy play.

Scared Isn't *Silly*

What were you afraid of as a child? Shadows? Something under the bed? The closed closet (what *is* lurking inside?)? Think about the things that frighten you still. Perhaps you shiver instinctively when you see a spider or harmless garden snake. A dark passage makes your heart race. Maybe you *still* prefer to leave a light on in your bedroom, or cringe during thunderstorms. Fears among toddlers are common, too.

WHERE FEARS COME FROM

Many fears are naturally based on self-protection. We constantly evaluate information about the threat and safety of every situation. The more the balance tips toward threat, the more fearful we generally become. That makes sense in explaining the genesis of some frights. After all, a darkened room *can* hide a real menace, not just an imaginary one. Some toddler fears spring from this same reasoned evaluation. He knows from prior experience that a situation is threatening. For example, young children generally fear pain. The doctor often needs to give your child an injection. No wonder he's afraid of the pediatrician. Or if a rambunctiously affectionate dog once knocked your child over, it's logical that he should want to keep his distance from canines.

Fear also springs from the unknown and imagined rather than

what we've personally experienced. A novel situation can scare adult and child alike. We know that true danger *could* lurk on the unfamiliar street, even if nothing has ever befallen us there. It gives us the shivers. Although a young child can't imagine gruesome consequences as we can, he might be scared merely by the unpredictability of a novel situation. A study at the University of Minnesota by Megan Gunnar, Kelly Leighton, and Raymond Peleaux found that, in a test situation, thirteen-month-olds appeared more fearful of mechanical toys that started and stopped haphazardly than those that played on predictable schedules. Some theorists suggest that stranger anxiety might have the same roots. After all, an unfamiliar person is likely to do unpredictable things.

Fears can be considered a sign of intellectual growth. After all, a toddler must be smart enough to remember that situations have been threatening, or wise enough to realize that an unknown situation might carry threat as well as benefit, in order to be fearful. Fears show that a toddler is generating mental "questions" about the way the world works; the trouble is, he lacks the knowledge or experience to answer them.

HOW TO HELP

A toddler's anxiety at the movements of a windup toy may seem silly to you. From his viewpoint, though, the toy might somehow harm him; he doesn't understand that it's not alive. (Most children don't really comprehend alive and dead until well into preschool age, which is why toddlers are often frightened of dead insects or animals.) Many a toddler is afraid of taking a bath. One reason is because he fears the sound of water being sucked down the drain. *We* know this can't happen, but he's not so sure. Many fears *do* have a real basis when seen from the child's perspective.

Rule one in helping a toddler is to accept his fears as legitimate.

Rule two: When your toddler expresses a fear, be careful how you phrase reassurances. Suppose he has climbed the first rung of the jungle gym—then cries out in fright. Because he's little and inexperienced, the danger of falling may seem very great to him. We've seen parents respond to this situation with what they mistakenly believe is reassurance: "You aren't scared. Go on—you're having fun." In truth, he *is* scared. Telling him he isn't does nothing to alleviate the fear, but it may make him feel badly about himself. Another common scenario: The doctor-fearing toddler starts to cry as he enters the waiting room, so his parent tries soothing with "Don't be scared. The doctor won't hurt you." Again, he *is* scared. And since the doctor *will* hurt him, the parent is in effect lying—which the toddler soon discovers.

Rule three: Offer physical and verbal reassurance. Lift him down from the jungle gym. Hold him comfortingly in your arms as you sit in the waiting room, or weather a thunderstorm, or protect him from a pooch. Remember, he often formulates questions that he can't answer. Tell him that you understand he is scared. Some brief statements help him realize that the episode isn't (or wasn't) truly threatening: "I know the thunder scares you. It can't hurt you, though—it's just a noise." Or: "I see you were scared. That doggie sure jumps a lot! We won't go any closer. Let's watch him play from here." In these ways, you acknowledge that he is scared while gently pointing out that there's nothing truly to fear. Remind him that you won't let anything bad happen.

Also keep in mind that forcing your child to do something that scares him seldom works to break the fear. A toddler who's afraid of the water is certainly not going to feel any more secure after being carried into the pool against his will. Thoughtful, gentle introduction to such experiences is a much better way to relieve your child's apprehension. One more thing. . . . Your toddler takes cues from you. You'll help soothe him if *you* remain calm and unafraid.

IN SUMMARY

Most fears should be dealt with in this fashion. Try to understand and accept a fear. Don't force your child to confront the fear-provoking situation if you can help it. Reassure him that you know that he's scared. Try to provide more information that helps him understand the situation or object that frightens him. Gradually help him become comfortable again. With your support, he'll eventually overcome what upsets him so.

Handling Common Fears

STRANGER ANXIETY

This pops up again and again throughout the early years of life, and the ways to deal with it remain essentially the same. Rather than trying to force your child to interact with the unfamiliar person, make contact yourself. Chat comfortably and show your child that this person is your friend—or at least isn't someone to fear. Help him become friends at a pace that he accepts. Remember that he learns a great deal from your reaction to a stranger. A hand-hold or hug can easily demonstrate your feelings and reassure your child.

Sometimes a toddler quite legitimately fears a specific person because of some particular trait. Perhaps the person's booming voice scares him. Or maybe she handled your child too roughly last time, or poked him with a gesture she thought was playful but your child viewed as aggressive. Sometimes an aspect of personal appearance—exaggerated hair style, beard, different skin color—panics a toddler. Accept these fears. Treat these situations thoughtfully and matter-of-factly, and you'll soothe both your child's and the stranger's feelings. Likewise, masks and similar disguises usually terrify a toddler. He can be all smiles watching Mommy put on her Halloween costume, then shriek when she dons the false face.

FEAR OF DOGS

This is absolutely one of the most common fears, and for good reason. Dogs can be big and bouncy and clumsy. They can swat a face with a wagging tail, or nip or growl or howl unexpectedly. Making a child pet the dog often intensifies the fear. Instead, hold your toddler in your arms and watch the dog from a distance. Point out how other people are petting it. You might give him a toy dog to play with, and talk positively about the dogs in his picture books. Work up to having him pet a dog while safely in your arms.

Keep in mind that fear of dogs isn't necessarily negative. After all, dogs *can* be dangerous. You need to decide how fearless you want your child to be around them. In fact, we think it's a good idea to instill a little skepticism, and warn your toddler not to pet unfamiliar animals unless you're there.

BATH FEARS

Fear of the bath, also fairly common among one-year-olds, seems to arise as a toddler becomes aware of potential bathing hazards. One is the inherent insecurity of this environment. It suddenly dawns on your child that he's vulnerable and unsteady in the slippery tub. At any moment he might slide under the water—and most toddlers hate wet faces. Maybe he has accidentally slipped already, and fears a repeat performance. Another hazard—illogical to adults but very real to many a toddler—is the drain. He has seen the noisy, swirling bath water whoosh down the open drain and suddenly fears that he, too, may be sucked through that secret opening. For this reason, it's best to remove your toddler from the tub *before* pulling the plug. This might prevent the sucked-down-the-drain fear from starting, or cure a mild apprehension once it begins. A bath seat, foam form, or bath mat on the tub bottom might ease his fear of sliding under the water, too, and make bathing safer in general.

Some children, however, seem so frightened that they refuse to get into a tub at all. This can be tricky to deal with; parents are seldom willing to let their offspring forego bathing altogether. If your toddler reacts this strongly, you might try bathing him in the kitchen sink or in a baby bathtub again. Or try giving him a sponge bath. Some children who resist baths are willing to shower if the spray is gentle. Then gradually ease him back into using the tub at a rate he accepts. Be gentle and reassuring; after all, this fear is very real to him, and your fighting it certainly won't make matters easier.

FEAR OF DOCTORS

Be truthful. Don't tell your toddler an injection won't hurt, because it will. Prepare him as you go into the examining room, emphasizing that the pain will last for only a little while, and that you'll be right with him at all times. Reassure that the doctor is his friend. Remember, too, that the pediatrician has been through this countless times. Don't be embarrassed. You won't be there for your child if you're worried about the doctor. And even if the other children in the waiting room look calm, chances are they're nervous, too.

Another Look at Pronunciation

Parents can become unnecessarily worried because their child makes "mistakes" that appear to fly in the face of logic. Pronunciation produces many such events. One parent recently asked why her toddler could pronounce some words correctly but had trouble with others that were almost identical—at least, in the parent's mind.

One reason a child mispronounces a word is because he lacks the physical skills needed to say it properly. Perhaps the word incorporates a new sound that's hard for him to make. Maybe he can't shape his lips correctly, or he's missing some vital teeth, or he doesn't have proper control over the necessary tongue placement. But then . . . why can he say one word correctly but stumble over another that's nearly the same? The answer could be that the two words aren't as close as they appear. *Boots* and *boost,* for instance, are nearly identical to adults, but the final word sounds are quite different. It's easier for a child to make the *ts* sound than the *st.*

A study by Stephen Camarata (Pennsylvania State University) and Laurence B. Leonard (Purdue University) suggests that pronunciation is also influenced by how easily the child *understands* the new word he's trying to say. These researchers found that the twenty- to twenty-five-month-olds they tested could pronounce the names of new *objects* more accurately than new *action words,* even when the object and action words were very similar in terms of syllables and consonant structure. (*New* means that the child was just beginning to use a particular word or word-sound spontaneously, or was using an unfamiliar word as part of a controlled test.) The reason? It may be that a child grasps the meaning of a new object word more easily, since the word refers to a concrete, visible item. An action word refers to a symbolic concept so it is harder to conceptualize. For example, it's easier for a child to understand *carpet* (an object he can see and touch) than *carry.* Camarata and Leonard suggest that because an action word has a more complicated meaning, or is more complex because it is not as concretely observable, it limits the ease with which the child understands it. Since the child has to put more mental effort into understanding and producing it, he has a greater chance of pronouncing it incorrectly. The increased processing required to say action words reduces a child's ability to use newly developing sounds in these words. From a toddler's point of view, therefore, *pig* and *pick* aren't as similar as you might think.

Twenty months isn't the time to be worrying about diction-clear pronunciation, anyway. Most toddlers have trouble with speech sounds that adults find easy. Rather, this is a time to enjoy your toddler's growing vocabulary, to talk to him and to listen when he talks to you, to share books and casually point out the names of objects in his environment. After all, he's still pretty young, despite all his apparent worldliness.

Food Fads

Yogurt and fruit at every meal—that's all your toddler is willing to eat right now. You entice him with a serving of luscious vegetable stew. No dice. No dice, too, to the crumbled hamburger, the cheese that last week he couldn't get enough of, the perennially favorite mashed potatoes. Don't fight it. Many toddlers go through temporary fads and binges, eating only one kind of food and refusing all else. We can only guess at the reasons. It may be that their bodies periodically crave a type of food, much as adults sometimes profess a craving that only chocolate or peanut butter may satisfy. It could be that they merely overindulge in a newly introduced food or food combination for a while before sliding back into a more normal and varied diet. Toddlers often go overboard: When given a new toy, they'll play with it *only;* when acquiring a new skill like walking, they forsake other activities temporarily. A food fad might sometimes be a deliberate way to assert their young wills with their parents, especially if you show anger or annoyance when your toddler refuses to eat what you've prepared for him. He learns that demanding just one type of food aggravates you, so he continues doing it until you tire of reacting, or he tires of its particular taste.

As we said several chapters earlier, you can't force your child to eat something he doesn't want, and pleading and anger will probably only increase his obstinacy. You might as well go along with specific food fads when they arise—as long as they are basically healthful foods. (It would understandably be unwise to feed your child only candy if that's all he's willing to eat.) A particular fad is almost always short-lived.

Growing through Play

FILL & DUMP CARD GAME

Many older toddlers love cards—not to play solitaire with, obviously, but to look at, scramble around on the floor, drop into a container and dump out again, and insert through a slot. Disappearance! Reappearance! Eye-hand coordination! Add a special box to a deck of cards and you've made a captivating toy. It's a tidy one, too, because the cards can be stored in the box between playtimes.

You need:

- deep adult-sized shoebox, with lid
- packing tape, at least 1″ wide
- scissors or sharp knife

1. Cut a slot in the shoebox lid. This slot should be at least a half inch wide, and at least one inch longer than the playing cards.

2. Line the slot with tape on all four sides; this helps prevent rips and tears over time. You might also want to reinforce each corner of the box with a strip of tape.

SAFETY NOTE: Supervise play to make sure your toddler doesn't chew on the cards.

Show your toddler how to insert the playing cards through the slot one-by-one; then how to open the box, dump out the contents, replace the lid, and start again. You might join in and help insert the cards. Make it fun, too. Pretend you're mailing postcards to friends ("Let's send this one to Grampa!") or putting bills into a bank ("Here goes more money into the bank!").

HINT: You might give your toddler just part of the deck. Inserting fifty-two cards can be an overwhelming prospect.

HINT: You might count the cards aloud as he inserts them. It helps introduce numbers. Don't expect him to learn numbers anytime soon, of course, but counting things aloud for him helps set the foundation for future numbers understanding.

HINT: Use three-by-five-inch file cards instead of playing cards. Decorate them with pictures cut from magazines and catalogues. Talk about the pictured objects as he plays with the cards. Or use greeting cards! Cut off the backs, so that they're simpler to insert. You'll probably need to use a larger container than a shoebox, such as a squarish gift box with removable lid.

IMITATION AND EARLY FANTASY

Your toddler has long taken a keen interest in imitating things that he sees his beloved and admired parents do. Even as a baby, he copied simple facial expressions (sticking out his tongue), gestures (waving bye-bye), sounds (babbling to your babbles), and actions (playing pat-a-cake, blowing a kiss). Usually you began the simple engagement; sometimes he did. But the game lasted only as long as you and he were directly copying each other. We might say that this one-to-one imitation is a first step toward fantasy play.

The next step toward fantasy play usually occurs between about twelve and eighteen months, when your child adds a new dimension to his basic imitation. Now he copies more complicated tasks he finds fascinating. He may "dust" and "sweep" as he's seen you do. He might pretend to drive a car "just like Daddy," or parade around the room clutching a play briefcase "just like Mommy." He also engages in other forms of imitative play, most commonly the caretaking routines with which he's most familiar. He "drinks" from an empty cup, for example, "feeds" himself with a bare spoon, "washes" his face with a dry cloth, and pretends to comb his hair. The big difference between these kinds of imitative play and his earlier direct imitation of you is more than just scale; *he performs these actions even when you aren't doing them.*

At some point usually between eighteen and twenty-four months, this imitative play undergoes an important shift: Your toddler may begin to perform such activities on dolls and stuffed animals as well as on himself. He'll give dolly a bath, put it to bed, feed and hug it; in short, do for his doll the sorts of things that you usually do for him. He might also take toy figures for rides in toy cars, just as he himself is often taken. This marks yet another big step in fantasy play. In the coming months and years, these scenarios will grow to include more complex plots, more abstract props, and other children.

We'll have more to say about this important aspect of development in future chapters. For now, you might want to foster fantasy by providing appropriate toys. A good, basic plastic doll with rooted or molded-on hair is a staple. The simpler, the better, because this "baby" will get washed, dumped in the wading pool, dropped in mud puddles, thrown against the wall in a fit of anger. . . . Simple doll equipment like a bed and push stroller are also good. Others: stuffed animals, toy cars and figures, play telephone, toddler-sized versions of adult possessions. . . .

SAFETY NOTES:
· When choosing a doll stroller, make sure you select one that's sturdy and has a wide base. Your toddler will occasionally rely on it for support, as he often does a real stroller or other pushable item.

Also, make sure it can't easily fold up or collapse. Folding strollers usually have X hinges where two pieces of the frame attach to one another. When the stroller folds, the hinge closes like a scissor; your toddler could get his finger pinched.

· When choosing small toy vehicles, make sure the wheels are securely attached. If they come off, your toddler might swallow them. Also, the exposed axle is usually sharp.

· Pay attention to the age recommendations on toys, especially play figures. The age range often reflects safety considerations more than behavioral appropriateness. Many figures that are acceptable for a child over three years are dangerous for a toddler because they're small enough to become lodged in his throat.

Research Update:
Sex-Stereotyped Toy Play

Several experiments have found that toddlers (some even as young as thirteen months) tend to choose toys and exhibit play behaviors that are stereotypically related to their sex. On the positive side, many researchers consider these behaviors as early evidence of gender understanding, which is a vital part of self-identity. Yet on the other hand, parents and experts who want to help children break through the boundaries of sex stereotyping find this limiting. Two recent studies, one by Barbara Lloyd and Caroline Smith (University of Sussex, Brighton, England), the other by Marion O'Brien and Aletha Huston (University of Kansas), add to this growing body of evidence that toddlers manifest early sex stereotyping. Some of their specific findings suggest ways that parents may help encourage less gender-specific play.

· When they studied the toys in toddlers' homes, O'Brien and Huston found, not surprisingly, that the boys owned many more "masculine" than "feminine" or "neutral" toys. Girls had the exact opposite. Lloyd and Smith found that boys engaged in more vigorous play than did girls—*when each sex played with his or her mother.* The differences weren't so great when a child played with a peer. It seems that parents directly or subtly influence this sex-stereotyped play, often without being conscious of it.

· O'Brien and Huston found that when boys played with a toy considered feminine, such as a toy house and play family, they were inclined to use it in combination with a masculine toy, such as tools. Mixing toy types might encourage freer play.

· Lloyd and Smith found that when two boys or two girls play together, the children predominantly play with toys traditionally associated with their gender. Yet in mixed boy-girl pairs, the children also frequently play with toys of the other gender. So playmates of the opposite sex can help a child break through his own imposed stereotyping.

24

YOUR TWENTY-ONE-MONTH-OLD

Overview

In discussion groups, parents of toddlers often express the most serious concerns about issues of *socialization*. On the simplest level, this refers to helping a toddler get along with others— friends as well as family members. We look at some aspects of these types of social skills on the following pages. But the issue is actually far broader and encompasses all kinds of abilities that allow a child

to function in society with some degree of autonomy. In this sense, socialization includes self-help skills like eating, dressing, and toileting (which we talk more about in this chapter).

Toilet Learning: The Next Steps

In reviewing how we suggest parents prepare a toddler for toileting up to now, let's assume that you have already

- started helping your toddler make the connection between the physical feelings of urinating and defecating and the resulting products;
- started helping your toddler understand how and why people use the toilet rather than diapers;
- casually introduced the potty chair and have talked about what it's for and how your toddler will use it later.

The next step is judging when *your* toddler is ready to begin actually using the potty for its intended purpose.

SIGNS OF READINESS

She'll start using the words for urination and defecation (or urine and feces) that you've taught her. She'll start telling you that she's urinating or defecating *when* doing so. These show that she's making the connection between sensation and product. She'll indicate that she's aware of a forthcoming bowel movement; she may clutch herself, or get a funny look on her face, or make sounds of anticipation. She might also touch her groin area when feeling the need to urinate. While clutching, she may look at you to "tell" you what's going on. Overt signals like these indicate that she realizes she needs to void *before* she actually does so, and maybe that she's trying to hold it back. She may also be dry after bedtime or naps.

In general, toddlers exhibit readiness signs between about twenty-one and twenty-eight months of age, with the average being twenty-four months. Remember: The age naturally varies from toddler to toddler. Some signs, like being able to hold back urine and feces, are governed by physical development; there's no way to speed these up even if you should want to. Let your toddler lead the way. Remember, too: Early readiness does not signal precocity in other areas of development and learning, just as later readiness in no way indicates a slow developer in general.

Some studies have found that girls, on the average, tend to show readiness a little earlier and learn toileting a bit faster than boys. This might be because girls mature faster than boys in many areas. Other studies, notably one by pediatrician T. Berry Brazelton, have found that these gender differences are fairly insignificant.

USING THE POTTY CHAIR

Now's the time to suggest that your toddler sit on her potty chair without diapers several times a day. Pick likely times: while you run her bath water, soon after a meal, following a nap, or any time she has been dry for a few hours. Many toddlers have bowel movements at about the same hour each day, so that's another good time. Talk about what you expect of her, using the words she has become familiar with over the past months. Keep this potty time short and cheerful, and let her feel free to leave whenever she likes. If she resists getting on the chair, just accept it. You can't really force her if she doesn't want to, and your persistent requests (or worse, threats) will just make her angry. Likewise, never demand she stay on the chair until she produce a movement or urine. Physically, she can't go to the bathroom on command, even if she wanted to, and her inability to please you might upset her.

Suppose she eliminates in the potty. Fine. Tell her how nice that she used her chair. Keep your approval pleasant but basically low-keyed. We suggest you avoid going overboard with praise. After all, it will be months—maybe even more than a year—before she uses a potty reliably. If you make a big deal the few times she goes successfully, she'll feel proportionately worse when she soils her diapers. Likewise, phrase your approval to make it clear that she's doing this for herself ("Aren't you proud of yourself?"), and not just to please you. Remind her how nice it feels not to wear dirty diapers. Should you emphasize that "I'm so proud you did this for Mommy," or "You've made Daddy very happy," she'll feel that she has greatly displeased you—even though she couldn't help it—each time she goes in her pants.

When your toddler first exhibits the signs of imminent urination like clutching herself, she most likely won't be able to hold it in long enough for you to remove her diapers and get her to the potty. That's OK. Gently point out that she has urinated to reinforce the connection between sensation and product, and mention that soon she'll probably urinate in the potty more often than in her diapers.

However, once she begins signaling her need to defecate, she is able to hold back her feces, probably long enough to deposit them in the potty. That is, if she wants to. One reason you should encourage your toddler to sit on the potty several times a day is to get her used to it, and used to voiding in it *if she happens to by chance* (and to give you an opportunity to praise these successes gently). Naturally, the sometimes contrary toddler won't take this seat every time you ask—only when *she* feels like it. So she won't always agree to use the potty even when it's clear to you, and maybe to her, that she's about to defecate. Again, don't argue and don't chastise. If you turn toileting into a battle, you won't win. But you will lose your child's cooperation, and you'll make toilet learning that much more unpleasant and difficult. Another thing. . . . Asking her if she needs to use the toilet when you see these signs is rarely successful. A child often doesn't really understand this question or is even entirely sure that she does have to go. It's better just to invite her to sit on the potty chair, or even guide her to it if she's amenable.

In fact, the best way to encourage cooperation is to let your toddler be in charge of as much of the toilet-learning process as possible. She's at a "*Me* do it!" stage, and she feels proud of her growing independence. To this end, once she successfully uses the toilet about half the time, you might switch from diapers to training pants, which she can pull off and on. (Continue using diapers during naps, though, until she shows reliable daytime control, and at nighttime and whenever you'll be away from the house for a stretch.) Training pants help her feel more grown-up, which might predispose her toward using the potty. Also, a toddler is more aware of urinating and defecating when wearing training pants than when in diapers. We suggest you make this transition without a lot of fanfare. Making a big deal about grown-up pants will likely cause her to feel demeaned when she's put into the diapers she still wears at naps and other times.

In time, your toddler will come and tell you in advance when she needs to use the toilet, so that you can help her undress (if she needs a hand) and so that you can ferry her to unknown toilets when you and she are away from your house. This big step signals that the end is in sight. Elastic-waist shorts and pants that she can pull down herself will help build her independence. Nonetheless, she'll still have lapses, especially when she's so involved in something she's doing that she ignores the signs until it's too late. Patience, patience, patience. . . .

SLOW BUT SURE

You may think that your toddler is ready for toilet learning in earnest only to discover that, after a week or so, no progress is being made. Successes on the potty are few and far between, and your child doesn't seem to understand what is expected of her. You might as well let her continue sitting on the potty fully dressed—or not at all. Try again later when you notice more signs of readiness.

Learning to use the toilet reliably usually takes several months, even when you wait until your toddler seems very "ready" before you start. Some studies show that bowel control generally happens first, since many children have bowel movements at similar times each day and since they can hold in a movement longer than they can control urine. Bladder control usually follows a month or two later. (However, Brazelton found that the toddlers he studied achieved reliable bowel and bladder control at roughly the same age.) Reliable nighttime control comes, according to Brazelton's study, an average of six months later, usually close to the third birthday. We repeat: These are just averages; each child has her own schedule.

ABOVE ALL, BE PATIENT

Your toddler's progress in toilet learning will be bumpy. Sometimes she'll improve more slowly than you like, other times she may seem to lose ground, apparently forgetting her new skills under the stress of illness, a move, a new baby, or some smaller change in her life. Also remember that your toddler is struggling with issues of independence that can work both for and against toilet learning. For, because she may want to handle things herself, and thus enjoys the freedom of not having to depend on you to change her diapers. Against, because she may sometimes defy you when you encourage her to use a toilet. Let these setbacks pass without negative comment. Keep telling yourself mentally that she *will* learn, in her own time and with your help in ways as we have outlined. Above all, be patient. One mother we interviewed had the perfect attitude about her daughter's toilet learning: "She'll do it when she's ready. I *know* she won't get married with diapers on."

Family Factors

Let's start with an assumption: Good marriages equal happier toddlers. It sounds logical, and, not surprisingly "the available

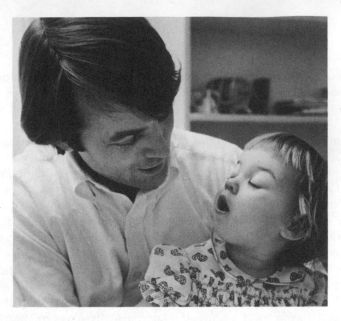

theoretical, clinical, and empirical evidence support a position linking positive marital quality with sensitive parenting characteristics and optimal child development." So say Wendy Goldberg (University of California at Irvine) and Ann Easterbrooks (Tufts University) in a study of how marital quality affects toddler development. Naturally, no study could ever look at all the factors regarding how family relationships affect a toddler, so researchers tend to focus on one or two factors that they can control in test situations. Here are some things they have found.

Goldberg and Easterbrooks looked specifically at how marital quality affects the toddler's attachment to her parents. Security of attachment was measured using a standardized procedure and rating system involving observations of brief separations of the child from her parents. Marital quality was measured using a parent questionnaire. The researchers found that secure attachments between toddler and parents are most common in families where husbands and wives describe their marriages as high in satisfaction, cohesion, and affection. Surprisingly, though, less "satisfactory" marriages seem to affect the child-mother attachment less than the child-father attachment. Other studies have also found that the relationship between a toddler and the toddler's father tends to be influenced more heavily by marital stress and changes in the family (such as the mother's going to work) than the child-mother relationship. No one can say exactly why. In a study of upper–middle class two-career families, Rita Benn (Merrill-Palmer Institute) confirms that mothers who rate themselves as highly satisfied—with work, marriage, and how they spend their time away from work—tend to have more secure relationships with their toddlers.

KEEPING IT IN PERSPECTIVE

Studies like these, quite understandably, can look only at particular behaviors at certain points in time. The findings are also extrapolated to represent general qualities of the family relationships, which may not be true if you studied these same families in their homes, day in and day out for weeks. (Such research would be prohibitively expensive!) Although the findings lean toward good marriages equal happier toddlers, this is merely a generality. Perhaps a stressed marriage increases the parents' attention toward the toddler, possibly to compensate for the lack of harmony between spouses. Perhaps a happy marriage actually impedes good relationships with the child; the spouses view their offspring as an intrusion on their togetherness. Suffice it to say, a shaky marriage doesn't necessarily doom a toddler, just as a strong marriage doesn't guarantee a happier, better-adjusted child.

All this *is* evidence that, positively or negatively, family feelings *do* affect a toddler. She picks up on what's going on around her, even if the emotional situations aren't directed toward her. Parents give us everyday accounts of how sensitive toddlers are to parents' feelings, from patting a mother's head when the she seems unhappy to pushing up the sides of a frowning Dad's mouth to make him smile.

LOOKING AT YOUR TODDLER

This information probably confirms what most parents already knew—or suspected. Yet such findings, general as well as specific, increase our awareness of family factors, and give us some clues about how we can help our toddlers in times of family stress.

- Try to shield your toddler from your personal problems as much as possible. Don't argue in front of her. If she does catch you at tense times, reassure her that you're not mad at her, and that your anger is not her fault.
- Your toddler can't express her feelings with words or ask you questions about what's going on when she senses problems. You can help her feel better by reassuring her and reflecting

her feelings—"I understand you're unhappy about . . ."
Even if she doesn't comprehend your words, she'll surely
absorb the intent of these explanations.

· If you and your spouse are at odds, this may affect your
toddler's relationship with her father more than with her
mother. Do everything you can to encourage a strong father-
child friendship.

In general, take your toddler's feelings into account. You
shouldn't—and probably can't—cheer yourself up in stressful times
just for your toddler's sake, but neither should you believe that she's
too young to be aware of family troubles.

Growing through Play

ACTION RHYMES

Nursery rhymes, those favorites of babies, haven't lost their
appeal. Try these. They're popular with many toddlers we know
because of the action involved.

Ten Little Wiggle Worms: A catchy rhyme to introduce the
numbers one to ten. (Don't expect your child to understand numbers for a while yet.) Hold up all ten fingers—these are the worms.
Now, each time two of them run away, fold them into the palm. At
the end—all the worms have disappeared! Make up your own
names for the worms, too. Don't like worms? Call them Silly
Snakes or even Funny Fingers.

> Ten little wiggle worms sitting on a gate.
> Good-bye, Jack! Good-bye, Jill! Now there are eight.
> Eight little wiggle worms doing dancing tricks.
> Good-bye, Tim! Good-bye, Tom! Now there are six.
> Six little wiggle worms in an apple core.
> Good-bye, Pat! Good-bye, Pam! Now there are four.
> Four little wiggle worms gliding on some goo.
> Good-bye, Ruth! Good-bye, Ron! Now there are two.
> Two little wiggle worms waving to the sun.
> Good-bye, Sal! Good-bye, Sue! And now there are *none!*

Jack Be Nimble: Lay a stick, broom, or similar item on the floor as the "candlestick." Chant this rhyme as you step back and forth over it, and encourage your toddler to copy you.

> Jack be nimble, Jack be quick,
> Jack jump over the candlestick.

Here We Go 'Round the Mulberry Bush: Follow each other around a chair or small table while singing

> Here we go 'round the mulberry bush,
> The mulberry bush, the mulberry bush,
> Here we go 'round the mulberry bush,
> So early in the morning.

This popular ditty lends itself to many applications. For example, substitute daily activities for the mulberry bush part, and pantomime them for your toddler to imitate.

> This is the way we wash our face . . .
> (drink our milk . . . pet the dog . . . use a spoon . . .)

Or use this rhyme to demonstrate simple actions that involve body parts—lots of useful vocabulary words!

> This is the way we clap our hands . . .
> (stomp our feet . . . touch our
> nose . . .)

Does your toddler like these activity rhymes? Then go out and get some rhyme books and records so you both can enlarge your repertoires.

ROCKING AND HOBBY HORSES

Rocking horses are winners, and many toddlers love them. If you buy one, choose a model that's hard to tip over; it'll get some rough riding. And to save yourself a lot of running to and fro, find a horse that's low enough for your child to climb on and off by herself. Good idea: Take her with you when you shop, then you can test the mount/dismount and the toy's stability. Sit your child on the horse and try to tip it both forward and backward. It should be very hard to flip it over. How hard is very hard? It's impossible to say. You just have to "feel" it. Also try to tip the horse sideways. Remember that your toddler won't always rock just forward and backward, and that when she mounts her steed she may put disproportional weight on one side.

A hobby horse on springs appeals to many toddlers, although some people think that this toy rocks and bounces too hard. If your toddler is the zesty sort and you think she'd enjoy a bucking bronco, keep these safety points in mind:

1. There should be sturdy handles rather than thin reins for your child to hold.
2. The base should extend beyond the horse in all directions, so that the toy can't tip over no matter how vigorously your toddler rides.
3. There should be solid footrests that she can reach when seated in the saddle. It's even better if these footrests are adjustable so that they "grow" with her.
4. The mount/dismount question is tricky. If your toddler can mount and dismount a hobby horse without help, she won't be frustrated when she wants to ride (or stop riding) and you aren't available with a helping hand. Yet, climbing on and off is probably the most hazardous part of riding a spring-mounted horse. Never forget that this toy can be dangerous. It's always best to supervise rides.

Research Update: When Playmates Disagree

It seems to adults that two twenty-one-month-olds rarely play together without an occasional shove and harsh "Don't!" "Mine!" punctuating the silly games and gleeful shouts. Several studies, though, have recorded that these disagreements are usually few (far fewer than most of us believe), and that they overwhelmingly involve toy disputes. Hildy Ross (University of Waterloo, Ontario, Canada) and Dale F. Hay (Institute of Psychiatry, London) confirm these findings. The pairs of twenty-one-month-olds whom they observed spent only 5 percent of the play sessions in conflict. Surely enough, nearly 90 percent of the conflicts were over possession of toys.

Many researchers have looked at the nature of these conflicts. Ross and Hay have a theory. Because of the way their particular study was conducted (see box on page 324), these researchers conclude that such struggles may not be what they seem.

The observations were made in a lab containing twenty-two toys, not in the toddlers' homes, so neither child "owned" the toys. With so many items to choose from, it's highly unlikely that both children would just happen to want the same object at the same time. Also, when toys were available in duplicate, the toddlers often struggled over one of them. As many parents have suspected, it appears a toy may become more attractive primarily because another child is playing with it. It also looks like toddlers don't always fight over a toy because one or the other really wants to play with it. Something else is at stake with these conflicts, at least at this age. Toy contests are one way that toddlers, with their limited speaking skills, approach one another and attempt to make social contact. They haven't learned the niceties of shaking hands.

Ross and Hay consider these conflicts basically positive experiences. On closer examination, they found that struggles between two children were methodical rather than random or disorganized, and had social rules that both toddlers followed. The behavior within each toddler pair remained remarkably consistent over the study, which suggests that the two children developed some sort of social relationship even in this short time. The toddlers also resolved conflicts rapidly, and in an orderly fashion, within twenty seconds in more than half of the cases. One child relinquished the toy and the dispute was soon over. No struggles lasted as long as three minutes, nor did parents need to intervene. You could interpret this as "might makes right," or "stronger wins." However, as the researchers say, it could just as correctly suggest that each child evaluated the worth of the object in dispute. One decided that it wasn't really worth fighting over so she refrained from extending the conflict.

EDITOR'S NOTES

• This study found that, on average, the toddler who initiated the dispute — that is, who tried to snatch a toy away — was successful in 56 percent of the cases. But it didn't make clear whether, in each pair, one specific toddler almost always won these toy struggles or whether each toddler was successful about half the time. So even though toddlers usually resolve conflicts themselves, you might need to step in if one child is always getting things snatched away from her. Encourage her to stand up for her rights. Remind her that she doesn't have to let go just because another child wants the toy.

· Although toddlers sometimes struggle over the same toy when an identical one is available, it still can be worth it to get duplicates for playgroup. This won't automatically end conflict, but it may cut down fights caused when two children truly *do* want to play with a certain toy. And it will give the children a chance to imitate one another, a favorite type of toddler play.

· Incidentally, the girl toddler pairs engaged in just as many toy struggles as the boy pairs.

Not every study of toddler conflicts has identical results, or even the same interpretations. Nonetheless, we think that the Ross and Haye experiment sheds some valuable light on the nature of toddler toy struggles.

How the Study Was Done

Ross and Hay videotaped twenty-four same-sex pairs of twenty-one-month-olds over four successive days. The children's mothers were present, but were instructed not to interfere unless help was truly needed. Each daily fifteen-minute observation period took place in a brightly decorated lab playroom containing twenty-two common toys. Several items were available in duplicate. Afterward, the tapes were examined and each episode of conflict was isolated and studied. The researchers defined conflict as "when the action of one child met with protest, resistance, or retaliation by the partner." A conflict was considered over when protest, resistance, or retaliation was followed by a thirty-second period free of such actions.

25

YOUR TWENTY-TWO-MONTH-OLD

Overview

In many ways, growing up is a journey toward establishing one's own individual identity. A newborn depends on parents for almost everything; things are done to, with, and for him. A twenty-two-month-old stands quite a bit apart. He feeds himself (sometimes, and sometimes more successfully than others), may try to dress—or more likely, undress—himself (at least with the

easier clothes), chooses his own playthings, may spend long periods away from parents, has his own friends outside the home; in short, he has more *control* over his own life. This self-determination grows as he does, and in a few years your child will go off to school in a flood of tiny age-mates, seeking his own fortune and unique place in society.

One vital ingredient along the various pathways to individuality is self-concept. This chapter looks at one set of milestones in this process. Identity is also defined by individual expression, and for a toddler, nowhere is this more apparent than in fantasy play. Over the next several months—indeed, years—your child will demonstrate his interests, admirations, wishes, desires, and questions through the make-believe roles he adopts at the drop (or donning) of a hat. The following section helps you understand better the importance of fantasy, and suggests ways you can encourage and enhance this dramatic skill. As he grows, your child also becomes increasingly better at expressing himself in words, and soon (if not already) forms plurals. In these and other creative areas (art, music, and so forth), your child both explores his potential and defines his individuality.

Fostering Fantasy Play

Your toddler ventures increasingly beyond the protection of his home and parents, encountering things that confuse or trouble him—the bullying child next door, the doctor who (although as nice as can be) gives him a painful injection. Family situations like the arrival of a new baby can be disquieting, too. Even parents come and go according to their schedules, not his whims. It's not surprising that he suffers occasional insecurities.

One way a child deals with insecurities is through *fantasy*. He becomes the big, brave, strong police officer who protects the world—and himself—from bad guys (including, not incidentally, larger neighborhood children). On a more familiar note, he's the mail carrier or nurse or delivery person, the helpful and respected adult he sees in his daily life. Most especially, he's the Mommy or Daddy who cares for a brood of assorted dolls, stuffed animals, and other nice and naughty children. He often plays the roles of any familiar adult who (in his eyes) is wise, powerful, or respected. These feelings of power and control, fleeting though they may be, help him feel strong and good about himself.

JUST THE BEGINNING

The foundations of fantasy play lie in the simple imitation games of infancy, which occur only while both parent and baby are present and actively involved. A young toddler imitates more complicated adult activities, *and* he performs them even when a parent is *not* playing with him. Rather than needing a direct role model, he mimics from memory. At some point, usually between eighteen and twenty-four months, he adds a dramatic shift. Now he performs familiar routines on dolls and stuffed animals as well as himself. In short, he assumes the role of a different person—usually an adult— and acts out what that familiar character does. This is an early form of the fantasy play you'll see over the next many years.

Because fantasy skills grow progressively, just like many physical skills, don't be concerned if your twenty-two-month-old doesn't spend hours pretending he's Doctor Dan or the ice cream man. A toddler this age usually engages in very simple make-believe, often centered around daily routines, his parents, and other aspects of home life. He also tends to slip in and out of roles quickly rather than to play elaborate characters. Then again, many twenty-two-month-olds are still more interested in exploring the mechanics of toys—how the different parts fit together, what happens when he pushes a switch—than in using them in make-believe. Each child starts when *he's* ready.

VALUABLE AS WELL AS FUN

When you watch your child master a puzzle—turning that last piece this way, then that, until it finally slips into place and he beams with pride—you can almost see the "learning" that takes place, and the value of puzzle play. Fantasy play has innumerable benefits as well, although they may be a bit more subtle to the casual eye.

A child sometimes works through bad feelings in fantasy play. He recreates an unpleasant experience, but changes it in an attempt to master it. If he's angry in real life at the needle-wielding pediatrician, in his play he might give the doctor a shot. This makes him feel more in control. Or he takes out his momentary jealous feelings about his new baby sister on his uncomplaining teddy bear. This helps alleviate the need to act them out on his real sibling. Naturally, you, his parents, are the most powerful people in your toddler's life, and the ones who exert the most influence. When your toddler becomes the parent to a doll or stuffed animal, he enjoys this power, too. These power fantasies are just that— fantasies. But the good feelings they bring are real, and they help to make your child feel more confident.

Jerome and Dorothy Singer of Yale University, longtime students of pretend play, point out some of its other benefits in their book *Partners in Play: A Step-by-step Guide to Imaginative Play in Children.*

Studies show that children who engage in lots of fantasy play usually have a good capacity for entertaining themselves. At home when things are slow, or in confined areas like waiting rooms where there is little to do, children who are adept at pretending tend to be less restless.

In make-believe, children take the parts of other people. This "trying on" the emotions of others fosters feelings of sympathy and empathy. Fantasy is also linked to that elusive term we call creativity. On the whole, children with active imaginations are more spontaneous, flexible, and able to adapt to new situations than less imaginative children. Although it's almost impossible to determine whether fantasy leads to this creativity, or whether highly creative children just happen to like fantasy play, the two are most probably connected.

HELPING FANTASY ALONG

You can't actually teach a child to be imaginative, but you *can* encourage his natural talent for fantasy. As the Singers state, "While the capacity for fantasy or pretending is inherent in all reasonably normal human beings, the degree to which it is used by children depends to a large degree on whether parents or other adults have fostered it." You can foster it by:

- enlarging your child's world
- encouraging your child's imaginative thinking through play suggestions
- providing toys and props that lend themselves to make-believe play

ENLARGING YOUR CHILD'S WORLD

- Read to your toddler. Favorite books will surely introduce plots he'll later act out. In the future, stories will also carry him into fantasy worlds populated by talking cars and engines that can make it over the highest hill with a menagerie on board (*The Little Engine That Could*, by Watty Piper) and teddy bears who live like children (especially *Corduroy*, by Don Freeman).

• Make up stories. Simple tales involving his doll or favorite stuffed animal. *Short* stories about the magic bus in front of you as you drive to the market. Fables about the family pet. Adjust the length and complexity of these tales to your toddler's age and level of comprehension.

• Go on outings. Trips to the zoo, the park, the library, special events like a parade—all inspire fantasy reenactment at home.

ENCOURAGING IMAGINATIVE THINKING

• When you see your toddler engaged in make-believe, occasionally offer encouragement and suggestions. Try not to intrude, or to direct his play too much. Just drop hints naturally. Elaborate on what your toddler is doing, and suggest a new direction when he appears to be stuck. If he's playing with dolly, you might add the logical next step to the scenario. "How nice, you're giving dolly a bath. Maybe she'd like you to wash her hair. . . . Oh, dolly looks so tired now. I wonder if she wants to go to bed." If he's pushing a truck around the floor, notice what he's doing and what sounds he's making. You might be prompted to offer "It sounds like an ice-cream truck." If he answers affirmatively, maybe continue with "I'd like to buy some ice cream. What kind are you selling?" Are some toy animals scattered on the floor nearby? You might suggest that his truck become a circus wagon that gives them a ride, or a zoo train. Is your toddler stirring some fantasy concoction in a pot? Ask if he's making soup. Can he give you a taste? Maybe teddy bear would like some, too. Again, take your cues from him.

TOYS AND PROPS

In general, toddlers this age favor realistic props for fantasy play. That is, they're more likely to "drink" from an empty plastic cup than pretend that a block is a cup, or to talk on a play telephone than on a receiver-shaped rattle. We give some specific toy suggestions in "Growing through Play," later in this chapter.

LOOKING AT YOUR CHILD

Your child's fantasy play is another reflection of his uniqueness. His themes may give you insights into his individual interests—as well as illuminate some particular unsettling time he's experiencing. Even how *much* he makes believe tells you about himself. Parents we consulted confirm that some toddlers are far more predisposed to fantasy than others. That's one reason we recommend you encourage by following his lead, rather than by trying to "control" his scenarios. It's the best way to help lay the foundations for the complex and fascinating imaginative play that's the hallmark of preschoolers.

Knowing "That's Me!"

Toddlers are fascinated by themselves. Who am I? What do I look like? What am I comprised of? What makes me unique? This process of self-discovery begins when he's born and never really ends. We grow and change and discover ourselves throughout life.

"That's Me!"

Psychologists have likewise been fascinated by how young children develop the concept of self. To tackle a topic so complex, researchers frequently break it into manageable, observable chunks that fit into the total self-concept mosaic. Michael Lewis (Rutgers University Medical School) and his colleague Jeanne Brooks-Gunn (Institute for the Study of Exceptional Children, Educational Testing Service), among others, have explored aspects of this field extensively. Since "One possible way to explore the concept of self is through the study of self-recognition," as they put it, they've examined when children typically recognize themselves—in mirrors, still photographs, and videotapes. All three are studied because each "medium" gives the child different clues. Here are some insights.

(Editor's note: Most of the studies described here looked at both babies and toddlers. For simplicity's sake, the term "baby" refers even to those participants over twelve months.)

WHO'S IN THAT MIRROR?

A natural place to start is the age children realize that they are seeing themselves and not "another" child when looking into a mirror. As we reported back in chapter 7, "Your Five-Month-Old," this appears between twenty-one and twenty-four months, on average.

WHO'S IN THAT PHOTO?

In another study, Lewis and Brooks-Gunn showed each nine- to twenty-four-month-old a colored slide of himself, of a baby the same age and sex, and of a baby the same age but opposite sex. Only the face and shoulders were pictured. In one phase of the experiment, the nine- to twelve-month-olds reacted about the same to pictures of themselves and the same-sex baby, but looked less at the picture of the other-sex baby. In another phase, the nine- to twelve-month-olds smiled more at themselves than at either of the other two babies. In both phases, the twenty-one- to twenty-four-month-olds smiled and looked most at their own pictures, and in one phase tended to frown more often at the pictures of other babies. It seems that just-turning one-year-olds are capable of some discrimination between pictures of self and others, but the ability becomes much stronger near the end of the second year. In a similar study, Lewis and Brooks-Gunn found that 25 percent of the eighteen-month-olds and 67 percent of the twenty-two-month-olds identified themselves in pictures by name (i.e., answered correctly when asked "Who's that?").

THAT'S ME ON TV!

Lewis and Brooks-Gunn also showed nine- to twenty-four-month-olds videotapes of themselves and of another same-age, same-sex child in the identical setting. Some of the fifteen-month-olds indicated that they could differentiate between themselves and the other child; most of the twenty-one- to twenty-four-month-olds could. Interestingly, these children demonstrated this ability by looking and smiling more at the other child, yet imitating their videotaped selves more!

So, when does the typical toddler reliably recognize himself? Most likely between twenty-one and twenty-four months. Probably not coincidentally, most children begin calling themselves by their own name at around two years, too.

PARENTS & TODDLER TOGETHER

As Lewis and Brooks-Gunn point out, the concept of self is formulated by an individual's interactions with the world—particularly with other people. There are lots of ways you help your child develop a strong and positive image of himself. One is by providing a solid sense of security, so that he feels the world is a safe, supportive place. Your caring, protectiveness, praise, sympathy, sensitivity to his needs—your love, in sum, fuels this. Another is by helping him learn about himself: the names and functions of parts of his body (through the naming games almost every parent instinctively plays), the range (and limitations) of his skills, indeed, even what he looks like. Mirror games almost assuredly contribute to this self-recognition. So does sharing with your toddler photographs of him. He'll probably dote on a special book containing just pictures of him, a homemade book with a theme like "Billy's Big Birthday," "Paul at the Zoo," "The Life of Daniel," "Sam's Super September." Just as he dotes on your love and attention.

Night Wandering

Once a toddler moves to a bed or can easily climb out of a crib, he may well start getting up again after you've put him down for the night. This refusal to stay in bed can understandably annoy parents. One reason you set a regular bedtime for your child is so that you can have some uninterrupted time in the evenings. So when your child arrives back in the living room a few minutes after you've said your (supposed) final "good night," we suggest that you *never* reward him—even mildly, with smiles or indications of how cute he looks or how clever he is to come down the stairs so quietly. Deal with the matter quickly and consistently, though not angrily. Carry your toddler straight back to his bed and tell him definitely, but lovingly, "It's time to sleep now. So stay in bed and go to sleep." If you act angry, he'll get upset and then you'll have two problems to deal with. Remember, he isn't getting up to be bad. He just wants to be with you and he can't understand why you don't want him around.

Wandering around the house can be dangerous, especially if a toddler does it in the dark or after parents themselves have gone to bed. If you have a night wanderer, be sure his entire room has been childproofed, leave on a night-light, and close his door. If he's clever enough to manage a doorknob, or if he doesn't like the door closed, a high safety gate across the open doorway makes him feel less shut in and isolated.

Growing through Play

MAGICAL SAND

Sand *is* rather magical. It scoops and pours like water, so it provides similar play opportunities and benefits. Like water play, too, sand play can be very soothing. But unlike water, sand can be dribbled into interesting patterns. It's great for drawing in (with finger, sand comb, or other utensil), for digging in, for hiding toys in. Add a little water and it forms a sort of dough that holds its shape when you press it, mold it, or make designs in it with cookie cutters (plastic, please, and no sharp edges!). Add more water and it becomes runny. Not really a solid, not really a liquid, sand is something else instead.

Safety Reminders
1. Always supervise sand play with toddlers this young. They'll try to throw it, or eat it.

2. Plastic cups and sieves and similar water toys are great for sand play, too. So are wooden and plastic kitchen utensils. Remember: No pointed ends that might poke into an eye, no sharp edges that might cut. Remember, too, that half-buried toys will be stepped and sat on. Objects with any kind of rigid protrusion (such as a funnel turned upside down) could injure.

HINT: Because sand scratches most plastic objects, it makes sense to buy your child his own set of kitchen items rather than having him use yours.

3. When you visit a neighborhood sandbox, sift through it before your child plays (use an old mesh-wire kitchen strainer). Neighborhood cats, and occasionally other animals, have a habit of using a sandbox as a toilet. Keep your home sandbox covered between playtimes with a sheet of plywood or other appropriate lid.

Simple sand "box": Fill a large plastic tub or dishpan about half full with sand. Your child sits or kneels beside this to play. *Idea!* Set this tub (and your child) inside an empty wading pool or on a plastic tablecloth. Then any sand he spills won't get lost in the grass.

MORE FANTASY TOYS

Housekeeping props: A set of toddler-sized housekeeping props lets your toddler participate in your domestic duties, or "clean" whenever the whim hits. Fill a small plastic bucket with a dustrag, a scrub brush, dustpan, maybe an apron to wear if you wear one. Cut down the handles of an old mop and broom to toddler size (be sure the cut ends are sanded smooth). Or purchase a junior play housekeeping set. If your child demands authenticity and his wet mopping indoors is too messy, let him take his pail of water and junior mop outdoors. You can supervise his cleaning the porch or sidewalk.

HINT: When he does mop indoors, put very little water in the pail so that spills won't be a problem.

Cars and trucks: Toy vehicles of all kinds are favorites because they suit both fantasy and action play (toddlers *love* action). Small cars and trucks can also fit into your purse or diaper bag for play on outings. Always make sure wheels and other small parts are securely attached. Larger vehicles offer more dramatic play on the floor. As of this writing, there are a few sturdy plastic trucks on the market that are specifically designed for a toddler. They're large and easy to push, and have special features like a cargo hold for storing things, and removable parts that can be fitted onto the truck various ways; these also serve as additional props in fantasy play. Such vehicles offer stacking/fitting play for the younger toddler, fantasy play for the older, and action for both.

Disguises: Toddlers this age aren't ready for elaborate dress-up, because most articles of clothing are simply too difficult for them to put on. But they do love things like sunglasses (or lightweight glasses frames with the lenses removed), adult-sized mittens, and (the absolute favorite) hats. Look into the mirror together as he tries on various things. Talk about who he is now. A fire fighter? Pediatrician Pat? Daddy?

SAFETY NOTE: Some dress-up disguises can be dangerous. Glasses can get poked into an eye, especially if your toddler should fall while wearing them. Necklaces—another favorite—can get caught on something and cause choking. It's best to supervise and never to let your child run around while wearing such items.

Research Update:
Using—and Misusing—Plurals

One language development theory says that children don't learn to speak by merely parroting the language that they hear; rather, they grasp certain principles that allow their language to proceed. Moshe Anisfeld, language specialist at Yeshiva University and author of *Language Development from Birth to Three* (New Jersey: Lawrence Erlbaum Associates, 1984), sees evidence of this theory in a child's speaking vocabulary. A toddler learns new words slowly when he starts to speak. Many of these early words are names of objects: *car, mama, dog.* However, once he understands that such words are symbols for the objects they represent—that is, once he grasps the *naming principle*, Anisfeld and other theorists say—his vocabulary shoots ahead.

We can see further evidence of this "rule" principle in how children use plurals. A small study by Courtney Cazden of Harvard University found that the toddlers she followed used few plurals at first. But at some point (and in her study it was on average around twenty-four months), their use of plurals shot up dramatically.

Anisfeld interprets the initial slow growth as a time when toddlers merely repeat specific plurals that they have heard. But once the children mentally grasp the principle of how to form plurals (and that plural means more than one), they're no longer limited to those plurals they hear. They can—and do—construct plurals on their own, and plural use blossoms.

Dr. Anisfeld finds additional evidence of the rule theory in the fact that children often make "mistakes" with plurals. For instance, most regular English nouns become plural by adding an "s": _car, cars; dog, dogs._ At some point, many young children use incorrect plurals for irregular nouns; they may say _foots_ instead of _feet,_ or _mouses_ instead of _mice._ Dr. Anisfeld and other theorists believe this happens because the child has grasped the general rule for forming plurals and is applying it—even if incorrectly—to all nouns. After all, unless his parents commonly say _foots_ and _mouses,_ he most likely isn't just parroting things he hears. In addition, once children learn that certain words take "es" (or "ess" sound) to make a plural—_box, boxes; peach, peaches_—they sometimes overapply this other rule as well. They may say things like _handes_ (instead of _hands_), or even apply both plural rules to one word and come up with _footses_ for the plural of _foot._ So don't be surprised if your child makes up some pretty strange plurals himself. It's a sign of growth: He is learning one of the rule systems that govern our language.

Should you correct these "mistakes"? Some theorists say not to bother because a child will eventually learn the accepted form anyway. (In fact, he may even resent your correction, because he really can't comprehend that he has made a mistake.) But other experts point out that children don't necessarily pick up correct grammar without guidance, as evidenced by the large number of adults who still use words like _feets_ and _mices._ We suggest that you wait until the new rule system is securely established, then "correct" by rephrasing your child's sentence with the acceptable form. He: "Foots cold!" You: "Yes, I bet your feet are cold!" Don't draw undue attention to either the mistake or the correction, and don't expect him to follow your example immediately. With time, experience, and your casual guidance, your child will learn the acceptable plural forms.

26

YOUR TWENTY-THREE-MONTH-OLD

Overview

This chapter looks at another influence on your toddler's behavior: television. There's no question that most children enjoy it; yet, even with all the research conducted in recent years, there are few answers to the question, "How does television

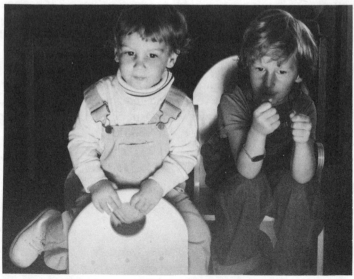

affect toddlers?" After reviewing some research focused on television and children under thirty-six months, we conclude that television may not be as benign as parents have been led to believe.

As this second year draws to a close:

· Your toddler continues to express her desire for autonomy by taking a larger role in dressing herself.
· She is outgrowing the board books so favored by babies and younger toddlers, and looks forward to real stories in real books.
· She is playing more and more with friends (when she has the chance); and the little games they devise tell a lot about her social abilities.

We explore these topics—and play—in this chapter, too.

Toddlers and Television

It is estimated that by the age of eighteen, a child born today in the United States will have spent more time watching television than in any other single activity besides sleep.

This statement has been trotted out in so many books and articles that, like other often-heard statistics—the budget deficit, the number of hamburgers sold by a restaurant chain—it has nearly lost any power to amaze. But *think* about it. This means more time than in play, more even than in school. We can surmise that television must have an astounding impact; yet, surprisingly, researchers have reached no specific conclusions about its actual effects. And no one can state scientifically how television affects toddlers. Even so, what we've learned about television research on older children, and what we know about toddlers in general, prompted us to look more closely at toddlers and television.

WHAT TODDLERS UNDERSTAND

Most television experts believe that a toddler comprehends very little, if any, of what she watches. This general assumption is largely based on two beliefs.

1. *Most toddlers usually pay attention for only a few seconds or minutes at a time.* They may watch a short sequence, or dance or croon a bit along with a song or advertisement jingle, and then they're off doing something else.

2. *Toddlers are too young to assimilate the kinds of information typically presented on television.* No shows are specifically designed for a toddler's limited attention span and mental abilities. Even *Sesame Street* is aimed at three- and four-year-olds.

Let's examine each of these beliefs.

1. *Most toddlers usually pay attention for only a few seconds or minutes at a time.* This assumed viewing behavior is based primarily on what parents report to researchers. It would be prohibitively expensive to monitor long-range exactly how a large sample of toddlers interact daily with television in their homes. One study of fifty-one toddlers by Daniel Anderson (University of Massachusetts) and Stephen Levin (Johns Hopkins University) did look at toddler viewing in a laboratory setting. The researchers found that children eighteen months and under spent only about 16 percent of the test period actually watching the show. Their viewing was also sporadic; they attended to the television a little more than once each minute on average, and each single, separate attention period lasted about five seconds on average. Between eighteen and thirty months, the television viewing—frequency and duration—roughly doubled. These children seemed far more interested in playing with toys or interacting with their parents than in watching television in the laboratory. The researchers also interviewed each parent about the child's viewing habits at home, and found similarly that television only sporadically captured the toddlers' attention.

However, these toddlers were studied while watching, one child at a time, a black-and-white "test edition" of *Sesame Street* in a laboratory playroom setting with lots of toys available. The results might have been quite different if the show had been in color. The results might well have been different, too, if the study had been done in homes. Toddlers like to model their parents' behavior, and therefore sometimes watch television in imitation of their parents. Parents we consulted report that their own twenty-three-month-olds appear to pay far more attention to televised shows than the above study suggests, especially if the segment contains some or all of the following features: music, repetition, animation, puppets, and frequent picture changes.

2. *Toddlers are too young to assimilate the kinds of information typically presented on television.* This is generally true, but it appears that young children *can* understand certain things if the content is

geared specifically to them. Robert McCall (University of Pittsburgh) and two colleagues studied ninety-six toddlers in three age groups—eighteen, twenty-four, and thirty-six months—to see how the children would react to toy play behaviors demonstrated both live and on television. (See the box on this page for a description of how the study was done.) The researchers found that, on average, children twenty-four months and younger were twice as likely to imitate a behavior shown live than to imitate the identical behavior shown on television. However, at thirty-six months, the children were equally as likely to imitate a televised demonstration as a live one. Since every child imitated *some* behaviors she viewed on television, she must have comprehended some of what she watched. This comprehension appears to increase with age. Also, each child saw the toys demonstrated one at a time—four live, four on television. Afterward, she was given all eight toys at once to play with any way she liked. The twenty-four-month-olds played about the same amount of time with the toys they saw demonstrated live and those demonstrated on television. Yet the thirty-six-month-olds spent more time with the television-demonstrated toys.

How the Study Was Done

Each child was tested one at a time. Her parent was in the room, but not involved in the experiment. The child sat in a chair at a table; the demonstrations (live or televised) took place across the table. An identical procedure was used with each toy: (1) The child was allowed to play with the toy undirected until she lost interest; then (2) A research assistant (live or on television) twice demonstrated a *target behavior*—the specific actions he wanted the child to imitate with the toy; (3) After viewing the demonstration, the child could play with the toy any way she liked and her actions were carefully recorded. When the child either imitated the behavior she had seen or somehow indicated she was through playing with that toy, it was removed and the next item was presented immediately. After the separate demonstrations—four live, four televised—the child was given all eight toys to play with.

McCall and his colleagues conducted another study, this time with twenty-six-month-olds. Each toddler watched on television a child her same age play with four different toys, one right after another with no break between toys. This televised "presenter" demonstrated a specific behavior with each toy. Then immediately afterward, the toddler was given eight toys, four of which she had seen demonstrated and four that were similar but new to her. The result? The toddlers played more with the toys they had seen demonstrated than with the new ones. They also imitated the particular play behaviors they had viewed almost 60 percent more frequently and/or accurately with the demonstrated toys than with the similar but novel toys. The experimenters ran this same test with another group of twenty-six-month-olds; however, this time each toddler wasn't given the eight toys until a week after watching the tape. The findings were almost identical with the first group of twenty-six-month-olds. Thus, it appears that toddlers are capable of picking up at least some things that they see on television—and that particular simple sequences may stick with them for days after watching.

Again, parents we consulted agree. They report that their own twenty-three-month-olds seem to absorb a lot of what's being presented on television, especially the commercials. This isn't surprising; commercials often contain the features—music, repetition, animation—which draw the most attention from toddlers, and a single commercial may be repeated several times within a regular program.

SESAME STREET

Parents we know have the most questions about *Sesame Street:* specifically, does this show help improve skills like number and letter recognition? We've found plenty of studies on *Sesame Street*'s supposed impact; but none that we know have been conducted with toddlers. Nearly all focus on the three- and (especially) four-year-old. Most studies indicate that children who view the show regularly, especially disadvantaged children, do show advances in skills, like prereading, over children who watch less or not at all. Other studies, though, have found that the gains aren't nearly as dramatic as once trumpeted. We think *Sesame Street* is a fine show— particularly when compared to the alternatives—but that it's not proven as making a measurable "educational" impact on toddlers.

THINK ABOUT IT . . .

We have found no hard evidence that television either benefits or harms a toddler. On the positive side, shows like *Sesame Street* may lay the foundations for some later skills. Television in general does provide auditory and visual stimulation, and therefore may play a role in language development, especially when a child is older. And there are certainly times when it entertains.

But let's look at the other side. We agree with many experts that toddlers are probably too young to be picking up on programming content that becomes an issue in the preschool years and beyond: violence, commercials, racial and sex-role stereotyping, and the like. But no one can be completely sure, because it's impossible to know exactly what is sinking in. Some studies discussed in this section suggest that toddlers *can* pick up on things they see on television, especially if the behaviors are simple and fairly familiar (as they were with the toy demonstrations). Other studies that we've quoted in past chapters point out that toddlers are quite sensitive to angry outbursts that they view in person. They *may* somehow be affected by certain emotional things they glimpse on television, too. Toddlers may also be upset by sudden loud noises, scary monsters (even those puppet or cartoon ones that older children consider friendly), and movements they consider menacing (especially those shown by one character against another), even if they don't really "comprehend" what they're seeing. Also, television viewing habits *may* be set early; it's thought that children who watch a lot at the age of two or three tend to be more attached to television over the rest of childhood.

Two suggestions. If your toddler does watch television, please watch with her. That way you can talk—keep it simple!—about what she's seeing, and can turn off anything that seems to be bothering her. Finally, we don't recommend prolonged watching at any age in early childhood, especially if it replaces time spent playing or with parents. Learning through play is still the best way. And spending time with you probably beats everything.

Books for Older Toddlers

(Editor's note: Not all twenty-three-month-olds are ready for every specific title listed in this section. The parents whose responses are quoted here had children up to thirty-six months. Nonetheless, the guidelines for choosing books are appropriate.)

Reflecting her ever-growing worldliness, your almost two-year-old has increasingly sophisticated literary tastes. No longer a fan only of simple, brightly illustrated, name-the-object picture books, she also likes stories with a basic plot: beginning, middle, and end. She likewise enjoys text that sings with rhythms and rhymes and simple poems. You'll find a smorgasbord of titles in your local library or children's bookstore from which to choose. Which *do* you select?

Whichever ones you like, and think she will like. Each child has personal tastes, and with hundreds of new titles appearing each year—some excellent, some forgettable—no list of recommended books could ever be comprehensive. Yet there are some classics that have been known and loved for years. We asked parents to select from a list of acknowledged classics the ten books that they and their young children really like. Some titles definitely stand out as favorites, as reported below. But much more importantly, *the favorite books shared one or more very specific themes.* Keep these in mind as you evaluate books for your older toddler.

FEATURES OF SUCCESSFUL BOOKS

· The story is simple and repetitive; this makes it easy for a toddler to follow. Books parents and toddlers especially like:

Caps for Sale, by Esphyr Slobodkina; *Millions of Cats*, by Wanda Gág; *Goodnight, Moon*, by Margaret Wise Brown; *The Little Engine That Could*, by Watty Piper; *The Three Bears*, by Paul Galdone.

· The text is full of rhythms and rhymes, including both poetry and silly rhyming words. Books parents and toddlers especially like:

A Child's Garden of Verses, by Robert Louis Stevenson; *When We Were Very Young*, by A. A. Milne; Dr. Seuss books, the simplest ones.

· The story and pictures invite parent and child to play with sounds. Books parents and toddlers especially like:

The Train to Timbuctoo, by Margaret Wise Brown; *The Little Engine That Could*, by Watty Piper; *The Three Bears*, by Paul Galdone; Dr. Seuss books, the simplest ones.

· The main character has characteristics, behaviors, feelings, and emotions the toddler easily identifies with and understands. Books parents and toddlers especially like:

Tale of Peter Rabbit, by Beatrix Potter; *Corduroy*, by Don Freeman; *Where the Wild Things Are*, by Maurice Sendak; *Bedtime for Frances*, by Russell Hoban.

· The storyline presents situations and routines the toddler herself often experiences; again, this helps her identify with the main character. Books parents and toddlers especially like:

Goodnight, Moon, by Margaret Wise Brown; *Bedtime for Frances*, by Russell Hoban; *Curious George*, by H. A. Rey.

· The story has social-emotional lessons. For example, it presents strong family relationships, or has a powerful moral lesson, or shows a weak character overcoming adversity. Books parents and toddlers especially like:

Corduroy, by Don Freeman (that love endures even through adversity); *The Little Engine That Could*, by Watty Piper (the importance of perseverance and positive thinking); *The Maggie B.*, by Irene Haas (friendship); *Play with Me*, by Maria Hall (why and how to wait quietly); *Peter Rabbit* (family relationships, minding your parents).

THE CHAMPS AND THE CHUMPS

The specific titles listed above reflect the sixteen favorite classic books chosen by parents for children twenty-four to thirty-six months. The absolute favorite was—surprise! *The Tale of Peter Rabbit*. Second was *Corduroy*, and third was *The Little Engine That Could*. We also asked parents which books they don't like and why. One basic theme emerged: Parents rejected books whose story contains violence, killing, or cruelty. Tops on the loser list were *The Three Little Pigs*, *Hansel and Gretel*, and *Little Red Riding Hood*. These parents definitely felt that the two-year-old just wasn't ready for such stories.

There are other terrific books that embody the six favorite themes described above. For additional suggested titles, ask the

Growing through Play

SAVE THE FISHERMAN

Here's a silly-funny game suggested by a day-care teacher we know. Place two shallow buckets or dishpans on the floor, a few feet apart. Put a toy boat with figure in one bucket, and pour a few inches of water in the other bucket. Give your toddler a cup she can hold easily. Now, you start a tale about the poor fisherman stranded in an empty pond, and how he needs water to sail home. Then show your toddler how to scoop water from one bucket, walk to the other bucket, and dump it in "so you can fill the pond for the poor fisherman!" Back and forth, back and forth, until she has transferred enough water to float the boat—and has saved the fisherman! Keep going, too, if she wants to continue. We've seen some children play this game until they've transferred all the water from one bucket to the other. Some even drain the pond again, cupful by cupful. And, of course, some toddlers don't follow the rules so exactly, preferring to pour water right back into the bucket they're scooping it from, or occasionally on themselves. It's all part of the game.

HINT: Add funny sound effects. Make gurgling and splashing sounds when your toddler pours the water. Become the fisherman's voice and squeak "Thank you! Thank you!" each time your child delivers water to the pond.

ENCOURAGING INDEPENDENT PLAY

In the hundreds of families we've interviewed over the years, we've found a few toddlers who seem to depend almost totally on their parents for play. It's particularly common for children older than two years to go through such a phase. We don't know whether this is some general personality trait in these children, or whether their parents unconsciously foster this dependence. Whichever, it's very trying on the parent; and it's not very beneficial for the child, either. Since she can't depend on being around people every moment for the rest of her life, it's important that she develop the capacity for entertaining herself.

– 345 –

If this sounds like your child, you might try the "weaning" approach. For example, you and she start off playing together with a toy. Then, gradually wean your way out of the game until, unbeknownst to her, she's playing by herself and you're on the sidelines. If she seems anxious, reassure her that you're nearby. Also, casually drop hints and suggestions of other things she might do with the toy. Or she might start off alone. You give her a toy or suggest an activity and tell her that you are too busy to join in now _but you will in a few minutes._ Then do, and gradually slip away again. As before, reassure her that you are nearby if she truly needs you.

One more thing. If your child seems to require inordinate attention, it might be because you're always giving it to her. In such cases, it helps (rather than hurts) to tell her on occasion that you're just too busy and that she'll have to do something all by herself. Then even if she tags around behind you, ignore her as best you can (unless she becomes very troubled, of course). After a while, she'll realize that you're not so much fun and will (hopefully) toddle off after more interesting pursuits. As one of our consultants says, the world is inherently fascinating to a young child, and even the most tag-along toddler can be seduced by it if, as a parent, you clearly support her explorations.

Research Update:
Toddler Games—Silly or Savvy?

Toddler pairs delight in games like running round and round a tree, or taking hats on and off, on and off—things parents usually enter into with much less enthusiasm. Silly fun, you say. Well, maybe. Trivial as these activities might seem, they reflect advanced social skills.

Behavioral scientists like Hildy Ross (University of Waterloo, Ontario, Canada) feel that social games tell us a lot about children's growing abilities to relate to their age-mates. Many of our adult social exchanges are governed by unspoken rules—making an introduction (such as shaking hands), waiting turns to speak, responding to a person's cues, and the like. These are the niceties that lubricate human interaction. When closely examining the simple games that twenty-four-month-olds play, Dr. Ross found that toddlers likewise appear to follow their own set of unspoken rules. (By definition, "Games consisted of sequences of at least four turns, two by each partner in alternation.")

- Toddlers can be sensitive and responsive to one another's invitations to play. (Dr. Ross found that, on average, 42 percent of the play-inviting overtures one child made to her partner received a positive response.)
- They can spontaneously adopt simple roles (such as the tosser and the retriever in ball games).
- Perhaps most importantly, they can take alternate turns, depending on the play context. For this to happen, a toddler must be able to indicate to her partner that it's time for the partner to act, and then give the partner enough time to both start and complete his turn. This takes, among many other social skills, patience and respect for the partner's rights. And, naturally, once the partner takes his turn, the first toddler must respond appropriately to the partner's behavior—whatever it is—to keep the game going. This takes flexibility!

Just as significant, Dr. Ross found that these games-playing twenty-four-month-olds weren't merely copying specific play behaviors learned from adults. In one phase of the study, a researcher demonstrated certain behaviors to and played specific games with each toddler before the pairs played together. Yet during the social playtimes, the twenty-four-month-olds almost never copied what they had been shown or had played previously with the adult. Rather, they made up their own games and responded spontaneously to one another, devising their own roles within a game. (Incidentally, in two different studies conducted by Hildy Ross, a ball inspired more—and more varied—toddler games than any other toy.)

Even if they aren't imitated exactly, parents have certainly contributed to these game-playing skills through all the games they and their toddler have played since she was born. Yet just as obviously, older toddlers are creative enough to draw from those experience banks and devise their own pastimes in collusion with pint-sized age-mates. They *are* becoming their own persons. So next time your child and a pal hold a fake-laughing contest or take turns tossing Teddy at the wall, look closely. You might discover a method in their madness.

27

TWENTY-FOUR MONTHS—AND BEYOND

Two years old! Your toddler is well on his way toward becoming his own person. Over the next six to twelve months, he'll most likely master toilet learning, which in both his and your eyes will make him seem even more mature—and independent. His ever-increasing physical and intellectual skills allow him greater autonomy over feeding and dressing and most other

areas of self-care. As his abilities come better into line with his desires, he'll have less need to rebel against parental control. And as he develops a better understanding of who he is (or self-concept), he'll definitely feel less need to express his newly independent self by fighting authority on almost every front.

Issues for the Coming Months

BIG ADVANCE IN LANGUAGE

As we said in previous chapters, the ability to express oneself in words can help reduce the need to act out frustration physically, and you'll see dramatic language development over the next year. Consider the following typical statements:

Two-year-old: Daddy go store.

Three-year-old: Daddy is going to the store to buy me shoes.

They illustrate some of the great linguistic strides a child makes between twenty-four and thirty-six months. One is length; the average two-year-old speaks in two- or three-word sentences, with the occasional longer utterance. By three years, nine- or ten-word sentences are common. Even more important is the complexity of the older child's statement. Throughout this year, children gradually build complex sentences out of the component parts so typical of the two-year-old's simple utterances.

The average twenty-four-month-old speaks very much the way we write telegrams—just the important words. Then, according to David Crystal, a noted linguist at University College, Bangor, Great Britain, "The 'little words,' such as *is*, *in*, *the*, and *do*, begin to make their presence felt. At first, a sentence might consist only of the 'main' words, such as *man kick ball*. Then the different parts 'fill out,' to produce sentences which sound more correct and adult: *The man is kicking that ball*."

Dr. Crystal stresses that this expanding happens gradually. Children simultaneously add more parts to the simple sentence structures common at two years *and* make each part more complex. They usually extend the *predicate*: the part of the sentence containing the verb and whatever else commonly follows it, like the object. The *subject* remains simple—as it is in adult conversational English. Dr. Crystal says that over half the sentences we say in everyday conversation have just a single word—a noun, proper name, or pronoun—before the verb.

The best way parents can encourage language development is by talking to their child and encouraging him to talk by asking questions, and rephrasing correctly and expanding what the child already says. Dr. Crystal gives an excellent example of this in *Listen to Your Child: A Parent's Guide to Children's Language* (Penguin Books, 1986):

CHILD: (coming in from garden): Daddy knee.
MOTHER: What's that, darling? What about Daddy's knee?
CHILD: Fall down Daddy.
MOTHER: Did he? Where did he fall down?
CHILD: In garden fall down.
MOTHER: Daddy's fallen down in the garden! Poor Daddy. Is he all right?
CHILD: Daddy knee sore.
MOTHER: Daddy's fallen over and his knee is sore? I'd better come and see, hadn't I?

In this way, the mother fills in the missing parts of her child's language, and encourages him to continue with the story. Over time, the child develops this "filling-in" ability himself. The progress is gradual, and your child won't be free from grammatical errors such as incorrect verb tenses and plurals. However, if you speak correctly, ask questions, and unobtrusively rephrase his utterances with correct grammar and word forms, he'll learn proper language without formal "instruction." And he'll enjoy the process!

SIBLINGS OR ONLY CHILD?

One issue that's likely to arise this year, if this is your first child, is whether to have another baby. Most American families with children do have two or more. Yet the number of single-child families is on the rise. Research suggests that about 30 percent of families forming in the 1980s will have only one child, either out of choice or because of economic necessity or other factors. Research also finds that parents of a single child aren't necessarily comfortable with that decision, largely because an overwhelming majority of families still believe that the only child has an innate disadvantage. Does he?

There are easily hundreds of professional papers on this topic. And after reviewing scores of studies and reviews of studies, we've come to the same conclusion as Dr. Toni Falbo of the University of Texas at Austin, recognized as the leading expert in the field:

> The question is so complex, the factors so hard to isolate, and the findings so contradictory, that on the whole, researchers just don't have any definitive answers.

Are single children smarter than children from larger families, especially first-borns? Some studies have found evidence supporting this supposed superiority, others have found the exact opposite; still others have found, on the whole, no differences between the two groups. Are onlies more selfish and less social? Not necessarily; some studies find that they're more sociable. And one study found that although single children do tend to have fewer friends and join fewer clubs than children from larger families, they have just as many close friends and are just as likely to hold leadership positions in the clubs they do join. Are onlies more prone to psychological problems? There's no concrete evidence that only children have more or fewer problems than other children. And no one has proven that onlies are any more or less happy than children with siblings. In fact, solely in the area of achievement are there some fairly consistent data. Only children tend to go further in school and achieve higher status in business and society. The reason for this above-average achievement, says Dr. Falbo, "may be related to the greater ability of one-child parents to finance the education of their children . . . [or] the special relationship only children have with their parents. The unbroken attachment between onlies and their parents, their more adult-oriented home environment, and the high standards set by one-child parents probably all contribute to the facilitation of achievement among only children."

Back to the big question: Are only children at an automatic disadvantage? We have found absolutely *no* conclusive evidence. Are they better off than children with siblings? Again, no evidence. The one fact we can point out is that their lives tend to be different from those of children with brothers and sisters. Not necessarily better (except, statistically, in terms of family affluence) or worse, just different. We think that the fears you may have about the oft-heard (but often unsubstantiated) "negative" effects of only-child status should not be a major factor in deciding your family size.

How you raise your child is far more important per se than whether or not he has siblings.

STARTING SCHOOL

Another issue many parents confront this year is school. When parents ask whether they should send their just-turned two-year-old to school, they usually mean: Does my child need formal schooling at this age? Will he be at a disadvantage later if he doesn't start school now? The answer: Probably not, depending on how he spends his time during the day.

Make no mistake; nursery schools can offer a toddler plenty: hundreds of building blocks instead of dozens, entire playground gym sets, messy art activities—like finger painting—that many parents would rather not handle at home, and the social atmosphere of several children his own age. However, many toddlers gain these experiences anyway through playgroups and day care, trips to the playground, and the like. What about the "learning opportunities" a school offers? Parents can—and do—offer them as well, except, perhaps, the somewhat formal curriculum associated with certain schools. Yet, there's a question whether children this young benefit any more from structured learning tasks than they do from all the experimenting and exploring and playing that characterize a normal day—if they have a stimulating home environment with well-chosen play materials and a supportive parent or caregiver. We don't think that toddlers _need_ to attend school to give them a learning head start. But neither do we feel that school is a bad idea (except for very rigid ones, which are inappropriate at this age). Should your toddler go to school? It's up to you. We do suggest, though, that you wait until he seems ready.

Is he self-sufficient—at least in some areas? Does he often play by himself without constant adult supervision? Does he stay willingly with the baby-sitter rather than always fuss after you? Does he generally enjoy new experiences rather than depend on you strongly for support? Do you feel that he's independent enough to enjoy being away from home a few hours each day? If not, he may not be autonomous enough to set out with confidence. That's fine— many twenty-six-month-olds haven't gained this autonomy.

NOTE: You might wait until your child is toilet trained before enrolling him. Many schools require that a child be out of diapers and know how to use a bathroom with a minimum of assistance.

PROVIDING ROOM TO GROW

Toileting, self-care, school, and expanding social network—these are all signs that your child is growing up. To nurture this independence, you must provide room to grow.

It's natural for parents to feel inclined—even overinclined—to give almost too much help. After all, you love your child. You want to do everything in your power to ensure that he's happy and healthy, that he's developing well. Almost paradoxically, this demands that you occasionally pull back the reins of your good intentions. You're bound to feel like jumping in when he hits a snag. Yet it's usually better to wait until he asks for help—and then to assist *his* efforts rather than taking over totally. It can be agonizing to watch him struggle with a puzzle that's beyond his skill level or suffer the third collapse of a tower he seems driven to construct. But doing too much for him defeats the learning inherent in the task—and robs him of the supreme satisfaction of mastering a challenge that he imposes on himself. Yes, you should offer suggestions when he seems to be getting frustrated, but the key is contributing suggestions ("How about if you start with this large blue block?") and responding to what your child does rather than directing ("Put the large blue block on the bottom and the smaller red block on top of it.").

Parents often feel most inclined to direct when two toddlers play together. Yet research is finding that toddlers generally do quite well by themselves. They usually solve minor disputes without parental intervention, and they devise their own games. You should, of course, provide toys and keep an eye on toddlers for safety's sake, but you needn't take over as a play conductor or referee. Likewise, you needn't—and shouldn't—entertain your toddler all day long. He should have time alone. Constant attention prevents him from developing the capacity to entertain himself. Keep an eye on him to make sure he's safe, though.

We suggest you keep this advice in mind for the rest of toddler-hood—and on into preschool years. Because your toddler is becoming his own person, you should treat him like one. By doing things *with* rather than *for* him. Not by running his life. By sharing it.

28

LOOKING FORWARD

First, look backward for a minute, back to when your child was born. Now look at him today. The changes that have occurred in these past two years are probably the most dramatic you and he will experience throughout your lifetime together. He has progressed from that tiny, virtually helpless, and almost totally dependent newborn into a walking, talking, climbing, self-asserting, beguiling, sometimes exasperating, and overall charmingly remarkable and unique person. Your relationship with your spouse or partner has undoubtedly changed as a result of having this child, and your child's relationship with each of you, his parents, has grown into a mutually rewarding love. All in two years—less than 750 days. Astounding.

Although the changes throughout the remainder of early childhood will be less abrupt, in toto they are no less profound. The coming years will see an abundant flowering of skills. Your child will become bigger, stronger, and better coordinated: able to run smoothly, race around a corner and stop on a dime; able to hop, jump, and skip; able to throw a ball accurately, swat it with a tot-sized bat or racquet, and catch it when it's tossed to him; able to erect elaborate constructions with blocks; able to solve puzzles with many pieces; able to scribble simple pictures and make fantastic (if somewhat crude) objects from clay. Physical, mental, and psychological advances will combine to help him be ever more independent. Already he can largely feed himself (provided someone else prepares the food for him!), and maybe help you undress him. Over the next several years he'll begin to dress himself, wash his own face, brush his teeth, wash himself in the tub, use the toilet reliably—in short, to look more competently after his own self-care needs. His social skills will grow by leaps and bounds, too, as his life moves progressively outside of home and family. He'll spend increasing amounts of time both with age-mates and with neighborhood children a few years his senior. He'll form a few close friendships. He'll probably have a best friend.

The most vivid developments, though, will likely be in the areas of language development and thought. Your child's vocabulary will grow almost daily, so that by about three years it will include almost 900 words. And these are just the words he uses; he understands many more words than he says. His sentences will become longer and more complex; he'll start using conjunctions. And he'll ask lots of questions in attempts to learn more about the world around him. His statements and questions give clues to his expanding cognitive abilities. So does his play, particularly the rich and complex fantasy play that's characteristic of the preschool years. The roles your child plays, the symbolic uses he gives to his toys, the scenarios he acts out—all reflect what's going on in his mind. And it will soon become clear that this fertile, questioning, challenging mind doesn't necessarily work the same way as does an adult's mind. In many ways, the toddler-preschooler doesn't interpret things or reason the ways that adults do.

So as your child grows, you'll continue to face new challenges related to his care, development, and education. How you deal with many of these will undoubtedly grow out of the foundations laid these first two years. How you support his developing skills, how you help him learn, how you play with him, how you discipline, how you handle family conflicts, how you express your love—these already have ground rules that you've begun establishing since your child was born. You'll undoubtedly have to adapt some basic rules to the changing situations occasioned by your child's growing older, wiser, and more competent, but by and large you've crossed many of the parenting hurdles. If you've raised your child thoughtfully and compassionately, chances are you and he both have a sturdy bedrock on which to build your futures.

INDEX